ABOUT THE AUTHOR

Klaus Dodds is Professor of Geopolitics at Royal Holloway, University of London and a Fellow of the Academy of Social Sciences. He is one of the UK's leading authorities on geopolitics and has written a number of books for a variety of popular and academic audiences, including for OUP's A Very Short Introduction series. From 2006 to 2020 he also wrote a monthly geopolitics column for *Geographical Magazine*. He gives frequent talks on border issues, is an expert in the geopolitics of international terrorism, and is often invited to join panels at events and in the media on the subject of border issues. He is a recipient of the Philip Leverhulme Prize, awarded to 'outstanding researchers whose work has already attracted international recognition and whose future career is exceptionally promising'.

KLAUS DODDS

BORDER WARS

THE CONFLICTS
THAT WILL DEFINE
OUR FUTURE

2

Ebury Press, an imprint of Ebury Publishing,
20 Vauxhall Bridge Road,
London SW1V 2SA

Ebury Press is part of the Penguin Random House group of companies
whose addresses can be found at global.penguinrandomhouse.com

Penguin
Random House
UK

First published by Ebury Press in 2021
This edition published by Ebury Press in 2022

www.penguin.co.uk

A CIP catalogue record for this book is available from the British Library

ISBN 9781529102611

Printed and bound in Great Britain by Clays Ltd, Elcograf S.p.A.

The authorised representative in the EEA is Penguin Random House Ireland,
Morrison Chambers, 32 Nassau Street, Dublin D02 YH68

Penguin Random House is committed to a sustainable future
for our business, our readers and our planet. This book is made
from Forest Stewardship Council® certified paper.

MIX
Paper from
responsible sources
FSC
www.fsc.org   FSC® C018179

CONTENTS

President Ronald Reagan standing at the podium speaking as West German Chancellor Helmut Kohl (R) and US Ambassador Richard Burt (L) and wife sit next to him at the Brandenburg Gate in Berlin in June 1987. In the speech, the president urged his Soviet and East German counterparts 'to tear down the [Berlin] wall'.

Introduction

IN JUNE 1987, PRESIDENT RONALD REAGAN TRAVELLED TO THE
divided city of Berlin. Standing at a podium, with the iconic
Brandenburg Gate as backdrop, Reagan did not mince his words. On
the formal occasion of Berlin's 750th anniversary, the former actor
turned two-term president made a remarkable appeal to his Soviet
equivalent, General Secretary Mikhail Gorbachev:

> Mr Gorbachev, open this gate. Mr Gorbachev, tear down this
> wall!

The effect of the televised speech was arguably more striking on the
other side of the Berlin Wall, with East German and Soviet media
claiming that Reagan's demand to tear it down was incendiary. But
there was no question in West German Chancellor Helmut Kohl's
judgement that Reagan's impassioned appeal anticipated a shift in the

public mood. In November 1989, East German border guards failed to prevent surging crowds from opening the Brandenburg Gate, and the iconic Berlin Wall, built in the early 1960s, was broken and battered by crowds armed with hammers and pickaxes. A piece of the wall sits on my desk. In this respect, I am not alone.

It was a momentous time. Very few of us who experienced those events in person or even via television and radio could have failed to be moved by the desire to open gates, tear down walls and destroy the formal border between West Germany and East Germany – the Democratic German Republic (GDR). For four decades, ice, iron and bamboo curtains separated capitalist and communist worlds in the Arctic, Central and Eastern Europe, and East and South-east Asia. Relatively few people breached those barriers, but those who did escape were household names to many North Americans and Europeans – such as Czechoslovakian tennis player Martina Navratilova, who defected in 1975 after participating in the US Open at the West Side Tennis Club, Forest Hills, Queens, N.Y. Navratilova was embraced by her country of choice and became a US citizen in 1981. Her adoption of the US was a propaganda victory for Reagan's America. She had rejected publicly the constraints enacted by the Czechoslovakian regime and its tennis federation. The rest is history and geography, as she travelled around the world winning grand slams and accumulating prize money. She is now a well-respected sports commentator and political activist, especially for LGBT rights.

Tearing down communist walls and 'red fences', and opening those borders and barriers, reflected post-Cold War optimism in the righteousness and robustness of liberal, democratic and 'Western' countries. The 'end of history' and 'end of geography' was upon us, and the stark division between capitalist and communist worlds would soon disappear. Global mobility and trade would be freed from pernicious geopolitical barriers. Between the late 1980s and early 2000s, the dominant talk was of 'our' free-flowing globalisation and the rise of 'our' geo-economics: the hyper-mobility of finance, the transnationalism of trade and investment, and the global diffusion of liberal freedoms. A classic Cold War military technology, the internet began in the 1990s to enable near instant communication, virtual trading and data transmission. The obituary for Manichaean geopolitics – in which everything was reduced to a struggle between good and evil – was being written, and it was not uncommon to read that authoritarian governments would be held to account by an online community, empowered by shared democratic norms and liberal values around the world.

The European Union (EU) embarked on a phase of new member-state expansion and, in North America, the US government signed the North American Free Trade Agreement (NAFTA) with Mexico and Canada. In South America, a new trading bloc – Mercosur (Southern Common Market in English) – was initiated in the early 1990s and taken to be a sign that previously authoritarian and military regimes were prepared to negotiate over a common economic future rather than compete over contested borderlands and resources. In the European case, however, lingering fears about a post-Soviet Russia meant that Eastern European members such as Estonia and Poland wanted the additional security reassurance of NATO membership. Poland joined NATO in 1999 and then the EU in 2004. Article 5 of NATO's 1949 treaty states that an attack on any one NATO country is considered to be an assault on the entire membership.

Hollywood might have envisioned new perils in the form of alien invasion but the mood in the 1990s was decidedly optimistic. Aliens could come for us but under American leadership we would prevail. Either tough mothers would prevent the end of humanity (*Terminator 2: Judgment Day*, 1991) or, as in *Independence Day* (1996), the United States – led by a visionary president – would save the earth from extraterrestrial invasion. In the 1990s, borders still acted as regulatory barriers in fiction and fact, but the dominant impulse was to encourage faster flows of products, professional services and highly skilled migrants. The predicted disappearance of 'the closed border' was a lodestar of this era of optimism. Other movies such as *Traffic* (2000) warned viewers that 'free trade' and 'open borders' offered opportunities aplenty for drug cartels and criminals to profiteer, but these were in the minority.

The 9/11 attacks on the United States decisively altered feelings, and action, around open borders. Borders were re-purposed to fit new ideological prejudices and psychological needs. Hollywood changed as well, with film companies eager to capture the new, more sombre geopolitical mood. The very symbol of transnational mobility, the jet plane, was repurposed as a weapon of mass destruction on the morning of 11 September 2001. Immediately afterwards, the George W. Bush administration closed the southern border with Mexico but not, notably, with Canada. Looking for danger southwards was no accident. For much of America's post-independence history, the south and west have functioned as frontier lands populated with stories of rapacious bandits, intent on abducting white women and propagating bedlam. Later on, drug cartels and illegal immigrants have at various moments been blamed for rampant lawlessness and endemic violence.

Mental maps can be quickly repackaged to position where we think our friends, enemies and strangers lie. Escapism, however, remains a luxury for the most privileged. The highest grossing films of the 2000s were semi-historical fantasies such as the *Pirates of the Caribbean*, *Harry Potter* and *Lord of the Rings* series. There were for others a number of ugly truths behind 9/11 and the 'War on Terror' that deserved public exposure. Agitprop filmmaker Michael Moore used his film *Fahrenheit 9/11* (2004) to confront the American public with the previously lax attitudes towards American national security, including a failure to monitor the the cross-border comings and goings of third parties – from those attending a flight school in Florida to the use of private jets by the Saudi royal family.

The legacy of 9/11 continues to inform contemporary geopolitics and reverberate across international borders. The 'Costs of War' project hosted by Brown University in the United States estimated that US spending on the War on Terror (2001–19) had reached $6.4 trillion. They also calculated that more than 800,000 people have died due to violence directly associated with wars in places such as Afghanistan, Yemen and Iraq. More than 20 million people have been internally and externally displaced. Social, political and economic reverberations continue in those aforementioned countries. Borders were routinely violated in the conflicts and American drone strikes in Pakistan caused enormous human suffering and resentment. Meanwhile, other states such as Russia simply invaded, annexed or occupied territories, such as Chechnya, Crimea and parts of Georgia respectively. What many countries did in the midst of the War on Terror was opportunistically use the threat of terrorism and third-party attacks to settle long-running geopolitical scores and capitalise on any military and strategic advantage available. Borders were securitised in some places and violated in others.

'Open borders' were re-cast as a security threat. Having resisted pushes towards further democratisation in the 1990s and 2000s, Russia and China had different views about borders from the United States. In China's case, large segments of the indigenous Muslim-minority population have been detained and subjected to detention and extensive surveillance, accused of fomenting extremism and separatism by the government. It is worth noting that Xinjiang province, where around 11 million Uighurs live in the far west of China, is resource-rich and strategically positioned between Central Asian Republics and Mongolia. China is determined to prevent any attempts to create a breakaway republic, and the Uighurs are bearing the brunt of this. Russia has also waged wars on regions such as Chechnya that Moscow judges to be separatist. In this instance, the US-inspired War on Terror emboldened both countries to re-purpose a globalised fear of terrorism to double down on minority communities and separatist groups that 'threatened' their national territories. Beyond China and Russia, civil societies around the world have been squeezed by surveillance and security impulse of national governments, and Western companies and countries have enabled and exported new forms of digital authoritarianism. Borders act as rallying cries for political leaders eager to re-energise national self-purpose, manufacture fears of migrants and cherry-pick what constitutes an actionable 'border violation'. The 'Make America Great Again' mantra called for Americans to adopt a frontier spirit that stretched to infinity and beyond. But this kind of border language ends up destroying empathy for others. The most famous fictional Vietnam vet, John Rambo, travels south to rescue his adopted daughter from a vicious gang of Mexican bandits (*Rambo: Last blood,* 2019). In a script that could have been written by a Trump supporter hellbent on vigilante justice, Rambo's SUV drives through security fencing somewhere along a porous Arizona–Mexico border, with precious little of the surveillance-military capacity that the US authorities can muster when they wish to.

While impugning Mexico and other Central American countries for imperilling American borders, President Trump observed in his 2018 State of the Union Address that, 'Over the last year, the world has seen what we always knew: that no people on earth are so fearless, or daring, or determined as Americans. If there is a mountain, we climb it. If there's a frontier, we cross it. If there's a challenge, we tame it. If there's an opportunity, we seize it.' John Rambo did that for sure. But what President Trump failed to note in the speech was that it works both ways – Americans are not the only ones who can cross, climb, swim and walk over things and places. Migrants and refugees from Central America might wish to seize their opportunities and head towards the United States. Such a spirit might also be shared by others.

Borders have taken on a new salience in the last 15 years, with militarism, terrorism, climate change, migration and, most recently, pandemics fuelling this resurgence of interest. There are four drivers of this profusion of borders: constriction, expansion, deflection and expulsion.

Governments around the world have also actively encouraged 'hostile environments', which are less accommodating to migrants, asylum seekers and refugees, for a whole host of reasons. First, *constriction..* Hostility to outsiders is not new, but what makes the current era so striking is that domestic institutions, public employers and private citizens are being corralled into this border business in an unprecedented manner. This is not to claim that racial and housing discrimination was not already endemic. In the UK, private landlords can be served with heavy financial penalties if they fail to inform the Home Office about 'illegal migrants' seeking to rent accommodation.

University examiners have to prove their citizenship before they are employed by another university. Citizens are expected to play their part in the control and patrol of borders. In India, the Modi government stands accused of using the Citizenship (Amendment) Act and National Register of Citizens to wage 'border wars' on indigenous peoples and non-Hindu citizens. Undermining citizenship acts as a proxy for land theft, marginalisation and resource extraction – all done in the name of securing 'Mother India'.

Constriction means embedding 'hostile environments' in bureaucratic-legal systems and everyday life. It places a heavy burden on those who have to be ever-ready to prove that the work visa and the accompanying paperwork is in order. Sociologists such as Nira Yuval-Davis produced pioneering research on this 'internalised' border and reminded us that these experiences and practices have mushroomed in recent years. This sort of bordering can also get outsourced so that fellow residents take it upon themselves to tell others to 'go home' and threaten to report visa irregularities. The everyday border – underpinning 'hostile environments' – has inspired artists, novelists, journalists, filmmakers, former border guards, immigrants and citizen-activists to put pen to paper, to document real-world realities and to curate those experiences. For the privileged, borders can be largely invisible in our lives and barely monitored, except in times of emergencies such as pandemics, civil disorder, natural disasters and wars.

Next, we have *expansion*. In the United Kingdom, a series of high-profile cases, including those involving people who had arrived on HMT *Empire Windrush* in the late 1940s, revealed capricious examples of detention and deportation of elderly and vulnerable residents. In her 2019 book, *The Windrush Betrayal, Exposing the Hostile Environment*, Amelia Gentleman exposed the devastating consequences for those who felt the expanded administrative grip of the border. Lives were turned upside down with grievous consequences for physical and mental health. Colin Grant's *Homecoming: Voices of the Windrush Generation* (2019) reminds us that for many of those affected in recent years by the Home Office's legerdemain, there is always a longer history of racism and everyday struggle. The border, like a river, has meandered in and out of people's lives, sometimes simply deluging them. All the while, nativists, racists and xenophobes warn repeatedly about Britain being 'flooded' by immigrants.

In the European Union, the 'border region' is part of an expansive EU territorial classification ranging from level 1 to level 3 territorial units. Level 3 units are border regions that share a land border and where half the national population lives within 25km (15 miles) of the said border. This system appears apolitical because the EU promotes itself as a borderless bloc of like-minded nations. Other countries take a different view of their borders. The US–Mexico, India–Pakistan and Israel–Palestine borderlands attract a corpulent body of reportage and creative work seeking to explore and exploit stories of 'the border'. In large part, this heightened level of interest is due either to them acting as migratory chokepoints or being animated by prevailing geopolitical tension. The US–Mexico land border is commonly regarded as a line of division not only between two independent countries but the global north and south. On closer inspection, the line is not quite as clear-cut as some might wish. American business opted to invest in cheaper manufacturing plants in Mexico, while illegal migrant labour plays a crucial role in the agricultural and service sector north of the border. Some welcome migrants, others want to deport them. Meanwhile, migrants from the south travelling north see the border as an obstacle to cross or an opportunity to make money. Your view of any border tends to reflect relative power, country of origin and racial privilege – it can expand, expel, contract and deflect.

It is, however, often at 'the border' where contemporary and future geopolitics reveals itself. Shortly after worsening tensions between Iran and the US in January 2020, around 200 American citizens of Iranian descent described how they were detained at the US–Canada border for up to ten hours. Detainees complained that they were being asked about their 'political allegiances and views'. The inference appeared clear to those detained – some residents and citizens were not to be trusted because of their family heritage, an experience that many Arab-Americans spoke about after 9/11. Elsewhere, in the literary world, Mexican and Mexican-American authors and journalists took to the airwaves – and social media platforms – to criticise a white American woman for writing a novel about the experiences of a mother and son trying to leave Mexico and head towards the United States. Jeanine Cummins's *American Dirt* (2019) attracted huge interest from publishers and controversy about whether she was right to try, in her words, to humanise 'the faceless brown mass' by depicting struggles to cross the border without herself having had experience of these challenges.

Then we have *deflection* – the desire to use borders to deflect attention away from other issues such the shadowy role played by migrants in a host of activities from agriculture to hospitality and food service sectors. The political left has railed against the moral depravity of borders, while the political right argues that borders are vital to control those who would wish to enter from elsewhere. Both sides argue about the legality, morality and profitability of borders and regimes of control. It turns out in many countries, including much of Europe and North America, migrant labour is crucial to virtually every sector of society. While new measures have been put in place to make it even harder for migrants to claim asylum status in the United States and many parts of Europe, distinguishing between the migrant, the asylum seeker and the refugee is something which some political leaders don't want to bother with. The Trump administration has pushed for Central American refugees to remain in Mexico while they wait, sometimes for months, for their claims to be adjudicated. Other countries such as Guatemala have been declared 'safe third countries', which means that migrants entering into that country are expected to claim asylum there. The Trump administration signed new migration agreements with Guatemala, Honduras and El Salvador (the latter two famously went to war over border and migratory tensions in what was termed the 1969 'Football War') in return for the US not imposing further economic pressures on those countries. Mexico is also under pressure to do more to deter migrants from travelling north.

Finally, we have *expulsion*. Successive presidents and prime ministers in countries around the world have invested in securing their homelands, spying on domestic and foreign populations, and manning the external borders of their respective countries. They have not been alone in this 'border theatre' – a way of looking tough and purposeful without actually being honest and straightforward about what might drive these impulses. They include worries about immigrants overwhelming settled populations (what might be termed 'replacement anxieties') to an outright dread towards anything and anyone who disrupts 'business as normal'. Like a highly contagious winter flu or, worse, a COVID-19 infection, other governments around the world – both liberal democratic and authoritarian – have embraced the border frenzy. Walls, fences and barriers alongside digital surveillance and tracking are commonplace. Thanks to countless TV reality shows, fly-on-the-wall documentaries and a gamut of films and video games, Western audiences have been virtually immersed into border security. It is now possible to watch shows about Australian and New Zealand customs officials, British and Irish airport security teams, and scores of American and Canadian shows following border guards, police officers and homeland security staff. We now talk about 'border security TV' as a distinct type of reality show, which captures this re-enchantment with border control and security.

Wendy Brown, in her book *Walled States, Waning Sovereignty* (2010), made the compelling case that a great deal of this is simply about governments and publics coming to terms, slowly and reluctantly, with the fact that having exclusive control of one's territory including its border is simply a fairy tale. Brown's assessment spoke of 'waning' not 'disappearance'. Even when the television cameras are not around, there are plenty of examples of nations around the world that continue to embrace the promise of beefed-up border security strategies. The intersection of the physical and psycho-geographies of the border matter. In August 2019, the small oil-rich state Equatorial Guinea provoked outrage in Cameroon. The source of the irritation was its plan to erect a near-200km (125-mile) security wall along the two countries' mutual border. The wall itself, however, was not the only source of tension. Cameroonian officials were concerned that the markers being deployed to outline the positioning of the wall were crossing the recognised international boundary between the two states. The markers were, by their very positioning, deemed provocative. The two countries have a history of frosty relations. Ever since Equatorial Guinea became an oil exporter in the 1990s, it has accused Cameroon of doing little to deter illegal migrants eager to seek new employment in the smaller country. Equatorial Guinea's offshore oil and gas production makes it one of the biggest players in the African energy market, and it is classified as a middle-income country compared to its immediate neighbours such as Cameroon and Gabon. The border-wall project comes at a time when the incumbent Equatorial Guinean president Teodoro Obiang finds himself condemned for human rights abuses, embezzlement and endemic corruption. It is widely regarded as a diversion strategy that helps to inflame domestic public opinion while simultaneously appealing to his supporters, many of whom worry about the scale and pace of social, economic and cultural change.

When then US presidential candidate Donald Trump told American audiences in February 2016 that he was going to 'build a beautiful wall' and get Mexico to pay for it, he was ridiculed by many. But he mobilised for many voters a persistent fear that America's borders were in peril and by association the nation itself. The southern border became, yet again, a fertile ground for invasion fantasies. A century earlier, border security consisted of four strands of barbed wire and was largely designed to keep out rogue cattle. Over the decades, the rhetoric and practice of border patrolling and management hardened, as fears of Latin American illegal migration grew. The 'war on drugs', inaugurated by the Nixon administration in the early 1970s, reinforced the drift towards the militarisation of the border. Drugs, crime and later terrorism left their mark on the people of southern United States and northern Mexico. The growing fears of Latin American illegal migration simply add further nourishment to what have been termed 'white anxieties' about how to secure borders and restore waning sovereignty.

ON THE GROUND

While borders are something to be exploited by politicians, they are also grounded somewhere. While the everyday border can make itself felt in our towns and cities, we should not forget that the lines we draw on maps are to be found etched on and in deserts, plains, mountains, rivers, lakes, seas, jungles and even subterranean environments. Air is partitioned up into parcels of national and international airspace, and third parties are expected to secure permission before entering into airspace above national territory as well as 12 nautical miles (22km) from any corresponding coastline. In areas of the world where there is prevailing tension, such as the South China Sea and in and around Syria, it is common to hear rival militaries accusing one another of violating their national airspace. Given the speed of military jets and the nature of air space, these 'violations' might be measured in mere seconds with nothing more than a vapour trail left in the violator's wake.

On terra firma, rivers, mountains and deserts have long provided physical opportunities to impose borders and hardwire partition/separation. Sometimes it works and sometimes it doesn't. The Pyrenees have long been thought of as a natural border between Spain and France – defined in 1659 by the respective kingdoms – but people and animals have found ways of criss-crossing the mountain ridges and valleys. It was not until 1866–68 and the Treaty of Bayonne that Spain and France agreed on a defined national border, using watersheds and summits to weave their way around a shared mountainous environment. As Chapter 2 reveals, the border rules we use for mountains end up being undermined by natural change. Ridges and crests get eroded and denuded over time, and a retreating glacier, in all likelihood, will provoke fresh opportunities to re-border.

Border infrastructure rarely does the security work that some might hope. Rules are made, procedures are put in place – but then something else happens to expose the fragility in all of this. In January 2018, CCTV captured images of a curious elephant approaching a security post on the China and Laos border. The elephant calmly lifted its feet and walked over the security barrier. Within two hours, the elephant returned to China after some late-night foraging. No one was brave enough to try to stop it. It serves as a harmless example of nature rebelling against human borders.

Climate change, including more extreme weather events, is raising the stakes, however. The earth does not remain passive in the face of human intervention. For years, environmentalists and affected communities have warned that local walls and barriers worsen natural hazards such as flash flooding. Border-security paraphernalia interferes with cross-border migration flows of animals, large and small. Border communities, often made up of indigenous peoples in many parts of the world, have had their lives turned upside down by border fortification. Governments compound matters by re-engineering landscapes. It is not uncommon for tunnels to be dug, river courses altered, canyons filled in and hilltops flattened. Moving dirt and diverting water (to enable the building process itself) are integral to border-security projects around the world but these rarely come without substantial social and environmental costs.

There have also been circumstances in which physical features such as rivers become points and lines of disputes between neighbours. Arguments ensue about who is responsible for change and what happens when the ground itself alters. Rivers and marshlands are ideal candidates for this war of words. Countries end up arguing over the ownership of riverbanks, the course of a river, the source of a river, flow dynamics, resources, water extraction, waste management, river crossings, drainage plans, shipping, canal-building and river basin dynamics. While rivers might appear to be a natural line of division, they wax and wane.

Bolivia and Chile brought a case before the International Court of Justice in 2013 about the status of the River Silala. The disputed area is on the mountainous border between the two countries, and Chile argued that the river is an 'international watercourse' and wanted to secure water rights for its mining sector. Bolivia argued that Chile had interfered with a spring in order to artificially manipulate river flow. Both countries depend upon Andean water supplies, and this dependency has been made more fraught due to prolonged drought. In addition, lower water levels have interfered with downstream hydroelectrical power generation. These factors, combined with a prior history of border conflict (including Bolivia's loss of access to the Pacific Ocean due to past wars with Chile) and glacial recession, have all fuelled this legal argument. Highland communities, often inhabited by indigenous peoples, have found themselves on the frontline of this high-altitude border drama.

Remoteness is no barrier to border conflict. Just because something is out of sight to the vast majority of domestic populations does not mean that it will be spared the spectre of conflict. If anything, the literal edge of a country is often a locus for tension. Military stand-offs are common in the high-altitude unpopulated glacial environments of India and Pakistan. Thousands of soldiers on both sides have had to serve their country and suffer permanent ill health thereafter. Avalanches have claimed the lives of scores of men charged with patrolling and watching their nations' highest and remotest borders. Retreating glaciers not only interfere with water supply but can incentivise rival states to secure territorial and resource advantages. Land appears and new scrambles to claim and colonise follow. In the past, ice and snow might have acted as a prophylactic agent – warming in mountains and polar regions makes them both more unstable but also paradoxically more likely to attract concerns that any improvement in accessibility will embolden others to take advantage.

In many parts of the world, the history of borders is intimately tied to the history of civilisations and empires, and later the emergence of the modern nation-state in the sixteenth and seventeenth centuries. While the Romans are often credited with introducing the first passport, the capacity of people to move was either restricted on the basis of privilege and power or made possible by the mass expulsion of Jewish and other minority communities and trans-continental slavery. Borders in general were meant to keep people in place. But the experience of the border within Europe and beyond varied enormously. The Treaty of Westphalia (1648) is often noted as a milestone in the creation of the nation-state – a territory with a recognised community and system of governance within established borders. The treaty helped to pave the way towards the establishment of international borders, national sovereignty and national self-determination. It came about after a conflict spanning three decades, and the treaty was meant to establish peace and secure autonomy, independence and territory for some polities. Switzerland became independent of Austria, the Netherlands from Spain, and others such as Sweden expanded their national territory.

But this was not the experience of others, who had their tribal and communal borders violated. Millions of West Africans were transplanted to the Americas between the sixteenth and nineteenth centuries by Europeans for the sole purpose of enabling slave labour. The plantation, the gulag and the concentration camp all remain horrifying examples of capture and enclosure. Beyond slavery, colonial powers were eager to impose controls on who else could settle in their colonies. Fears of over-population and food shortages at home led to some Europeans being dispatched to overseas colonies. In the nineteenth century, those same European states became concerned that migrants were trying to enter their territories and used stricter border controls. The passport was reintroduced in the early twentieth century. Even after the formal ending of slavery and colonialism, indigenous and black people around the world found that their lives were constrained by legal, political and financial barriers and controls. The establishment of native reservations in the United States in the eighteenth and nineteenth centuries was underpinned by the forced re-location (known as the 'Trail of Tears') and resettlement of thousands of indigenous peoples and tribes. The bordered nature of the reservation ensured that these Native American tribes were trapped in places that were considered of marginal value to settlers and government.

Empires, states and governments past and present have wrestled with this age-old conundrum – how to control flows of people and things in a world parcelled up into territorial units with associated borders and fuzzy frontiers. What the last 300 to 400 years have witnessed are attempts to impose rules and procedures to identify, demarcate and delimit national and international boundaries. While there are plenty of cases where a field, a river or a gap in the forest might serve to mark the presence of an international border, the human demarcation of the world's borders follows a four-stage process: first, the identification of a border area; second, a survey of local landscapes; third, the physical demarcation of border; and finally, the definition and administration of border via agreement and treaty. The Native American reservation and the *apartheid* system of South Africa are examples of two of the most grotesque schemes designed to constrain and de-socialise communal lives.

When we look at our map or atlas, and we see lines dividing one country from another, we might assume that in the main this has been a fairly orderly and technical process, but very few places in the world have been spared tension and conflict in the demarcation of borders. Dividing up the world's land surfaces always involved some combination of tense negotiation, rising tension and outright conflict ranging from world wars to civil strife. There have, of course, been peaceful land swaps and treaties of friendships but they don't detract from the general point – borders reveal some fundamental truths about humanity. We are perfectly capable of devising complex rules for allocating land and resources and instituting regimes of co-operation, while retaining a well-honed capacity to breach, ignore and remove those borders when questions of power and authority come into play.

Managing those borders is hard because historic schisms may never disappear. They have an uncanny ability to make their presence felt in affected spaces. Many people in Bolivia still resent the fact that their country lost access to the Pacific Ocean because of a conflict involving Chile in the nineteenth century. Argentina begrudges to this day the loss of the Falkland Islands (Isla Malvinas) in the 1830s. Pakistan and India cannot agree on a shared border in Kashmir. While the British, Spanish, German, French, Austro-Hungarian and Ottoman empires, to name but a few, have come and gone, their borders, lines and zones of influence have a way of making themselves felt despite being trodden on and written over. Around the world there are examples of land territories plagued by the complex legacy of imperial and post-imperial borders.

Former British colony Cyprus remains deeply affected. Violent anti-colonial struggle and communal unrest punctuated the 1950s, and independence in 1960 did not deliver a new era of peace and stability. An invasion by Turkish military forces in 1974 hardened the schism in response to fears that Greek nationalists were planning to integrate the island with Greece. Since the invasion, the island has been divided along a 'green line', which separates Greek and Turkish Cypriot communities. United Nations peacekeepers continue to monitor and patrol a no man's land that runs through the centre of the capital city of Nicosia and beyond. Attempts to reunify the island have yet to prevail.

In May 2015, courtesy of the United Nations Peacekeeping Force in Cyprus (UNFICYP), I visited the deserted international airport in Nicosia and saw abandoned ordnance and a civilian Trident Sun Jet. My guide was a major in the Slovakian Army who explained the role that UNFICYP plays in monitoring activity in and around the UN Buffer Zone. Turkish security guards in their border towers started to whistle and shout warnings as I approached another segment of the Buffer Zone. There are two British sovereign base areas, with a total area of some 256km² (99 square miles), and a host of so-called retained sites in the city. Border fencing and security signage can be seen everywhere.

Cyprus is about 260km (160 miles) from Lebanon and even closer to Turkey. Since 2015 there has been a steady increase in migrants arriving in the unrecognised Turkish Republic of Northern Cyprus. However, with no asylum system in the north, asylum seekers have made their way towards the buffer zone and the British sovereign base areas. The UK government has found itself having to accommodate Palestinian and Syrian migrants in its military base areas. The Republic of Cyprus subsequently agreed to process the claims of those held at the British base of Dhekelia, but overall, around 3,000 people were seeking asylum and refugee status in Cyprus in 2019. The island's vegetation and undulating landscapes provide opportunities as well for migrants to discreetly slip through the border zone. Tensions can and do easily build.

Borders and 'lines' get breached, ignored and corrupted. They encourage all the activities that nation-states aspire to control, such as illegal smuggling, trafficking, bribery and corruption. In Estonia, the national border guard uncovered a series of plots in 2018–19 involving illegal smugglers being paid by the Russian secret service (FSB) to collect intelligence on border-security operations. Evidence presented to an Estonian court suggested that the FSB was also using the illegal smuggling operations to generate its own independent sources of revenue for further covert operations. For a country that has invested substantially in border patrolling, electronic countermeasures and surveillance, Estonia's physical borders remain vulnerable to an unsettling combination of bribery, coercion and extortion.

Indeed, borders act as a catalyst for money-making opportunities. Demand for property in the settlements and rural areas alongside Korea's Demilitarised Zone (DMZ) have received a boost whenever there has been speculation of cross-border rapprochement and improved cooperation. If ties between North and South Korea were renewed, investors from the south were hopeful that the border zone would become a place for economic activity and net immigration. According to Reuters, a 'buying frenzy' was making itself felt alongside the heavily fortified border. Aided and abetted by Google Earth satellite photos and nationally produced maps, investors were acquiring land plots in and around the DMZ. All of which sounds rather optimistic in the circumstances. The DMZ is one of the world's most militarised border zones, punctuated by landmines running into the hundreds of thousands, roving border patrols, surveillance towers and razor wire. For now, the DMZ continues to separate two opposing sides and their allies, and acts as a daily reminder that the border between the two sides reflects military stalemate not peaceful resolution.

In our new era of climate-change emergency and the COVID-19 pandemic, border shutdowns and even wars are all the more likely as states and communities seek competitive advantage while isolating themselves from 'viral others' and 'invisible enemies'. From the synthetic polymer fibres found in face masks to rare-earth minerals necessary for batteries and telephonic technologies, intrigue and interest in resources is going to remain intense. In the first six months of 2020 alone, there were plenty of stories exposing shady trade deals, double-dealing and grabbing of medical equipment. The United States in particular stood accused by its NATO allies of using superior financial power to outbid and out-buy when it came to vaccines.

As a result, we are not going to lose interest in borders any time soon. Remote spaces such as the polar oceans, seabed and moon attract attention from China, Russia and the United States. They are not alone. Elon Musk has dreams of building a new civilisation on Mars. The hunt for resources is far from over and will increase as populations continue to grow in Africa and Asia. Energy transition and 'net zero' targets notwithstanding, electrification and renewable energy growth will not be possible without continued reliance on coal, oil and gas around the world. The demand for strategic minerals is not going to diminish and that might bring fresh tension to ever more remoterparts of the earth such as the oceans and Antarctica. One thing is clear: we tend to overestimate economic growth and underestimate the amount of work required to mitigate climate change. A warmer and wetter world will force many countries to think harder about the effects of climate change, with elevated ground more sought after, with heightened flood and heat risk and loss of biodiversity all likely. In the past, native communities around the world would have relocated and adopted a seasonal model of community governance such as transhumance – moving their livestock to the lowlands in winter and highlands in summer. Borders, internal and external, interfered with that capacity for mobility and what we would now term climate adaptability.

The term 'Anthropocene' is gaining public and political traction as a useful indicator of the cumulative human impact on planetary change (*anthropos* being the ancient Greek for 'human'). Our oceans are acidifying, our glaciers are melting, our rivers are shrinking and our forests are diminishing. While arguments continue to rage over timing, drivers and future impacts, we continue to divide up the natural world, often in the pursuit of maximising yield and output. However, the impulse of the powerful and privileged to grab land, sea and vital resources such as food and water is not likely to diminish. The world will in all likelihood witness fresh conflicts over rivers, glaciers, aquifers and forestry. Areas ripe for cooperation, such as water sharing, disease prevention and pollution control, could provoke 'border vandalism', and countries could simply give up working with one another. In the meantime, indigenous and other communities are already turning to legal personhood (having rights, responsibilities and privileges) for rivers and tribal habitats in order to resist further environmental degradation and insisting upon restitution and compensation for damage. The Anthropocene will in all likelihood exacerbate international and inter-communal conflicts: rivers, deltas, marshes, mountains, lakes, forests, islands, coastline, and plains will be caught up in its wake. The myths of exclusive sovereignty and the fixed border are dangerous. We need to cultivate a radically different view of borders that is alive to the complex realities of earthly change and the likely mass migration of people in an era of intensifying climate change and conflicts.

As may be evident from this introduction, the sheer scale and complexity of border issues make the study of them a challenge for any author. In this book, I will discuss three kinds of border conflict that will dominate future agendas: borders shifting because of landscape change (often exacerbated by climate change), the stubborn border regions of continuing impasse, and the evolving and sophisticated borders enabled by technological innovation. *Border Wars* takes the reader on a journey through these landscapes and places shaped by history and geography. Never divorced from fables and legend, borders are microcosms for national and international geopolitics. In our audit of borders, we discover how the shifting geography of borders matters and how our hyper-mobility as a species creates opportunities and dangers for those charged with protecting the border. Climate change is complicating matters. Things are melting, sliding and disappearing. The once rigid distinction between land and sea is alter-ing. Islands and low-lying environments are in danger of disappearing from sight, and for all the improvements in the human condition our cumulative impact on the planet is immense.

We will also encounter the seemingly insoluble, such as unrecog-nised borders and no man's lands. It is in these highly unusual spaces that the myth of sovereignty gets exposed as far from exclusive and settled. Indeed, lines on the map and ground get scrambled when states and other stakeholders declare emergencies and impose excep-tional measures. As we will see, conflict and resource competition are powerful drivers of the non-recognition of borders and territorial grey zones. Even though it's very clear that epidemics and pandemics have a nasty habit of being indifferent to borders, frontiers and zones, the imposition of emergency public health measures in the midst of the 2020 coronavirus outbreak has gone hand in hand with airport shut-downs, border closures and severe travel restrictions around the world. Viruses without borders are not something which any of us want to see more of. Finally, we will take in new borders and frontier tech-nologies such as outer space and so-called 'smart borders' respectively. Border work is likely to become more automated, digital, remote and virtual in the future. In Ruben Andersson's terms, we have a highly profitable globalised border business, far removed from the optimism of that chilly November night in Berlin.

If we want to understand the foundations for future conflicts, we need to understand all three versions of border conflict – the physical, the unorthodox and the novel. But first, we need to understand why borders, often mired in dispute, generate activity, controversy and profitability.

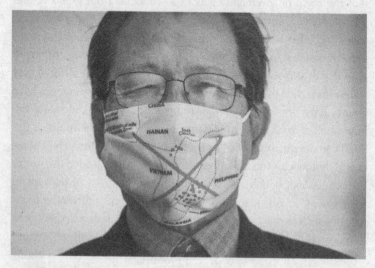

Quan Dinh, a volunteer at the Project Vietnam Foundation, wears a protective mask depicting Vietnam and the South China Sea at the Miyoco Medical Center in Fountain Valley. This face mask is an example of popular geopolitics. Using a now common item, a cloth face mask, the red cross on the map of the South China Sea rejects Chinese sovereign claims over highly disputed islands and surrounding waters. In April 2020, the two countries clashed over fishing rights and Vietnam accused China of sinking a Vietnamese fishing vessel near the contested Paracel Islands.

Chapter 1

Border Matters

BORDERS AND THE ARCHITECTURE THAT ENABLES THEM HAVE BEEN with us for thousands of years. The oldest walls built for defensive purposes date from 12,000 years ago in the Middle East, and the earliest recorded city wall was Jericho's in the Jordan Valley. Built either for defence or flood protection, these walls serve as a reminder that the instinct to fortify has a lineage stretching back thousands of years. Defensive walls found favour in ancient Athens but not in Sparta where the cultivation of warriors was judged to be a far more powerful deterrent than brick and stone. In nearby Constantinople, the famous Theodosian city walls lasted for nearly a thousand years. Built in the fifth century, they were only breached by Ottoman forces in May 1453, aided and abetted by gunpowder and siege cannons. Walls and fortified borders eventually fail due to human ingenuity and determination, while natural disasters such as sandstorms, volcanic eruptions, floods and earthquakes continue to reveal the limits of city walls and security fences.

Attitudes to bordering, however, ebb and flow over time. In the 1990s, there were far fewer border walls and barriers as governments around the world consumed globalisation Kool-Aid – calling for reduced barriers, increased trade, and the spread of democracy. Two decades later, it is commonplace to read of new investment in border security, including barriers, fences and walls. With funding and logistics in place, contemporary construction crews in the southern borderlands of the United States are reporting that they can build around a quarter of a mile of fencing a day. The land border with Mexico is over 3,000km (around 2,000 miles) long. President Donald Trump's ambitions for a 'beautiful wall' will take plenty of time and money.

Fences and walls, however, are just one element of border matters. Countries can register their state of border readiness in different ways. Governments might choose to spend millions of dollars and related currencies in introducing drone squadrons and re-engineering landscapes for the purpose of improving situational awareness and border surveillance. Alternatively, they might choose to alter prevailing visa arrangements and restrict the entry of citizens from countries judged to be dangerous, insecure, threatening or hazardous to health.

We should not forget that there are other bordering options too. Countries can choose to 'open' their borders for strategic reasons. They might decide *not* to prevent the flow of people and goods. For much of the migrant crisis affecting south-east Europe and the near Middle East from 2015 onwards, the relationship between Turkey and the European Union has pivoted around the question of the land and sea border between Greece and Turkey. Hosting millions of Syrian refugees and others from countries such as Afghanistan, Ankara and Brussels have been locked in acrimonious disputes about how those refugees and migrants are accommodated. Angry with apparent European indifference to its strategic interests on the Turkey–Syria borderlands, the Turkish government in February 2020 simply encouraged thousands of migrants to make their way towards the Greek border. In contemporary Turkey, the southern border is highly militarised and securitised while the integrity of the western border depends on the strategic calculations of the political leadership. Fearful of yet more migrants to accommodate and redistribute within the European Union bloc, Turkey has used the state of its borders to leverage financial aid and political support.

We always come back to bordering as an *activity* rather than simply the static border wall or the inert line on the map. Why might this be? In reality, there are many drivers that underpin investment in border security and, on the other hand, there are reasons simply not to bother ensuring their inviolability. Those drivers might be cultural, economic and political such as fears and worries about migrants overwhelming indigenous cultures, hostile third parties enabling conflict and terrorism, and third parties carrying disease. There are also financial imperatives as well, which are often less discussed. The European and North American experiences of border infrastructure and security illustrate a sprawling industrial-legal-political-military complex, involving a cast of characters such as defence personnel, border guards, lawyers, policymakers, smugglers, private contractors, civil society groups and political leaders. Here, border security and control is highly lucrative. In a report released in March 2019, the business analytical group Frost and Sullivan estimated that the border security market will be worth at least $168 billion by 2025. New investment will target real-time data analysis, as border security agencies attempt to improve their capacities to detect and prevent the irregular movement of people and goods.

Countries with mature border security industries are seeking to export their security technologies and digital surveillance capabilities. For example, the global military drone market is projected to grow in the 2020s and be worth upwards of $500 million per year. It is proving highly profitable in migratory hotspots such as Europe and North America, as well as other locations where border disputes are 'live'. In South America, fixed-wing drones have been deployed in an ever greater number in disputed areas between Venezuela and Guyana. Fixed-wing drones have greater endurance and can cover larger areas that may be disputed or in need of border surveillance. The drone industry is in rude health and countries such as Switzerland are actively marketing themselves as a 'drone nation'.

The European Border Surveillance system (EUROSUR) creates its own business opportunities for member states. In 2019, it awarded Greece a grant of around $60 million to develop a new surveillance system for the Aegean Sea, in effect the EU's eastern border with Turkey. The money will be used to provide a 24/7 monitoring system for the Greek coastguard and navy, and thus help improve situational awareness, the aim being to intercept illegal smuggling operations. Information will be shared between the Greek authorities and the European border security agency FRONTEX, based in Warsaw.

Border building and investment, however, bring with them costs – to taxpayers, to migrants, to border guards and to wildlife. The Sierra Club in the United States has highlighted the damage done to southern border ecosystems. The Santa Ana national wildlife refuge in Texas is a ground zero for ecological impact. Around the proposed border fencing route, vegetation will be removed, landscape is due to be re-engineered so that it is flat and even surfaced, and bright lighting will be installed throughout the night. Any border building project is going to require property to be bought, exclusion zones to be established and new laws introduced to allow the federal government to overturn any national wildlife refuge status. Environmental impact assessment and review could be simply dispensed with or downgraded. Appeals to national security often end up trumping all other considerations.

Border security projects generate political frustration the world over. In March 2019, the Kenyan government committed itself to building a new border fence at a cost of $35 million for a 10km (6-mile) stretch of fencing. The original plan in 2014 called for a new 700km (435-mile) wall to be established in the light of the dire security situation to the east of the country. Kenya has in recent years been rocked by terrorist incidents, including the 2013 Westgate mall shooting in the Kenyan capital of Nairobi and the Garissa University College attack of 2015. More than 200 people perished in those two attacks alone. The attackers were identified as being members of the Al-Shabaab terror group based in southern Somalia. In his 2019 State of the Union Address, President Uhuru Kenyatta stated that the government was 'strengthening border security and management'. But Kenyan parliamentarians, despite the threat posed by terrorism and cross-border militancy, demanded a cessation due to spiralling costs. The building of the wall has now stopped with the 10km stretch left incomplete.

The Kenyan experience is not unique. Persistent financial overspend is endemic to the implementation of border hardware. The millions of dollars and other currencies spent on motion detectors, drone patrols, fencing and surveillance technologies rarely produce positive cost-benefit assessments. By the time the Obama administration assumed office in January 2009, spending on border security and immigration policing was running into billions of dollars. In 2012, it was announced that $18 billion was being spent on immigration policing alone, some $10 billion more than on the Federal Bureau of Investigation (FBI). As more money was being spent on the southern border in particular, migrant detention facilities were privatised and the number of migrants rose steadily. The immigration detention sector became a huge industry with more people being detained and deported than ever before. It is now worth billions of dollars annually. In combination with detention centres, the cost of further state and federal investment in technological infrastructure, including drone patrols, radar facilities and ground-level surveillance, is not insubstantial. Border hardware is big business.

As well as being big business, borders are political dynamite. They are integral to political campaigning across the world, with national leaders promising their citizens that they will be tough on the causes of border insecurity. Nowadays, their pledges often capture the news cycle because border stories are rarely out of the media. At least the sort of news stories that address walls, fences and the experiences of those who attempt to cross them or defend them. It is often the shocking pictures of dead migrants that garner the most public attention. Few readers will forget the terrible pictures of a dead Syrian-Kurdish boy, Aylan Shenu (Alan Kurdi). He was found on a beach in September 2015 after drowning somewhere in the Mediterranean. The image of the stricken child quickly went viral and provoked a backlash against the immigration policies of the EU. Social media and the 24-hour news cycle have combined to ensure that the cross-border stories of refugees, migrants, humanitarian organisations and reception communities receive far more attention than in the past.

Borders, and border stories, retain considerable allure for many ordinary people – often leading to demands for them to stop being 'violated'. Autocrats and populist leaders around the world have leaped upon the border bandwagon and have used and abused that allure to promote their claims on expanded territory or to demand pernicious controls on some people and things trying to enter those same territories.

COMPETITIVE ALLURES IN HIGHLY DISPUTED AREAS

In China and Japan – though not only in these nations – maps of national territories cultivate not just allure but also anxiety about them being breached. Designed to show Japanese citizens the true extent of their national territories, in 2016 the Ministry of Foreign Affairs in Tokyo produced a map showing the 'shape of Japan', in which the country is seen to incorporate the contested Senkaku Islands in the East China Sea. The map aims to reassure the Japanese public that these islands are considered Japanese but also it serves to remind citizens that the country's territorial integrity depends on having investment in naval and military forces capable of deterring three nuclear-armed states – China, Russia and North Korea.

This is clearly a tall order given the conventional military capabilities of all three neighbouring states. The task matters all the more now that US support is a great deal less assured than it was during the Cold War. The maritime boundaries are depicted in bold and no distinction is made, visually at least, between land and sea. Japan is shown as a seamless continuum of land and sea territories, where everything is considered vital to national security, including the remotest and most thinly populated islands. The 'dots on the map' matter.

An accompanying video informs viewers in English about the islands to the south of Japan and how they were 'returned' to Japan after the post-war occupier, the United States, signed the 1971 Okinawa Reversion Agreement. The video notes, optimistically, that Chinese maps and newspapers depict and acknowledge the islands to be Japanese territory rather than Chinese. The reality is a great deal more worrisome for Japan – China does not acknowledge Japanese sovereignty over these disputed islands.

South Korea and Japan clash over their mutual maritime borders, they dispute ownership of Takeshima (and the fishing grounds around the small islands) and even the term to describe the waters that separate them is a source of disagreement. Japan insists the waters are part of the Sea of Japan while South Korea prefers the East Sea. Japan has lobbied the International Hydrographic Organization, which produces official maps of oceans and seas, to persuade the South Koreans to accept the name the Sea of Japan. What makes the issue of the islands – and the naming of the sea – toxic is that relations between the countries have been punctuated by conflict, and South Korea insists that the term Sea of Japan was popularised during the hated era of Japanese colonial occupation (1910–45). Both countries accuse one another of inflaming the situation. Provocative maps of their respective national territories are often seized upon as evidence of malfeasance.

Maps are used aggressively to support China's geopolitical interests. Its use of what is called the 'Nine Dash Line' (sometimes referred to as the Ten Dash Line) on its official maps of the South China Sea to depict a large area of sea, island and seabed under its effective control has become widespread in recent times. The Nine Dash Line has upset all of China's regional neighbours. In Vietnam, social media was abuzz in October 2019 about a joint American–Chinese cartoon animation film called *Abominable*, a heart-warming tale about a young Chinese girl called Yi and her friends who encounter the legendary snowman in the mountains of Tibet. What caught the eye of Vietnamese viewers was a scene in the film involving a map on the wall in Yi's house. In between postcards and photographs, there is a brief glimpse of the controversial dash line. As soon as it was remarked upon, the government of Vietnam ordered the movie to be withdrawn and movie posters were taken down across the country.

The South China Sea is a prime example of how Chinese technological investment in border expansion has been matched by visual campaigning, which uses new maps of Chinese maritime sovereignty in individual passports and public information videos to inform citizens about how the country is protecting its national territories. This is of increasing concern to the Philippines, Taiwan and Malaysia, as well as to Vietnam, as they all have their own maritime claims, resource interests and strategic visions. The expansion of Chinese territorial control and border protection is driven by resource potential and strategic access. In 2018, the United States Energy Information Administration released its estimates of potential energy resources in the region, which included over 190 trillion cubic feet of natural gas and 11 billion barrels of oil. As a vital sea lane for its near neighbours, and a rich fishing ground with accompanying hydrocarbon potential, the maritime borders of the South China Sea will be mired in controversy and possibly conflict.

Chinese media is good at reminding citizens why all of this is integral to the country's future. Artificial island building, security patrolling and surveillance of others is all considered to be vital given that 80 per cent of its oil imports travel through the South China Sea. As well as maps and promotional videos, drilling rigs and fishing vessels contribute to a portfolio of activities that make up border culture. Legal judgments against China don't seem to make much difference. China uses military and commercial levers to persuade countries such as Vietnam and the Philippines to work on joint exploratory projects or bully them into not doing things even within their own waters.

The Philippines has been caught between a desire to move away from long-standing subservience to former colonial power the United States and unease at its exposure to Chinese land and resource grabbing. Recognising the power imbalance in their relationship, the Philippines chose to work with China and announced that it was 'allowing' it to fish in the West Philippine Sea. The consequence is that President Rodrigo Duterte has had to spend considerable time and effort reminding his domestic audiences that the Philippines has not given up on border protection, as the Chinese vessels fishing in Filipino national waters are doing so with his personal permission. He has to resort to near constant linguistic gymnastics as he repeatedly downplays incidents involving Chinese vessels harassing Filipino fish-ermen. Meanwhile, Duterte has been told by opposition politicians that he cannot give away the country's fishing rights, with arguments raging about whether the Filipino constitution forbids the government to allow others to exploit the country's marine wealth.

These examples from the United States, Kenya and the heavily disputed waters of East Asia and South-east Asia illustrate that border matters have multifaceted implications. Border investment is being used by presidents around the world to reassure their citizens that national sovereignty is in safe hands. The edges of the nation, how-ever, reveal tensions and weaknesses. Border infrastructure, including walls and fences, is expensive. Their effectiveness is uneven. Very few border fences and walls have prevented people and goods finding ways of entering into those territories that are being guarded. Large-scale border projects often prove disruptive for local communities and ecol-ogies, causing local resentment. Offshore, maritime regions such as the South China Sea reveal that the promise of resources and the need for access drive geopolitical tension. But the lesson is clear: pub-lic opinion is crucial to ensuring that the stakes remain high, and that governments can maintain confidence.

BANAL BORDERS

In schools around the world, geography and history have often been informed by patriotic ideals. School children are instructed about their national territories and learn more about the formation and evolution of the nation-state. Special events and circumstances might also trigger renewed investment in patriotic education. After the Tiananmen Square protests in 1989, the Communist Party leadership doubled down on public education and nationalism in an attempt to ensure that the country did not get caught up in post-Cold War democratic revolution. Citizens were warned again about the dangers facing China, some of which were to be found in disputed borderlands with India but also a more general medley of international forces seeking to humiliate the country. In nearby Japan, school children still do not get told about the violent legacy of past Japanese occupations of Korea and Manchuria.

Teaching history inevitably involves geography and vice versa. Do children discover about their country's prior record of invading and occupying third parties or not? In Japan they don't learn about their wartime history. Do children learn that their homeland is in fact territorially incomplete? In Argentina, they do learn about British imperialism and the 'theft' of the Falkland Islands. And, finally, do children get to find out more about places where their grandparents might have once been born? In Armenia, children do learn about the Armenian Genocide and the loss of territory to Turkey and the Russian empire. In stark contrast, Turkish textbooks are far more likely to refer to the 1915–16 genocide as the 'Armenian matter' and speak little about the Soviet and Turkish defenestration of Armenia. The word 'genocide' is not be used anywhere, and children are taught that Armenia uses the 'matter' to imperil Turkish territorial integrity and seek financial compensation. Armenian schools operating within Turkey have to use textbooks approved by the Turkish Ministry of National Education. Border education, in short, is a matter of national security.

We can learn a great deal from a country's public education system and its attitude towards national geography and history. Emerging in the nineteenth century from the yoke of the Spanish empire, newly independent nations incorporated remote lands into their own national territory. The national elites had a story to tell their citizens. In Argentina, for instance, newly written history and geography books were telling an extraordinary saga: the country was expanding southwards and westwards and incorporating remote lands such as Patagonia. Military campaigns were making possible the so-called Argentinian 'Conquest of the Desert'. As with the United States, the framing of the country's expansion was highly opportunistic. If the territories were called a 'desert', then it was possible to cultivate a story about an empty space and a frontier-like spirit of engagement. It was a lie and designed to disguise the fact that the territories mapped, surveyed and occupied were not empty at all. They were inhabited by established indigenous communities. The spread of disease and the disruption caused by new soldiers and settlers were devastating. The indigenous communities were wiped out.

The central government in Buenos Aires, eager to ensure that new Argentine citizens, immigrants from Italy, Spain and elsewhere, had a shared sense of their new history and geography, was content to spread 'fake news' about both the country's gains and its losses. That 'lost' territory amounted to the Falkland Islands when the British established a permanent presence in the 1830s. Before the 1830s, an assortment of British, French, Spanish and Argentine communities were stationed there. After the British occupation, Argentine children began to be taught that there was a portion of their country that had been 'stolen' from them.

The 1982 conflict between Britain and Argentina over the Falkland Islands added further to that educational dogma. In more recent times, this has meant that young children are told that their country is also composed of a number of South Atlantic islands and a portion of Antarctica. From an early age, children are expected to be able to draw the country's outline and identify where boundaries lie between neighbours such as Chile and Uruguay. Every citizen should be able to draw an outline of East and West Falkland. The 1994 Argentine constitution reminds citizens yet again that Argentina is an incomplete nation with unsettled borders. The recovery of 'lost territories' is integral to the fulfilment of its national mission. This does not make a new conflict over the Falklands inevitable. What it does ensure is that there is an educational and cultural latency to borders in the country. Any visitor to Argentina will know that maps, stamps, public monuments, murals and posters have a way of broadcasting that basic message – it is a country with unsettled borders.

Argentina is not alone in taking its national territories and disputed borders very seriously. This desire for territorial completeness is ingrained in cultures around the world. Sometimes it is just nostalgic. It is commonplace for states and citizens to hark back to a 'golden era' when the territorial borders extended a great deal further. While Argentina obsesses about 'lost' islands in the South Atlantic, others dream of recapturing an imperial past or simply a time when their country had the epithet 'Greater'.

In Hungary, for example, it is not uncommon to see visual depictions of a 'Greater Hungary' (and there used to be a 'Greater Armenia' as well), a regional area which does not coincide with the formal boundaries of contemporary Hungary. In 1920, the Treaty of Trianon ripped apart the Hungarian element of the Austro-Hungarian empire. The borders of post-1920 Hungary were redefined so that the country shrunk to about a third of its original size. It became land-locked and areas of territory were reallocated to other countries. Millions of ethnic Hungarians were left stranded in states such as Romania. With the 100th anniversary of the treaty imminent, Hungarian nationalists speak of 'lost territories' and lingering national humiliation. Sometimes nationalists even point to national television in Hungary and approve of the use of weather maps that show the prevailing conditions across the wider Carpathian basin. One might do that for entirely understandable reasons such as acknowledging that weather does not respect national boundaries. Weather conditions are also shaped by wider physical geographies such as mountain ranges, continental plains and large water bodies. All of that might not matter to the patriot who just wants to be reminded that their country once prevailed over a far greater territory and might yet do so in the future.

The sociologist Michael Billig wrote in his 1995 book *Banal Nationalism* that nationalism was not merely the preserve of *sensations fortes* – strong feelings. He argues there is another side to nationalism that is more mundane, and part of our everyday lives. He uses the example of the daily weather map on national television to make his point. Weather maps are particularly eye-catching because wind current and rain patterns don't concern themselves with international borders. Talking about 'national weather' is a fiction that might resonate with viewers and listeners, even though we appreciate that we can quickly consult the weather maps for other places within and beyond our immediate milieu. It is worth remembering that Billig was writing at a time when the internet was in its infancy and terrestrial television channels such as the BBC were dominant. Weather maps, as older British viewers will recall, were focused on the British Isles. While weather symbols covered the Republic of Ireland and continental Europe, temperature readings were not shown beyond the UK. It seemed to me at the time a subtle way of recognising the national and transnational qualities of weather. As a British viewer, I could know that it was rainy in Dublin and probably guess the prevailing temperature was close to that of Belfast.

Outside the classroom and beyond the daily weather reports, the banal qualities of borders can be experienced in multiple ways. I recall, for example, my mother returning from a trip to Venezuela in the mid-1990s and showing me a tea towel with the map of the country depicted. On closer inspection, the national border of the country had been extended and covered a great deal of Guyana. The two countries have had a long-running border dispute. In essence, Venezuela believes that its national territory extends all the way to the western side of the River Essequibo. If this was ever to become the new internationally recognised border, Guyana would be drastically reduced. Two-thirds of its land territory would disappear, as well as, crucially, its sovereign rights over the sea. The Venezuelan constitution declares that the republic is composed of a number of administrative divisions and official maps make reference to what is termed officially as a 'zone of reclamation'. Venezuelan school children are taught from a very early age that the continental territory extends further than the official boundary between Venezuela and Guyana: the zone of reclamation (or *Guyana Esequiba* in Spanish) is Venezuelan territory and will eventually be reincorporated into the Bolívar and Delta Amacuro states.

This border dispute has been simmering away since the independence of Guyana from British colonial rule in 1966. Both Guyana and Venezuela even dispute the origins of the border conflict, although they do agree that a river is integral to the its genesis. The River Essequibo was at one stage a major artery for Spanish, Dutch and British colonial trading, and in 1899 a court in Paris issued a decree that awarded the river area to the British empire. Venezuela later challenged the validity of the territorial award but in 1966, under the Geneva Agreement, the Guyanese government was awarded control. Venezuela has never relinquished its claim to sovereignty over what would be the far-eastern portion of its national territory. My mother's tea towel is a good example of this territorial mindset. She purchased it at a time when the two countries were in low-level dispute.

What changed things in the region was the discovery of oil and natural gas. Twenty years on from the earliest musings on banal nationalism, the world is now digital. In 2015, Exxon Mobil declared that it had discovered commercially significant deposits of oil and natural gas in an area that is adjacent to the disputed territory. The Guyanese government approved further drilling licences; the Venezuelans were furious. A banal nationalism was transformed suddenly into hot nationalism. On the other side of the disputed border, Guyanese citizens were sharing stories on social media sites about Venezuelan criminal gangs and acts of murderous ruthlessness against local residents. The border took on heightened significance.

Since the initial discovery, Exxon Mobil and partners have announced further findings with claims that as much as 750,000 barrels of oil per day could be extractable. For a relatively poor nation such as Guyana, oil revenue could be transformative, with billions of dollars entering the government coffers in Georgetown. The population of the country is around 800,000, with GDP estimated to be around $5–6 billion per annum, much of which is based on the export of bauxite, gold and sugar. Oil and gas revenue could double national GDP in the first years alone. The president of Venezuela, Nicolás Maduro, was never shy in mobilising nationalist sentiment against

Guyana, but in 2015 he established the Office for the Rescue of the Essequibo and instructed a former army colonel, Pompeyo Torrealba Rivero, to redouble efforts to 'organise a process to recover that geographical space that belongs to Venezuela'. Educational and public information campaigns were to follow, along with a plan to issue up to 200,000 Venezuelan ID cards to residents on the Guyanese side of the disputed river.

The moral of the tea-towel story here is that a dormant or simmering border dispute can be suddenly transformed into something far more explosive. Opportunistic political leaders keen to stoke nationalist fires will point the finger at opponents and accuse them of land or resource theft. In the case of Guyana, there was some prior evidence for the potential for trouble. As early as 2000, Guyana and Suriname clashed over a maritime border dispute, which was triggered by the positioning of a Guyanese exploration rig. Then, in 2013, a Venezuelan naval vessel clashed with a seismic vessel charted by the Guyanese government. What is interesting about the recent discoveries is that Exxon Mobil and other international partners were able to convince Guyana to continue despite the dispute with Venezuela. Thanks to their technical support, Guyana is now considered to be a world leader in offshore crude oil discovery.

In 2019, Qatar Petroleum and the French company Total acquired new offshore exploration blocks off the coast of Guyana. In a tweet released by Qatar Petroleum on 29 July 2019, the company posted that they had acquired 40 per cent of the share of Total's two blocks. The state-owned oil company added a map to its announcement, which depicted the offshore blocks and highlighted Guyana as the controlling government. No other country was labelled on the map of the northern part of South America. The national boundary of Guyana was clearly depicted but there was no reference to any border dispute with either Venezuela or Suriname. In other words, the geopolitics of a disputed border could be outsourced and performed by others, including foreign investors. The government of Guyana would not have been unhappy with that tweet. Meanwhile, the government in Caracas must have been fuming.

Longer term, it is not hard to imagine the two countries clashing. An indebted and chaotic Venezuela is going to find it hard to accept that Guyana is reaping the rewards of offshore oil and gas in a disputed maritime region. The International Court of Justice will be hearing the case sometime in 2020–1, a move that Guyana has welcomed but Venezuela has not. As of 2020, the US has been more supportive of Guyana, but it will be interesting to see whether Russia gets involved. A highly indebted Venezuela borrowed money from Moscow in 2009 to purchase fighter jets and tanks but struggled to pay back the loan. Venezuela's oil production, in the meantime, has faltered and its international creditors have struggled to get paid. It owes money to China as well as Russia, and the collective debt exceeds $100 billon. Luckily for the country, Russia regards Venezuela as a useful regional ally, hence its willingness to financially support the country as a bulwark against US military and political leverage. All of which makes US support for Guyana more likely and Georgetown all the more confident that it can resist Venezuelan calls for the return of two-thirds of its national territory to a western neighbour.

It is clear, then, that border awareness and conflicts can ebb and flow for a number of reasons, whether there is a shift in business interests, territorial expansion, regional geopolitical dynamics or claims on newfound resources. The 'contested border' is a common concept to most cultures. What is abundantly clear is that the expression of this nationalism is not always banal. As we have seen on countless occasions throughout history, it can become violent, and disputes can endure indefinitely. Two examples in particular loom potently in our collective consciousness.

PARTITION AS PERMANENT BORDER CONFLICT

The partition of British India in August 1947 stands as one of the most dramatic and enduring examples of what happens when borders are imposed on the ground. Described as a late compromise between the relevant parties, the scale and pace of change were electrifying. British India was divided into two constituent parts: a Hindu-majority India and a Muslim-majority Pakistan (composed of West and East Pakistan, the latter renamed Bangladesh, securing its own independence in the early 1970s). While the origins of partition are complicated and mired in controversy, communal violence and political tension, the line on the ground was based on the recommendations of the Boundary Commission led by a British official, Cyril Radcliffe. A distinguished scholar and lawyer, he was given the job following the passing of the Indian Independence Act. He had never been to India and only visited in July 1947 when about to tackle the task in hand.

Radcliffe's Boundary Commission was a comedy of errors. But the legacy was far from amusing. Working with out-of-date maps and fronted by a man who had no formal training in boundary demarcation, the commission was amateurish. Paradoxically, maps and surveys were long regarded by the British as integral to imperial control. Volume 26 of *The Imperial Gazetteer of India*, titled *Atlas*, was one such publication used for those ends. Although Radcliffe was a lawyer, the process of partition would not necessarily have been any better if he had been a trained surveyor or mapmaker instead. The 'facts on the ground' would inevitably make partition a social catastrophe. There was and is considerable linguistic, religious and inter-communal diversity in the region. And although the British were eager to leave in a 'dignified' manner, at a time when the country was bankrupt and exhausted by a brutal world war, Radcliffe was given only five weeks to complete his task. On leaving India, Radcliffe was known to have been well aware that he was bequeathing a terrible legacy for Punjab and Bengal. Worried about his public reputation, Radcliffe destroyed his personal papers.

On the stroke of midnight, 15 August 1947, partition came into force. The line on the map became a line on the ground and provoked mass rioting, migration and immense loss of life. Up and down the new border between independent India and Pakistan, millions of people left one country for another. Muslims travelled to Pakistan and

Hindus, Sikhs and other minorities left for India. Lahore and Amritsar became divided border cities. The death toll resulting from partition is unknown, with estimates varying between hundreds of thousands to several million. Rape and murder were widespread, and the spread of disease accounted for further civilian suffering.

Some parts of India and Pakistan remained bitterly contested, including the Punjab and Kashmir. The first border conflict between India and Pakistan occurred shortly after partition. The high-profile Indian nationalist leader Mahatma Gandhi was assassinated in January 1948, blamed by some Hindu nationalists for giving away too much to the Muslim community. Many refugees thought, incorrectly, that they might even be able to return to their ancestral lands in a calmer post-partition era. Financial compensation or recompense was not forthcoming either.

The 1947 Partition Archive is a non-profit organisation seeking to collect and curate the testimony of survivors of the partition. Professional historians and concerned citizens continue to archive and curate the memories of those termed memorably by the Anglo-Indian writer Salman Rushdie as 'Midnight's Children'. He continues to warn his global readership about Prime Minister Narendra Modi and what he terms the 'unfinished business of partition' – the enactment of an identity politics that uses the 'border wound' as an opportunity to persecute enemies inside and outside the body politic. Born in September 1950, Modi is part and parcel of the Midnight's Children generation.

Thousands of stories on both sides of the borders between India and Pakistan and India and Bangladesh have been recorded and preserved in the archive. It describes the 1947 split as the world's largest mass-refugee crisis. At least 14 million people were directly affected. Each of the witnesses interviewed for the archive has had their migration and resettlement history mapped. In 2017, on the eve of the seventieth anniversary of partition, a large number of testimonies were released for public consumption. Many of the survivors who talked about their memories were young children in 1947. Indian-based oral

historians such as Aanchal Malhotra have highlighted a sense of dis-
belief among those affected:

> You know, people always say in interviews that there was a
> madness in the end. Nobody understood what was happen-
> ing. One day you were in India and the next day it was called
> Pakistan, but you had to leave. I think that the sense of mis-
> information is quite staggering.

In the first few years post-partition, counter-intuitively, the border was
reasonably open to cross-border traffic. Things started to change in
the 1950s as attitudes towards and activities around the partitioned
border hardened. Earlier plans for evacuation and migration control
were overwhelmed by the sheer numbers involved and the outbreaks
of violence. The border was militarised as both countries prepared to
consolidate their national territories. In highly disputed areas such as
Kashmir – a Muslim-majority princely kingdom, the line of partition
in 1947 effectively divided the region into two parts – the international border between the two countries transmogrified into a Line of
Control (LOC) via the 1972 Simla Agreement.

Originally a ceasefire line after several border conflicts, the LOC
is a de facto border. India later constructed a long security barrier
(over 550km/340 miles in length) along the LOC, citing concerns
about terrorist attacks from Pakistan-sponsored separatist militants.
This wall was started in the 1990s and eventually finished in 2004.
Noticeably, India was swift to embrace the War on Terror rhetoric and
argued, as the United States and Israel have done, that it faced ter-
roristic foes. Each of those three countries continues to embrace border walls and associated security projects.

The partitioned border continues to be a source of tension between
India and Pakistan. India has long accused Pakistan of facilitating
Kashmiri separatists. Kashmiri separatists, meanwhile, want to
reunite Kashmir and remove the Indian security forces – a tall order
but one that has become more urgent in the passing years because of

the intensity of the Indian military occupation. Both sides have popular geopolitical cultures, which are highly attuned to border violations and outrages. In February 2019, tension erupted after Indian jets crossed into Pakistani airspace and attacked a camp, which was suspected of housing separatists. This followed an attack on Indian military forces resulting in the death of 40 paramilitary police. Prime Minister Modi is highly nationalistic and seemingly tries to exploit as thoroughly as possible any border crisis. As for the people of Kashmir, a recent UN report made clear that they have suffered widespread human rights violations, much of which implicates the Indian security forces.

Can we be optimistic that this partitioned border won't be the source of future conflict? The answer is no. India and its allies are convinced that Pakistan continues to harbour terrorists and separatists, and India's media continues to report that Pakistan cannot be trusted in relation to terrorism and financial laundering. Pakistan's armed forces are blamed for fermenting aggression against India and for undermining any attempts by India and its allies to secure any geopolitical influence over Afghanistan. At the same time, India is worried about Pakistan's relationship with China. Pakistan has secured funding from China's ambitious Belt and Road Initiative (which provides strategic funding for investment and infrastructure) and is likely to pursue a closer strategic relationship with the country.

The trauma of partition continues. Ceasefire violations are common, with Indian and Pakistani troops firing their guns at one another in sporadic border incidents. Each side counts what it considers to be cross-border ceasefire violations and monitors 'calibre escalation' – in other words, when the encroachment escalates from, say, small-arms fire to a mortar attack and eventually heavy-artillery bombardment. In the first six months of 2019, the Indian government recoded more than 1,500 ceasefire violations. The reality of the border is very different to what tourists might witness at official crossing points. Many residents don't want Kashmir to be split between the two countries and wish for the border region to be demilitarised. What is less clear is what the future will hold – independence, a permanent split between India and Pakistan or some sort of compromise. It is worth remembering that China also occupies a part of Kashmir, so any future outcome is dependent on the realisation that there are three nuclear-armed parties involved in actual and potential border wars. India, for the moment, controls the largest portion of Kashmir.

In the middle of this border complexity, President Trump declared in July 2019 that he had been asked by Prime Minister Modi of India to mediate with Prime Minister Imran Khan of Pakistan. This claim was denied by both nations. India would never agree to third-party mediation on this issue. And China is hardly likely to agree to that proposition either. What we can say is that the partitioned border has the capacity to provoke low-level military tension and even to spark wars. On the other hand, it can also on occasion generate confidence-building measures such as cross-border train and bus services. Despite the latter, both sides remain in the grip of what has been called a 'cartographic anxiety', which makes compromise difficult to imagine.

PARTITION AND THE BORDER AS 'MOVEABLE FEAST'

Partition demonstrates the potent way in which ordinary people are caught up in geopolitical conflict between warring states. Another such situation that continues to dominate the public consciousness can be found in the Israel–Palestine struggle, where border conflict takes on added significance because an entire city lies at the heart of deeply disputed territory. The split city of Jerusalem, at the western edge of the West Bank, is a telling example of how the border dispute has taken hold of everyday and public life between Israel and Palestine. Since the creation of Israel in 1948, the Israeli–Palestine dispute has been extensive and bitter. At present, the Palestinian authorities exercise control over parts of the West Bank and the Gaza Strip. However, the West Bank is also occupied by Israeli settlers, although their presence is judged to be illegal under international law. Up to 400,000 Israelis occupy the West Bank and another 200,000 live in East

Jerusalem. While 2.5 million Palestinians live in the West Bank, the future viability of any independent Palestine will depend in large part on the fate of Jerusalem.

Jerusalem's multi-ethnic and religious character makes it a flashpoint for both sides. Israel and Palestine consider the city to be their respective capital city. In 2017, President Trump declared that the US Embassy to Israel would relocate from Tel Aviv to Jerusalem, and there is speculation that a British government under Boris Johnson might also choose to relocate, while Australia has said it will do so as well. All of which helps to legitimise Israeli claims on Jerusalem at the expense of Palestine. In March 2019, another disputed territory, the occupied Golan Heights (captured from Syria), was recognised as Israeli by President Trump. Recognition by powerful third parties can disrupt the fixed geographies of partition. Political terms such as 'Greater Israel' capture what political geographers term irredentism – a desire to recover either historic and/or desired territories.

For Palestinians, the status of Jerusalem is existential. East Jerusalem is the epicentre for Palestinian hopes for an independent future, as it was the part of the city that was left under Jordanian control following the 1949 armistice between Israel and its neighbours. The Green Line (a term used to reflect lines of demarcation on the map – during the 1949 armistice talks between Israel and its neighbours green ink was used by the negotiators) divided Jerusalem into two parts, the Palestinian East and the Israeli West. The meaning of a line of demarcation here is not the same as a border – its genesis lies in the aftermath of a ceasefire or armistice. In the wider international community, it is not a legally recognised division between two states. This line of demarcation changed again in 1967 when Israel extended its territorial control over areas beyond the 1949 armistice line. After the 1967 Six-day War, Israel occupied the Sinai Peninsula, the Golan Heights and the West Bank. The Sinai was returned to Egypt in 1979 following the agreement of a peace and friendship treaty between Israel and Egypt. Since that point, there have been further territorial readjustments, with a nascent Palestinian authority eager to establish East Jerusalem as its capital.

Since the 2000s, there have been various initiatives to link the recognition of Palestine as an independent nation-state with various agreements between Israel and its Arab neighbours. It is important to recall that Israeli settlement building in the West Bank and East Jerusalem is regarded as illegal under international law. These struggles are not just strictly diplomatic and political in nature. In March 2020, the Palestinian authorities achieved a small but highly significant victory regarding Amazon and its delivery charges. Until that point, Palestinian customers had to pay a delivery charge if they did not declare on their shipping forms that they lived in Israel; while if they selected 'Israel' they qualified for free shipping. Postal services in Palestinian territory are often affected by Israeli security checks and suffer long delays. After being threatened with legal action, Amazon declared that Israeli and Palestinian customers living in the West Bank would be treated on an equal basis. The UN Universal Postal Union reaffirmed that Palestinian citizens should not have their access to postal services interfered with by third parties. The proof in the pudding, however, will be how things operate in practice. The shaming of an American company is, nonetheless, notable.

The status of Jerusalem has proven particularly difficult to resolve because it is caught up in a medley of intricate territorial divisions that affect the West Bank. For critics of Israel, East Jerusalem stands as a poignant example of how border infrastructures can be used to create physical, administrative, military and psychological barriers for Palestinians. The charge sheet is a lengthy one: land has been annexed, the primacy of Israeli planning law, including building regulations, has been asserted, homes have been built by and sold to Israeli settlers, and city boundaries have been manipulated so that the demographic composition of Jerusalem is more securely Israeli. Visitors to Jerusalem will be struck by the proliferation of national flags alongside the coexistence of trilingual signage (English, Arabic and Hebrew) across the city.

Palestinians living in East Jerusalem have been given the status of 'permanent resident', but this means they are subject to greater restrictions. They are not allowed to secure similar permanent residency for family members who were not born in the eastern part of the city, which means that their capacity to buy and inherit property is compromised. Permanent residents choosing to leave the city for whatever reason run the risk of not having their residency renewed. The end result is that the state of Israel stands accused of using the disputed border to generate a confusing and complex infrastructure designed to entrench Israeli dominance.

In recent times, the demolition of homes has been another source of tension between Palestinian and Israeli residents. The Israeli Supreme Court ruled in favour of the decision to destroy homes that were deemed to be built too close to the Israeli security barrier. For Palestinian residents, construction permits can be subject to long delay and thus there is a constant battle between municipal authorities and residents about whether a building is legal or illegal. Everyday life becomes shaped by the negotiation of what is legal or not, what is judged to be too close to the operational security of the Israeli military and where the Israeli security wall is positioned in Jerusalem. In the case of the emotive demolition of the apartment blocks, their location was transformed by the route of the security wall. The placement of the separation barrier was altered in 2003 and ended up incorporating parts of the city that had been under the remit of the Palestinian Authority (PA). Even if residents secured legitimate permits from the PA, they were unwittingly caught up by a demand by the Israeli Defence Forces that residential buildings should be at least 250m away from the barrier for operational security reasons.

The housing demolitions of July 2019 are the latest example of a highly controversial policy, which brings into sharp focus the power of the Israeli state to mobilise planning law, civic authority, military directives and border security. International observers have been critical of the demolition of Palestinian housing, and the United Nations Office for the Coordination of Humanitarian Affairs has produced new maps recording housing destruction, land confiscation and creeping Israeli control in Palestinian Authority-controlled areas. Palestinian residents caught behind the security wall have complained that the de facto border/barrier now means that they live under the threat of their homes being demolished again as well as being isolated from the PA.

While opposition has been expressed to Israeli occupation of East Jerusalem, placing the city under international control is not likely to find any favour with Israel and the PA. The histories of international control of cities such as Berlin and Trieste are not happy ones. Internal opposition and external rivalries soon complicate expressions of earlier optimism. When the Trump administration declared that the US Embassy should move to Jerusalem it did so in part because it ruled out the possibility of the city ever being divided into two parts. Everyday life in Jerusalem, however, is bordered. The old city is home to religious sites of local, national and global importance: the Temple Mount and Western Wall, the Church of the Holy Sepulchre, the Dome on the Rock and al-Aqsa Mosque. Tension has flared up repeatedly over access to religious sites and a new Israeli-run tunnel that runs underneath a Palestinian neighbourhood, opened in July 2019, sparked further controversy.

Israel's border intransigence and infrastructural planning is rooted in a past history of conflict with near neighbours and shaped by a strategic perception that it has contested borders everywhere. For example, it remains locked in a dispute with Lebanon over their shared maritime boundary. Meanwhile, along the Gaza border, Israeli planes use pesticides to destroy cropland and vegetation to ensure that the 'strip' is kept as clear as possible. While the planes operate on the Israeli side of the border, the effects of the herbicide spraying affect Palestinian farmland.

The London-based Forensic Architecture research group and scholars such as Eyal Weizman have been at the forefront of research into the Israeli–Palestinian borderlands. They have also pioneered work using satellite imagery, on-the-ground testimony, in-depth investigation and geo-location tracking to investigate border infractions. Forensic Architecture has developed a website that includes short videos and interactive mapping to trace the ramifications of state-control strategies, which are described as 'conquer and divide'. Indirectly, the work of Forensic Architecture reminds us how

Jerusalem's underground spaces and infrastructure such as roads, buildings, security walls and drainage systems can and do become objects of conflict. The border can affect the air that some communities breathe, it can affect the food consumed, and it can interfere with where and how lives can be lived. Border creep is a reality for many people.

The capacity of cities to become contested and deeply bordered is not unique to this holiest of cities. As humanity becomes ever more urbanised, cities will be flashpoints for conflict and tension. In Jerusalem, access to the city and essential resources such as water reveal how deeply divided the city is for its Palestinian inhabitants. Across the Middle East, not just in the city of Jerusalem, any further population growth will promote more uncomfortable truths.

The border becomes akin to a moveable feast because partition is never straightforward. The lines on the ground that separate opposing communities are never entirely static. Families continue to cross over and trade, and political cooperation ebbs and flows. Dominant parties may wish to press home their post-partition or armistice advantage while weaker parties opt for delaying tactics or disruption to the dominant order of things. All four parties in our examples, Israel, Palestine, India and Pakistan, accuse one another of malfeasance and bad faith along the Green Line and the Line of Control.

THE HUMAN COSTS OF BORDER CONFLICT

Sometimes a border will be recognised by states under duress, but people and communities either side of that border remain dislocated and terrified. For example, members of the Muslim-minority Rohingya community living in Myanmar (formerly Burma) have fled in their hundreds of thousands to neighbouring states as a consequence of repression and violence on behalf of the Myanmar military. Persecuted viciously, they have settled in refugee camps in Thailand and Bangladesh. In November 2017, Bangladesh and Myanmar agreed a repatriation deal whereby refugees would return across the border to Myanmar. Many Rohingya did not wish to return because Myanmar will not recognise their community as an ethnic group deserving of constitutional protection, instead classing them as 'Bengalis' (in other words, foreigners). And those forced to flee are left in a world of painful dislocation and trauma. In December 2019, the International Court of Justice began its preliminary hearings on the fate of those refugees forcibly removed from Myanmar. The court will be given documentary evidence about atrocities carried out by the military forces of Myanmar including mass murder, rape and destruction of community villages.

Contested borders are unsettling and painful. Borders underpin and empower nationalist ideologies and ideas of who belongs and who does not. Radio broadcasts, newspaper columns, creative drama and videos designed for social media platforms, among other things, bombard us with information and opinion about the necessity and wisdom of borders on an almost daily basis. This is popular or even populist geopolitics, because it occurs outside public education and civics lessons. Border stories and television shows are transnational so that viewers around the world can watch, for example, the fictional struggles of the Polish border guard to prevent illegal Ukrainian migrants from crossing into eastern Poland (*The Border*, 2014). These everyday lived and invented experiences reflect a simple reality that borders generate opportunities for some and mortal dangers for others.

Indeed, for all the broader political implications of border conflict, we must not forget the human consequences, the people caught up in the bordering and re-bordering of the world. As we have seen in Partition and in Palestine, lives change dramatically – can even be lost – in ongoing border conflicts. But there are other kinds of human involvement that highlight, for better or worse, the vivid lives lived along border zones.

One case in point is the United States, where borders are more militarised and privatised than ever before. Federal authorities, as the American Civil Liberties Union (ACLU) reminds its supporters, are empowered to carry out searches and investigations at border crossings and ports of entry. This right to search and detain extends some 160km (100 miles) away from international borders and ports of entry such as airports. This extended border zone allows mission creep and encompasses large cities such as Los Angeles, New York and Chicago. It also means that southern states such as Florida are, in effect, an entire border zone. Customs and Border Protection officers can board vessels and vehicles within that zone, as well as establish roving patrols and checks at what are termed 'tactical and permanent checkpoints' as part of their checks on the immigration status of a detained individual or group.

These tensions are felt most strongly, of course, on the US–Mexico border. There are vigilante groups such as the Minuteman Project (formed in 2004) which keep up the pressure on government by maintaining a 'neighbourhood watch'-style border network. Described as an armed militia by some, they might be regarded as patriots by others. The membership, which included a couple of thousand volunteers at its height, continues to cajole federal and state governments to do more to protect the borders. Digital media is now integral to the generation of border news. Minutemen lobby congressional representatives and demand a stronger military presence, an increasing number of walls and barriers, harsher immigration laws and no amnesty for undocumented workers. They also work with foreign news crews to raise the profile of their cause. While the Minutemen are agitating, border towns such as El Paso in Texas are growing. It is a hotspot for migrants from Spanish-speaking Latin America and now record numbers of Brazilian migrants. Young Brazilians are leaving their homeland, just like their Central American counterparts, because of corruption, unemployment and gang-related violence. As migrant numbers grow, others will demand yet more action to stop it.

Harrowing accounts of those seeking to cross over have become commonplace and reflect the contemporary zeitgeist. Fortified borders may deter but they also incentivise risk-tasking and criminality. Refugees from Syria and Afghanistan in particular have shared their stories of how they left war-torn environments, paid people smugglers to take them to Turkey and climbed onboard precarious lifeboats, all in the hope that they would be intercepted by the EU/Greek maritime authorities. The fortunate ones escaped death from drowning and exhaustion and then discovered on arrival at Greek islands such as Samos that their fate was far from being determined. In overcrowded and poorly resourced camps, the refugees had to wait for months for their legal status to be evaluated. Life in the camps has been described as chaotic, unsafe and perilous to both mental and physical wellbeing.

There have also been legal and political battles worldwide involving those who seek to help. The humanitarian aid worker Scott Warren from Arizona was arrested in January 2018 for offering food and shelter to two migrants from Central America. His defence was simply that offering humanitarian aid should not be considered a crime. He faced several trials and eventually received a not guilty verdict from a federal courthouse jury. Had he been found guilty of harbouring and conspiracy charges he would have faced a jail sentence approaching some 20 years. What the trial proceedings revealed was how differently the border was framed by prosecutors and defendant lawyers. While Warren's legal consul emphasised humanitarianism, border-patrol officers were talking of the border as their 'areas of responsibility' with corresponding 'data points' for surveillance.

The Warren case exposed the complex web of emotions and interests at play. Borders are not only about walls, fences and surveillance. They also encompass the legal and political systems that enable and enforce borders. Borders involve, moreover, fundamental human encounters and will continue to do so as long as governments around the world pursue ambitions to seal off and repel. The urge of humanity to move will not be deterred and global drivers such as climate change will ensure that the fight for mobility justice – the stopping of discrimination in relation to the control of movement on ethnic/racial, religious or social grounds – will not abate.

More and more people around the world will push back against the proposition that it should be the wealthiest and most privileged scions of humanity who get to decide who moves when and where.

Even in the midst of 'lockdown' and border closures during the COVID-19 pandemic, there have been extraordinary stories of the super-rich attempting to use their private jets to fly to their second homes in overseas locations. In one infamous case, a multinational group of passengers on a private jet were detained at Marseille-Provence airport in France in April 2020. Three helicopters were waiting apparently to ferry the group to a holiday villa on the French Riviera. French police ordered the group to return to London, their original port of departure.

The super-rich are an extreme example of the way in which some communities can escape border conflict; at the other end of the spectrum, the most vulnerable are likely to be adversely affected. What is the future for Sea-Watch, the German-based group that has been locked in legal disputes with EU member states such as Italy about the legality of humanitarian assistance on the high seas of the Mediterranean? In December 2019, after six months of detention by the Italian authorities, their ship the *Sea-Watch 3* was finally released after the group won their appeal in an Italian court, a decision that was deeply unpopular with the government of Giuseppe Conte, which has expressed considerable unhappiness over the migrant burden being carried by Italy. Then, in January 2020, the Italian Supreme Court ruled that the captain of a ship effecting a rescue of migrants in the Mediterranean should not have been arrested by the Italian authorities. The COVID-19 pandemic will surely heighten the desire of coastal authorities to prevent the landing of irregular migrants, as public health measures add further cost and complexity to host countries. There is no obvious humanitarian dividend for desperate migrants, many of whom will decide that it is still worth risking their lives to escape an insecure or dangerous environment.

Before the pandemic we might have focused on transit countries such as Libya, which have been declared 'unsafe' by the UN High Commissioner for Refugees (UNHCR), and so the question becomes: can it be illegal for someone to offer humanitarian assistance in the midst of the Mediterranean and then seek a safe port of entry? The EU is trying to prevent those migrants and refugees from leaving Libya in the first place. The need to ensure the public health of EU citizens will compete with an international humanitarian imperative. The end result is likely to be that borders will tighten and receiving states such as Italy and Spain, which have been hard hit by the pandemic, will be even more unwilling to accommodate refugees and migrants.

All over the world, there are examples that exemplify the human costs of borders, some of which may not be disputed in the sense that states recognise lines on the map and ground as legitimate. What we are witnessing is the capacity of border conflict and tension to generate a myriad of human misery and desperation. In terms of human costs, migrants and refugees are discovering first-hand what happens when the authorities in control of your intended destination don't want you there. The machinery of the state is put to work, and it is wide ranging from outright military aggression to legal and administrative deadweight, which simply grinds down all but the most determined and resourceful. In open water and betwixt the border lines, there are examples of individuals and organisations trying to intervene in order to provide humanitarian assistance. Their very acts, in so doing, strike back at those who would wish to desist and deter. Somewhere in between there lies a medley of chancers and charlatans seeking to inflame, provoke and profiteer.

NEW BORDERS AND OCEAN GRABBING

For all the attention given to border walls and security fencing on land and sea-based encounters between migrants and national navies, the next generation of border security and surveillance is increasingly going to take place underwater in the world's oceans and seas. As will be discussed in more detail in Chapter 3, international maritime law and conventions provide a framework for dividing the world's seas and oceans into distinct zones. At surface level, this means that national coastguards and navies patrol their territorial waters and oversee fishing and other activities such as oil and gas exploration. What legal frameworks cannot necessarily do is keep pace with drivers of change, such as ocean warming, and how this creates challenges. In this instance conflict is likely, as local fishing communities cross maritime borders in search of alternative fishing grounds and national governments accuse their counterparts of doing too little to prevent ocean acidification, over-fishing and environmental degradation.

Below the surface things gets even murkier. During the Cold War it was common for US and Soviet nuclear submarines to enter one another's territorial waters on spying missions. The world has, however, moved on since that depicted in Tom Clancy's *The Hunt for Red October* (published in 1984 and followed by a film version in 1990). Novel technologies will make previously remote underwater spaces more accessible and exploitable. The world's seabed is integral to global communication networks – cables literally lie on top of the seabed and as they approach the coastline they are buried beneath the surface to avoid being snagged by fishing vessels and ship anchors. There are nearly 400 submerged cables, which carry 95 per cent of all data traffic between the continents, and China is becoming a major subsea cable provider through Huawei Marine Networks. Subsea cables are regarded by all states and corporate actors such as Google as critical infrastructure but are vulnerable to human and physical damage. And protecting sub-sea power and communication cables from accidental damage (e.g. typhoons) and sabotage (e.g. divers cutting cables) is of paramount importance to coastal states, and the wider international community.

The Pacific Ocean will be a major area of contention, with small island states not likely to ever match the capabilities of large powers such as China and the United States. Much of the Pacific Ocean is counted as international waters, giving opportunities for great powers to profiteer and interfere. Beyond 200 nautical miles (370km), plus what are termed exclusive economic zones, the sovereignty of coastal states diminishes as international waters take over. Protecting underwater borders is difficult and expensive and beyond the reach of small island states, who face their own existential dilemmas regarding sea-level rise. For larger and richer countries, a new generation of underwater sensors in combination with improvements in remote-operating technologies and drones mean that a country's capacity to act is being greatly enhanced. Traditionally, smaller states such as the Maldives have long been worried about protecting their fishing interests in their exclusive economic zones. Exploiting resources on the seabed depended on third-party involvement.

What is happening at present is a technological 'arms race' between the United States and China. China's underwater technology capacity is not beholden to international suppliers. New Chinese companies such as Tianjin Sublue Ocean Science and Technology are being actively supported by Beijing as part of a deliberate strategy to indigenise capacity under the banner 'Made in China 2025'.

New developments in China include ambitious underwater glider programmes, with a new generation of vehicles credited with ultra-low acoustic signatures. These gliders are small, about 2m (6 feet) in length, highly agile and capable of mapping and surveying underwater environments. The Chinese gliders are currently in use in highly sensitive regions of the world, including the Luzon Strait, a body of water between the Philippines and Taiwan. Shipping and submarine telecommunication cables are to be found in the waters and on the seabed respectively. It is a vital sea corridor and countries such as the Philippines are not in a position to contest Chinese maritime dominance.

Western military analysts have spoken about China's 'great wall at sea' and suggested that the next generation of autonomous underwater robots (AURs) will extend the depth and reach of the country in disputed waters in the South China Sea and the world's oceans. It has been reported that these AURs can operate in very deep waters and are designed for resource exploration and extraction of seabed minerals and sub-sea surveillance. If Chinese fishermen catch underwater drones in their fishing nets, they encouraged by cash rewards, up to the equivalent of US $10,000, to hand in the drones to the Chinese police and coastguard authorities. Media reported that the captured devices were capable of collecting information about ship movements and detecting submarines, and the state media agency, Xinhua, accused rival powers of elaborate plans to spy on China. The provenance of the foreign devices was not directly revealed, but three countries would seem to be the most likely culprits: Japan, Taiwan and the United States.

The western Pacific will also be an area of future tension. In July 2019, it was announced that the US Navy had awarded a $1 billion contract to two electronics companies to build and deliver more than 930,000 sonar buoys. The buoys are designed to not only detect third-party underwater vessels but also to transmit audio information to US submarines and ships. The detection system is being developed for the coastal waters of the United States and open ocean. The sonar buoys are airdropped and designed to be expendable. The challenge for defence planners in the future is to have at their rapid disposal a capability to detect ultra-quiet submersibles, supported by a network of underwater drones carrying out surveillance and information-collecting activities. While the underlying technology has been around for some time, what is striking is that demand has spiked in recent years as Russia, China and India have modernised and expanded their naval capabilities.

It is not inconceivable, then, that China and the United States will become engaged in underwater drone wars. Both countries will battle it out for control of the world's oceans and seas in the future. International law allows for third parties to conduct activities in other country's exclusive economic zones provided they don't interfere with the rights of coastal states to carry out their own activities. It leaves plenty of scope for geopolitical drama and role play. In disputed waters, the opportunities for mischief making increase markedly. China's kidnapping of a US underwater drone in December 2016 in the South China Sea might well be a sign of the coming times. The drone was snatched because China was concerned that the US was using the technology to spy on Chinese surface and underwater vessel activities. It might also have been taken to embarrass President-elect

Trump after he spoke to the president of Taiwan via telephone, a diplomatic move that China, which claims Taiwan as part of its territory, would have regarded as provocative. Whatever the motivation, we might well see not just drone wars but rival underwater mining projects in disputed spaces judged to be profitable by China and the United States.

As Chapter 3 details, a new scramble for underwater resources is likely, with the nightmarish prospect of major powers – and possibly non-state actors – using underwater drones and unmanned vehicles to destroy underwater critical infrastructure while simultaneously prospecting for mineral potential in the deep ocean. Repairing communication cables in the deep ocean is expensive and highly disruptive to affected communities.

In this first chapter, I have sought to demonstrate that the exploration of border matters is a diverse field of enquiry. We started with fences, walls and barriers and ended with underwater drones and new resource scrambles on the seabed. Human history is filled with examples of borders and barriers designed to protect against perceived threats as well as demarcate national territories and communal identities, demonstrating that the border can act as a geographical and cultural sealant. While borders cut across land and sea, the routes that they follow are integral to how nations and their citizens are positioned as an 'imagined community', using Benedict Anderson's framing in his book *Imagined Communities* (1983). Public education and medias around the world help to reproduce those bordered framings and play their part in inflaming perceived injustices and wrongdoing. For those experiencing the reality of partition and disputed borders, 'the border' matters because it is so integral to everyday life and future life chances. Countless lives have been lost over borders and border crossings can represent a last-ditch attempt by many to escape areas of the world where those borders don't protect but simply entrap. Now we have explored the wide boundaries of border studies, we will look at the changing shape of our physical world, and how this further complicates – and will continue to complicate – our borders.

Pakistani Army soldiers walk down to their command centre from a forward observation post, using rope lines for safety, on a spur of the Siachen Glacier at 18,655 feet on June 19, 2005 in what is considered part of the Northern Territories of Pakistan. The Siachen Glacier is highly disputed with India.

Chapter 2

Moving Borders

MOUNTAINOUS REGIONS HAVE PROVEN ELUSIVE AND FRUSTRATING FOR those charged with mapping, surveying and defining national or imperial borders. In British India, for example, it took years to map, survey and mark up the complex mountain regions. Carried out by imperial survey organisations, the aim was to leave cairns and trigonometric points on the ground in order not only to do the surveying work but also to act as physical memorials to British imperial sovereignty. The Great Trigonometrical Survey of India started in 1802 and concluded in 1871. Hundreds of people were involved in the formal surveying, which was not comprehensive even after 70 years of effort.

Following the professional career of a surveyor such as Sir Thomas Holdich (1843–1929) provides rich insights into the trials and tribulations of those entrusted with border demarcation. As a sometime Superintendent of Frontier Surveys in British India (1892–8), Holdich worked in the high-altitude environments of India, Afghanistan, Persia (now Iran), Argentina and Chile. He served on a variety of boundary commissions and was notably appointed by the governments of Argentina and Chile to help resolve their common boundary along the mountains and glaciers of the Andes. As he wrote in his book, *Political Frontiers and Boundary Making* (1916):

> Boundaries are the inevitable product of advancing civilisation; they are human inventions not necessarily supported by nature's dispositions, and as such they are only of solid value so long as they can be made strong enough and secure enough to prevent their violation and infringement.

He believed that whatever the determination of surveyors, borders needed to be defensible. If that failed then it was highly likely that they would become a source of contention in the future.

Mountains, Holdich thought, offered a straightforward opportunity to use 'natural borders' to establish the boundaries between northern India and neighbours such as Afghanistan. As he noted in his 1916 treatise, the Himalayas were exemplary in this regard:

> The Himalaya are the finest natural combination of boundary and barrier that exists in the world. It stands alone. For the greater part of its length only the Himalayan eagle can trace it. It lies amidst the eternal silence of vast snowfields and icebound peaks ... You would realise then that never was such a God-given boundary set to such an impressive and stupendous frontier.

With limited maps, surveys and no clear boundary lines, the idea that the mountain range might be a natural boundary marker was an appealing one.

As the published and unpublished accounts of surveyors and mapmakers in the nineteenth and early twentieth centuries often revealed, however, high-altitude mountain environments stretched the physical and scientific capabilities of the men and their instruments. Unlike Holdich's eagle, there were no opportunities to float above those mountain ridges and glaciated environments. Aerial surveys arrived at the tail-end of Holdich's life, in the late 1920s. But even then, flying in high-altitude environments was rarely straightforward, with the 'view from the air' compromised, at times, by inclement weather and prevailing cloud cover. Fundamentally, drawing border lines on paper involved a great deal of taxing work: establishing trigonometric points, erecting cairns and border pillars, and ensuring that your survey data was safely stored on returning to headquarters.

As border work took on ever greater importance in the postcolonial and independence era, geographer Richard Hartshorne posed an important question in his essay 'The Nature of Geography' (1939):

> Upon what basis then can we divide the intrinsically complex and indivisible world? One thing is clear; we can distrust from the start any simple solution. We are not looking for the one true method of division since there can be none; we are looking for a more or less suitable method.

Eighty years later, there would be few boundary/border experts who would disagree with the premise of the question. It has been answered over the years by technical, legal and political work.

While it made sense for many countries eager to establish their international boundaries to rely on mountains and other natural borders between two states, it also reflected a time when the presence of humans and their impact on landscapes were lower. Nowadays mountains and the resources they contain, in the form of glaciers and meltwater, are widely acknowledged to be integral to national security, and water supply and hydropower generation are vital for many countries that contain mountain ranges within their territories. But diminishing ice puts all of that in jeopardy and has also made landscapes more prone to flash-flooding, landslides and avalanches. Water infrastructure can end up being destroyed by mudslides, which can in turn affect water supply to downstream communities. The implications of this are profound because some 2 billion people directly depend on glacial water supplies around the world. The physical landscape is on the move, and what was once fixed has now become a source of contention and potential conflict.

DIVIDING UP HIGH PLACES

It is often in the world's remotest regions where the theory and practice of border demarcation and delimitation is put under the most severe stress. Demarcation as discussed here is the technical term used to refer to the physical marking of a boundary line on the ground via cairns, boundary pillars and cleared tracks of land – the kind of thing that the British were doing across the Indian subcontinent in the nineteenth century. Delimitation, on the other hand, is the legally binding description of the boundary, expressed via a treaty, map and/ or geographical coordinates. The officially recognised border depends upon demarcation and delimitation being aligned with one another.

Demarcation enables delimitation and vice versa. One common problem with mountains, therefore, is that border treaties and agreements contain details about delimitation but often in the absence of ground-level demarcation. Positional disputes are legion. Impromptu no man's lands emerge as a consequence of disputes over border demarcation and landscape change such as landslides, glacial melt and permanent snow-cover loss. In highly tense regions the scope for low-intensity and resilient conflict is immense. In the Chiatibo glacier region, which forms part of the poorly delimitated Pakistan–Afghanistan border, the Pakistan Army continues to battle a mixture of al-Qaeda and Taliban forces.

Using the natural watershed often made sense for those charged with boundary delimitation in mountainous regions. The watershed of a mountain is the area which collects snow and/or rain. The boundary of the watershed would be commonly defined as the watershed divide, a ridge or hill that distinguishes between a watershed on one side of the mountain and its opposite number. It separates and identifies drainage basins, areas of land where water and ice flows into a common outlet such as a river system. But snowfields and glaciers can complicate how borders get imposed. Ridges and glaciers appear and disappear. Natural watersheds might alter radically, revealing previously concealed ridges and presenting opportunities for new border demarcation. Countries might decide that the border has 'moved' and worry that a third party is seeking to gain some kind of territorial and resource advantage.

They can even generate squabbles over what those high places might contain. In September 1991, two German tourists discovered the remarkable remains of a man believed to have lived around 5,000 years ago. Nicknamed Ötzi because he was found in the Ötztal Alps on the Italian–Austrian border, the body was extracted from the ice and taken to Innsbruck in Austria. The location of the body, however, was not free from controversy. For that part of the Italian–Austrian border, the boundary line was defined as the watershed of two rivers, the Inn and the Etsch (known as the Adige in Italy). What made things more difficult was that the boundary line had shifted since the original treaty of 1918 because of glacial retreat. It was later established that the body was actually some 90m (295 feet) on the Italian side of the shared border. After some legal wrangling, the Italian province of South Tyrol successfully secured Ötzi and the mummified figure is now displayed in Bolzano at the Museum of Archaeology.

With glaciers and ice fields in retreat around the world due to global warming, the scale and rapidity of change in high-altitude environments is monitored in a way that surveyors such as Thomas Holdich could not have even imagined. While he did write about eagles floating high above the mountains, it would have required a remarkable leap in imagination to think that the eagle's eye would be supplanted by aerial surveying and later satellite photography. US satellite imagery from the Cold War is now being used by researchers to show that around 600 glaciers in the Himalayas are melting twice as fast as they were around the year 2000. As glaciers retreat, exposed ground gets colonised by plants and mountains turn green rather than white. At the same time, nations around the world worry about the long-term security of their remotest territories.

If natural environments are changing, then the borders that divide them are also going to change. As a consequence, melting and glacial retreat have done little to alleviate long-held fears that opposing sides will compromise any advantage they might have acquired. The experiences of Indian and Pakistani soldiers in the high-altitude environment of the Siachen glacier demonstrate the human costs of preventing the border from moving. Many serving personnel have lost their lives due to the effects of exposure to cold and high-altitude conditions, including devastating avalanches.

STUCK ON A BORDER

Elevated terrain has long been recognised as strategically advantageous. Height offers not only enhanced situational awareness but also potential control over accessibility and the movement of people and goods. In mountainous areas of the world, however, these advantages can become less obvious once you begin to factor in other concerns such as coldness, darkness, and the cumulative effects of altitude on the body and machinery. Mountaineers speak of the 'death zone' once one exceeds 8,000m (26,000 feet) above sea level but even before such heights have been scaled, the effects of cold and lower levels of oxygenated air are sapping. All of which might make the decision by Indian troops to seize control of the inaccessible and high-altitude Siachen glacier in April 1984 surprising.

Located in the Karakoram mountain range, it is the world's highest battlefield. Nearly 80km (50 miles) long, the glacier extends some 5,700m (18,700 feet) above sea level at what is called Indira Col and eventually descends to around 3,600m (11,800 feet). The geographical significance of the region was first recognised by British imperial surveyors at the turn of the twentieth century. The summit of the Siachen glacier was regarded as the northern boundary between British India and what is now southern China. At the time, British officials actually thought that they had established a boundary line that rewarded their mapping endeavours by 'giving' them control over mountains and river systems.

For over 30 years, Indian armed forces have occupied the glacier because it is located close to the Chinese border and is at the northern point of the Line of Control marker NJ9842. The point is significant because it is the last demarcation of the LOC agreed upon as part of the 1972 Simla Agreement between India and Pakistan. The agreement firmed up the ceasefire line between the two sides, after their earlier border skirmishes in the 1960s and the fallout from the 1971 Indo-Pakistani War. The Siachen glacier was not included in the LOC demarcation because it was considered to be too remote and inaccessible. The LOC just notes that it extended 'and thence north to the glaciers'. For the first ten years, between 1972 and 1982, India in particular did not worry unduly about the 'ceasefire line' north of NJ9842. Siachen and the Saltoro Mountains were no man's lands. The glaciers were simply assumed to be an impassable geographical barrier.

All of this was to change because of a chance encounter in the late 1970s involving a German mountaineer, a map and an Indian army colonel who was in charge of the army's mountain-warfare school. Colonel Narendra Kumar examined the US-produced map of northern Kashmir and discovered that foreign mapmakers had placed the ceasefire line between India and Pakistan further east than he expected. What alarmed him, and later the government of India, was that a line that had been left unstipulated by the 1972 Agreement was now imprinted on a map. Pakistan appeared to be the 'winner' in this impromptu demarcation of territory. Somewhere along the line it had become a cartographic convention elsewhere in the world to extend the line of control to the Karakoram Pass. Fearing the consequences of this publicly available map, Kumar's superiors ordered an expedition to be launched to ensure that Pakistan had not claimed territory north of the Line of Control.

There are further stories of other European mountaineers and tourists who had their maps inspected by Indian officials, which created an 'evidence trail' of how the Indo-Pakistani border was being identified. The message these maps told remained the same: they were not sympathetic to India's geopolitical and strategic interests. While it was not uncommon for India and Pakistan to publish their own maps depicting favourably their respective national territories, the US map caused particular alarm because it had been created by an influential third party. During the Cold War, Pakistan was a close military ally of the United States. At that time, China and Pakistan also had an agreement with one another over their border along the Karakoram, including a segment of the Siachen glacier region. China entered into agreement with Pakistan in 1963 and treated the latter as the de facto power. The border was not only identified in the text of the agreement, with reference to a network of mountain peaks and passes, but it also shifted sovereign authority over the territory to Pakistan. This mattered because the agreement made explicit reference to dispute mechanisms and parties of control.

This chance encounter highlighted the geopolitical importance of mountaineers and their expeditionary movements. Geopolitical analysts refer to 'oro-politics', a portmanteau term derived from the Greek for mountain (*oros*) and politics. The term was coined by an Indian mountain historian called Joydeep Sircar, who alerted his audience in 1982 that mountaineering was being used for strategic purposes. Writing in the *Telegraph* of Calcutta (now Kolkata), Sircar warned that mountaineering expeditions and maps of high-altitude regions were being used to shift the Line of Control in northern Kashmir. Climbing expeditions depended upon local authorities from Afghanistan, India, China, Nepal and Pakistan issuing permits to foreign climbers, and in doing so they were exercising a form of sovereign control over disputed territories. Those expeditions were often multinational and thus other countries were implicitly allowing their citizens to traverse mountains that might be fiercely contested. At the same time, as the British demonstrated with the ascent of Everest (named after the surveyor Sir George Everest, who was one of the superintendents responsible for the Survey of India's Great

Trigonometrical Survey in the nineteenth century), mountain climbing was also integral to expressions of national pride.

From the Indian point of view, the most alarming development was Pakistani-approved mountain expeditions. Pakistan had worked out that it was cheaper and arguably more effective to let foreign mountaineers do the geopolitical work for them. In the 1970s, they even incentivised high-altitude climbing still further by reducing the 'climbing fees' for those planning on ascending beyond 6,000m (19,700 feet). Every time a mountaineer climbed the Siachen glacier, or anywhere else in the disputed mountainous regions of South Asia, India worried that others would think of that glaciated environment as falling under the control of Pakistan and not India. The Line of Control was in danger of becoming a de facto border in its northern reaches.

Colonel Kumar and his team were ordered to launch an Indian Army expedition (disguised as a civilian expedition) in 1978. Kumar noted that there was no shortage of evidence of prior mountaineering: discarded rubbish. Three years later, he was ordered to carry out an extensive survey of the glacier. The expedition provoked Pakistan to issue a protest note, warning India to keep away from the Siachen glacier. In the meantime, Kumar published his findings in a mountain magazine, and specialist publications such as that one became another method of imposing geopolitical influence.

By the early 1980s, it was obvious to both sides that the Line of Control beyond NJ9842 was too important to leave to proxy parties such as foreign mountaineers. Having stocked up with gear at the same mountain clothing store in London, India and Pakistan were both ready to act. In Kumar's recollections, India decided that it needed to move swiftly and in 1984 dispatched another military expedition to the Siachen glacier. Operation Meghdoot used army helicopters to deploy forward-operating troops. They occupied the high ground and the all-important Saltoro Ridge, and a Kumar base was established. Despite a Pakistani counter-mission, the Indian troops were not dislodged.

The cost of maintaining the Indian military presence is now estimated to run to £400 million per year, and the extreme conditions are still testing to human health and wellbeing. In one disastrous year, in 2012, an avalanche swept through a Pakistani base and killed around 140 soldiers. It remains a dangerous and expensive operating environment. The entrenched nature of the conflict is an indication of what is at stake for both sides. Once India regained the upper hand, the incentive for it to shift was, in strategic terms, minimal, and the military lockdown of the area became semi-permanent.

India is unlikely to move from the Siachen glacier because the area is still coveted by Pakistan and China. The 1963 border agreement between China and Pakistan is a perennial complicating factor. In all three countries, maps of national territory assume considerable importance, and all three are prone to what has been termed 'cartographic anxieties', whereby domestic and rival maps can prompt nationalistic pride and unleash militaristic posturing. In terms of the Siachen glacier, India wants what it describes as the Actual Ground Position Line (AGPL) recognised on all maps of the region. On the other hand Pakistan, understandably, does not want the AGPL to be naturalised, because it wishes to move the de facto border. Despite successive rounds of diplomatic negotiations, no one expects the Indian Army to budge from its position any time soon.

Remote and inaccessible environments, such as the Siachen glacier, are also capable of generating a popular geopolitics of border nationalism. In India and Pakistan, films and television shows depict the heroic role of the border guard. It is not uncommon for Pakistan to ban the public screening of Bollywood films that address their shared border conflicts or reference any tension in Kashmir and the Himalayas. In February 2019, after yet another border skirmish, the film ban was imposed again.

Meanwhile, as one side wants the Line of Control to move and the other wants it to remain in place, the environmental and human consequences of this impasse are considerable. Environmental campaigners have drawn attention to the toxic legacies of the military occupation and proposed a trans-boundary peace park for the glacier, which would facilitate a clean-up operation alongside demilitarisation. However, there is little sign of any basic shift in strategic posture.

In 2019, India took a new order of Chinook helicopters to improve its capacity to move military supplies to those stationed on the Siachen glacier, after facing public criticism that it was not doing enough to ensure the wellbeing of its mountain troops.

Peace parks have been tried before on glaciers and mountains. From the US–Canadian border to the Cordillera del Condor transboundary protected area between Peru and Ecuador, there are over 100 examples. Often located in remote and inaccessible regions of the world, where borders are disputed and/or poorly defined, the logic of the peace park is straightforward: demilitarise the region, establish confidence-building mechanisms and promote cross-border cooperation in areas such as science and tourism. A similar idea might be to declare the Siachen glacier a World Heritage Site. But don't hold your breath: the Siachen glacier still retains a considerable grip on the collective imaginations of millions of South Asian citizens. Defensible borders matters and 'moving borders', in the sort of collaborative mode provided for by a peace park or World Heritage Site, is not something that territorial rivals want.

MOVING BORDERS

The post-unification history of Italy's Alpine border is varied: the mutual border with Switzerland was fixed in 1861; the shared border with Austria owes a great deal to the post-war settlement of 1919; and the Italian–French border changed after the Second World War. The Italian–Slovene border, meanwhile, mirrored that of the one agreed with the former Yugoslavia, a Cold War adversary. These changes due to post-war settlements notwithstanding, the Alpine border has more or less followed as a principle the natural watershed across the mountain ranges, along which it is estimated there are over 8,000 boundary markers, although some of the border is unmarked because it traverses snowfields and perennial glaciers. All of which would seem to be of lessening importance in a post-Cold War era in which there is no longer a shared border with communist

Yugoslavia and all Italy's neighbours are either EU members or closely associated with it in the case of European Free Trade Association member Switzerland.

Then, in the course of the last decade, a remarkable project by three Italian scholars, Marco Ferrari, Elisa Pasqual and Andrea Bagnato, discovered that the apparently natural border between Italy and its Alpine neighbours was on the move, with accelerating glacial shrinkage having an increasingly significant effect on the physical geographies of the border landscapes. By consulting nineteenth-century maps, campaign diaries, twentieth-century aerial surveys and photographs, the noted shifts were stark. Their aptly named project, Limes (Latin for frontier), began monitoring ecological change in the mountainous Italian–Austrian border in the spring of 2016. Having installed ground sensors, the team proceeded to record changes in the altitude of the watershed. As the latter shifted due to changes in ice and snow cover, so the border moved up and down and backwards and forwards as erosion took its toll on the prevailing landscape. Operating at over 3,100m (10,000 feet), access to the monitoring sites was severely restricted and only possible when it was safe to fly in a helicopter.

Glaciated landscapes can slip and reveal new features as ice and snow retreat or disappear, and this retreat was a catalyst for permanent landscape transformation. The old markers of the border, a matrix of ridges and watershed, were no longer performing their role. The Limes project used the sensor data to construct a real-time border line between Italy and Austria. It reaffirmed earlier work done via a ground survey, which was carried out by the Italian military in the 1990s. While they started to chart the scale of change at mountain level, the Limes project continued in more detail around Mount Similaun. Elsewhere in the Alps, at the Ubelalferner glacier (also known as the Ebeltal glacier), where the Austrian–Italian border extends to some 3,000m (around 10,000 feet) above sea level, ice melt exposed a new ridgeline, offering, as a consequence, opportunities to recalibrate the shared border.

In this way, the border is not permanently fixed. It moves backwards and forwards, depending on the height and extent of glaciers. As glaciers retreat and shrink, territories become bordered not by ice but by rocky outcrops such as mountain ridges. Depending on the physical geographies of Alpine environments, these shifts result in territorial gain for some and loss for others. Climate change in the European Alps will, therefore, determine the future size of Italy and its neighbours.

A heatwave in 2003 was also blamed for unprecedented snow-cover loss and permafrost thawing. Landslips were common at the time, and above freezing temperatures were recorded above 4,000m (13,000 feet) altitude. European Alpine glaciers lost an unprecedented amount of ice volume. The legacy of the heatwave was profound, with Swiss and Italian glaciologists warning that thousands of Alpine glaciers would disappear by the late twenty-first century. The natural boundary that was the mountain remains, but it is being forever changed by warming, melting, flooding and slipping terrain. Iconic areas such as the area around the Matterhorn were also found to be affected by the shifting border.

Since then, this and other mountain borders in the region have been subject to near-constant surveillance. GPS technologies have been established along the shared borders to provide terrain monitoring. The Italian Institute of Military Geography has assumed responsibility for this activity, and their GPS probes have revealed how the border 'moves' as watershed geometry undergoes change. The surveyors have discovered that the border moves by several metres, and sometimes by much more, depending on seasonal variations in snow cover and the ice volume of glaciers.

The news that Alpine borders were changing due to ongoing climate change, and corresponding shrinkage of glaciers and permanent snow cover, inspired legislative action. In 2006, the Italian and Austrian governments agreed to enshrine in law the concept of the 'moving border'. This was followed by a similar agreement with Switzerland in 2009. However, the concept of the 'moving border' is not free from the potential for geopolitical controversy. Depending on the long-term impact of climate change, a more nationalist or populist government might decide that the glaciers have to be 'saved'. Stories about territorial loss can quickly transform into existential angst that a country might be disappearing at the expense of its neighbours. It is not inconceivable that in the future countries could decide to invest heavily in the machines often used by ski resorts to preserve ice and snow for the forthcoming skiing season. Imagine a scenario whereby a country literally blankets a glacier (this has already been done by the Swiss on their Rhône glacier) and supplies artificial snow in an attempt to prevent a glacier from retreating and disappearing. While it might not result in armed conflict, resource-rich nations might decide that their glaciated landscapes are deserving of thermal engineering and even military protection.

For many countries, ice is a strategic commodity. It is easy to forget that for centuries ice harvesting and transportation was a global industry and highly lucrative for suppliers such as Norway. Stored ice played a crucial role for food preservation and water supply, and it was also a source of cooling in the hot summer months. Domestic fridges and freezers might have put paid to the ice trade of the nineteenth and twentieth centuries, but mountainous environments are still hugely important to the economies of many countries around the world. Geopolitically, the edge of countries, even in the remotest parts of the world, matters greatly. A 'moving border' can quickly turn into something that is securitised and militarised. And as Italy, Switzerland and Austria have recognised, it requires formal legal attention as well. When terrain changes, borders will inevitably be affected.

BORDERING MOUNTAINS

The collective contribution of glaciers to human civilisation is primarily in the form of supply of seasonal meltwater. Every spring and summer, glaciated regions around the world undergo melt. Meltwater replenishes rivers and streams, facilitating agriculture and supplying downstream communities with precious water supplies. Meltwater, while crucial to human and other living communities, can also be dangerous. Every season, there are peak flows from glaciers, and glacial shrinkage can paradoxically produce abnormal meltwater bursts, which happen when meltwater starts to build up at the terminal point of glaciers and forms lakes that sit behind what are known as terminal moraines. These act as natural dams that can burst when the volume of water exceeds the dams' capacity to hold it. The results can lead to devastating flooding and landslides. As warming temperatures cause glacial disruption, downstream communities face a double-edged hazard: too much water in the form of meltwater flooding and, over time, less meltwater flow as the glacier shrinks in volume.

China has experienced a marked increase in glacial bursts in areas such as the River Yarkand. With its origins in the Xinjiang autonomous region, the river is a geopolitically sensitive one for China. Beijing exercises an iron-grip on the Muslim Uighur population, while maintaining a careful watch over a territorial region that borders disputed areas with India. It is an oil- and gas-producing region and it is highly productive in terms of agriculture. China could, therefore, be faced with humanitarian crises in the future, as thousands of people decide that their lives have been rendered impossible due to devastating flooding and extensive periods of drought in the region.

Glacial recession is expected to worsen in the mid-twenty-first century. As a consequence of global population distribution and density, the fate of the glaciated regions such as the Himalayas is the 'ground zero' for analysis of glaciers and their contribution to water security for a multitude of states, including China, India and Pakistan. Disputed border regions, shrinking glaciers, water-catchment alteration and water anxieties are likely to be combustible in the future. As water supplies become more unpredictable and then subject to reduction, it is not hard to imagine tensions rising as states seek to secure their water rights in areas such as agriculture, hydroelectric power generation and drinking water. In the case of the Indus river system, India has established over 100 dams, and glacial meltwater is integral to maintaining river volume.

While dams are known to be triggers for international tension, the problems don't stop with those installations. Moving further upstream to glaciers and mountains takes us to the source. Without meltwater discharge, downstream dams would not be able to serve their full potential, including power generation. As a consequence of its geographical location and size, China is pivotal to all of this. There are ways of moving the border as part of a bigger strategic bargain. As the occupant of the so-called 'Third Pole', China in effect controls ten major rivers that flow downstream through a multitude of other countries. Borders could be made to move in areas that Beijing cares about in return for new negotiations over water supplies.

Put simply, India is dependent on China for its water supply. The Brahmaputra and Indus rivers, for example, have their origins in mountains that come under the Chinese occupation of Tibet. The Brahmaputra's catchment area is mainly in a disputed area of India. China has constructed a formidable number of dams in these glaciated regions and there are plans for more. India has an Indus Water Treaty with Pakistan but not with China, and there are no established mechanisms for water sharing. China has recognised the importance of the supply of water from its territories for Indian cities such as Mumbai, and for the country's food-production capacity, and has not done anything to jeopardise it so far. Water could be a pivotal factor in Indo-Chinese relations in the future and there are two potential flashpoints – India's policy on dam construction and China's use of river data sharing.

First, India has embarked on a 'dam race' in the hope that it can pressurise China to enter into discussions about the common management of shared rivers and catchment areas. India has expressed a willingness to ask the International Court of Justice to intervene on the matter, confident that the court would rule in its favour regarding downstream water-sharing obligations. But this confidence in a court ruling making a difference might well be misplaced. For one thing, China might not respect any International Court of Justice judgment that it regards as antithetical to its national security. Another factor is broader in scope. India's demands on China to share water responsibly will irritate others such as Bangladesh and Pakistan who have their own river-related gripes with New Delhi. Both countries have had testy encounters with India over water sharing, dam construction and environmental management. It is also worth recalling that China has been working with Bangladesh and Pakistan on water-related projects ranging from funding flood-control schemes (Bangladesh) to enabling hydropower schemes on the Indus (Pakistan) as part of the Belt and Road Initiative. India, on water management, might find itself hemmed in by China and its regional allies.

Second, water data sharing has been weaponised by China. Disputes over borders can migrate and find expression further downstream. In 2017, China refused to supply waterflow data to India with regard to the Brahmaputra. The genesis of the refusal lay in a confrontation between Indian and Chinese troops in Doklam, a plateau region located close to the highly sensitive border region of China, India and Bhutan.

India and Bhutan have long been sensitive to Chinese maps claiming portions of Bhutanese territory as Chinese. India and Bhutan have a close strategic relationship, with New Delhi acting as a guarantor of the latter's security. The underlying tension escalated in June 2017 because Chinese contractors began to extend a road further onto the disputed plateau. India and Bhutan protested at what they regarded as illegal intrusion. A stand-off resulted. It was then, in retaliation for what it regarded as an Indian military incursion, that China stopped sharing waterflow data with India. The information from China had helped India and, further downstream, Bangladesh shape their flood-control policies. China eventually relented in May 2018 after Indian and Chinese forces had withdrawn from their respective positions.

Longer term, this looks and feels like a dress rehearsal for something rather larger in territorial scope. If China secures enhanced access to the Brahmaputra then the capacity for strategic leverage will be extended. In essence, China is able to transfer water to the more arid regions in other parts of Tibet, extend capacity for hydropower generation and improve food production. With all that comes the incentive to invest further in infrastructure and military presence along disputed and controversial border lines. It is worth remembering that the Indian region of Arunachal Pradesh has been called 'Southern Tibet' by China for decades. China accuses India of violating its territorial integrity while New Delhi describes the region as integral and inalienable to India. What should worry India is that China has been proactive in investing in border infrastructure, in the modernisation of its armed forces, and in training and exercising along disputed borderlands.

While troops move in and out of disputed border territories, the surrounding landscapes continue to alter as well. Glacial melt, allied with monsoonal rain, not only delivers water to downstream communities but sediment flow as well, helping to improve the productivity of agricultural lands. Dams interfere with this flow of mineral-carrying silt. Mining can also be a game-changer, bringing with it a cumulative environmental impact on soil, air and water. China has developed new mining projects close to the disputed Indo-Chinese border near to Bhutan. Mining also brings with it demand for power and access to water. Yet again, rivers, resources and strategic access contribute to a prevailing culture of geopolitical tension.

Disputed border regions around South Asia are militarising at a pace, which brings with it all sorts of infrastructural investment in the form of roads, airports, dams and housing. This construction work and the subsequent military operations undertaken both contribute to landscape denudation. The need for strategic occupation trumps long-term ecological planning. The scale of the border dispute between India and China is huge, and the Line of Actual Control (LAC) along their 'shared border' goes to the heart of what matters to both countries: terrain, water and strategic access.

China is particularly entrenched in its control of river systems because they originate in Chinese-occupied Tibet, and Indo-Chinese relations are complicated by India's hosting of the Tibetan Government in Exile. As the physical geographies of the high-altitude areas of the Himalayas and Central Asia continue to change due to global warming, there is added incentive to double down on military infrastructure and strategic positioning, including military build-ups and operational planning. In June 2020, the two sides clashed again in a brutal conflict involving rocks, clubs and other improvised weapons which left scores dead. Indian media sources were thunderous in their response to Chinese 'border violations' (some of which were picked up via satellite image analysis) in and around the Galwan Valley. But it was a shocking reminder that the LAC, which criss-crosses remote and thinly populated mountainous regions, is shot through with geopolitical drama.

In our ice-covered and mountainous areas of the world, vague borders such as the LAC will continue to defy the definitive ambitions of national maps. The very term 'Line' is misleading because the LAC is really two lines – the Chinese one and the Indian one, with a mobile no man's land in-between. Numbered patrol points litter the areas in and around the LAC. In these contentious areas of the world, such as the Himalayas and Hindu Kush, we have scores of unsettled disputes between India, China and Pakistan, which often don't need much encouragement to escalate. The June 2020 incident was in part precipitated by accusations that Chinese troops had dammed a river in the disputed area, and then broke the 'dam' to strategically flood an area occupied by Indian troops. This small-scale river incident should not obscure a broader truism – up to 2 billion people are going to be affected by either flooding or drought depending on the scale and extent of increased meltwater and prevailing weather in these mountainous border regions. It is not hard to see why glaciers and upstream river environments will become ever more integral to national security planning on all sides. In the future, a larger border war could easily be triggered by a combination of natural change and the deliberate manipulation of water supplies and downstream flows.

The contrast with the Limes project along the Austro-Italian border and high-altitude dramas in South Asia could not be starker. A moving, mountainous border such as this does not have to be a source of geopolitical drama per se. When relations between two countries are cordial then there are ways and means of adjusting one's shared border. When there is an absence of cordiality then things become harder, particularly in regions of the world that are harder to access. They become a lightning rod for broader anxieties about the distribution and control of precious resources, the capacity of parties to move and long-term strategic advantage. But such shifting borders aren't just evident at altitude: we also find them below the water level.

A Soviet soldier guarding the border between the USSR and China in 1969. He is standing by the River Ussuri near Damansky Island (or what the Chinese call Zhenbao Island). In March 1969, the two sides clashed over the disputed island in the middle of the river. The conflict last some two weeks and the origins of the incident remains disputed. A ceasefire was eventually agreed. The island remains disputed.

Chapter 3

Watery Borders

As we have seen, it is estimated that billions of people will be living in areas of the world prone to water scarcity by 2050, but not just because of the impact of global warming on meltwater in regions of high altitude. Billions also depend on shared water supplies. Glaciers are frozen but they also melt and as such contribute to river systems around the world. Glaciers, rivers and lakes matter because governments recognise only too well the value of water sources for domestic and industrial use as well as for energy potential, public health, transport, agriculture and fishing. Controlling river flow and direction is also essential to national security planning and regulation of maritime transport. And local and national authorities want to control the movement of an assortment of mobile substances and people on the world's waterways, ranging from pollutants to migrants, traffickers and terrorists. The stakes are high. Hundreds of the world's rivers, lake basins and aquifers (underground layers of permeable rock, which are capable of storing water) do not have working cross-border agreements. There are over 270 trans-boundary aquifers spread out around the world, with the highest number located in Europe. The worst areas for conflict and tension over water sharing are in the Middle East and Africa in places such as Lake Victoria, the River Tigris and the shared aquifers of Israel and Palestine.

Disputes over river and lake boundaries can easily escalate into international crises. Even if the nature of the dispute is not a boundary line, other factors such as pollution and asymmetries in water sharing can swiftly mutate into conflict. While rivers and lakes have long been seen as 'natural borders', they are not static. A hostile state might decide to extract more water and cause environmental and public health chaos for a downstream neighbour. Dam construction and agriculture, even if done with a benign intention, can be deeply disruptive to others. Oil and gas prospecting, fishing and other activities such as hydropower generation in shared lakes and disputed seas is therefore a growing source of tension around the world. Aquifer usage might end up revealing profound inequalities, with studies suggesting that Israel extracts far more water per citizen than the Palestinian authorities do. West Bank Palestinians end up being dependent on Israeli water companies for essential supplies. The water supply in Gaza is precarious and hazardous to health. Not for nothing are aquifers described by UNESCO as 'blue gold'. Rivers, seas, aquifers and lakes complicate our ideas of borders. Hydro-diplomacy is a mainstream geopolitical issue around the world. Representatives from Pakistan, India and Afghanistan met at a 'Water Beyond Borders' conference in January 2020 for urgent discussions about water sharing in the future. Delegates noted that climate change, energy generation, agricultural expansion and population increase (with higher usage demands) were placing further pressures on all parties. Pakistan routinely accuses India of preventing it from extracting a fair share of water from the River Indus. Upstream states often stand accused of abusing their powers to interfere with downstream flow, and countries such as Ethiopia,

Sudan and Egypt have had a history of disputing their respective rights to the resource potential of the River Nile. In the 1990s, it was not uncommon to read that the next generation of conflict would be relatively local water wars that could trigger wider regional conflict. Former UN Secretary-General and Egyptian diplomat, Boutros Boutros-Ghali (whose UN term of office was 1992–96) warned in 1988 that 'the next war in the Middle East will be fought over water, not politics'.

While indigenous peoples and environmental activists are eager to assert the 'rights' of rivers and lakes to be managed and protected, governments and political leaders worry about opportunistic neighbours and unwanted interlopers. Sharing lakes, seas and rivers is never straightforward and will only become more fraught in the future thanks to increased conflict over resources and the cumulative impact of climate change. And armed with the UN Declaration on the Rights of Indigenous Peoples, we can expect indigenous populations around the world to add to demands that natural environments, including aquifers, deserve legal protection from those who cause damage. However, the record of national governments respecting the wishes, let alone rights, of indigenous peoples is patchy, especially when they declare that their actions are informed by national emergency planning.

WATER AS A NATURAL BORDER?

For those who study the international management of rivers a distinction is made between two different types of rivers: *through-border* rivers (ones that flow, say, from China at a point of origin and emerge eventually via a river delta located in Vietnam) and what are termed *border-making* rivers. A classic example of the latter would be the Rio Grande, which separates the United States and Mexico. This distinction can be used to underpin a wider point about the relationship between borders and water. Depending on the physical and political geography, our management of rivers, lakes and glaciers varies. Rivers might be entirely internal to one country or criss-cross numerous states. Lakes likewise might lie under the exclusive ownership of one party or be subject to sharing arrangements such as the Great Lakes between Canada and the United States. Glaciers might lie in a particular mountain range but on melting they might contribute to a river system that leaves an exclusively national jurisdiction.

Empires and nation-states have throughout history found natural barriers such as border-making rivers, mountains and coastlines to be useful and persuasive markers of territorial edges. When two imperial powers came into contact with one another, the contact zones were most often at a riverbank, lake edge, seashore or mountain pass. In the last 200 years, unprecedented efforts have been made to divide up land and sea through surveying, mapping, treaties and appeals to international legal frameworks. In the colonial occupation of Africa and Asia, European maps depicted water courses as border-making opportunities. They might not have been precisely defined but their mere presence meant that rivers, lakes and seas acted as natural accomplices to imperial control.

Later, international law, developed by Europeans in particular, became more useful to those eager to add precision to their borders. It developed a general rule that in dividing up a navigable river between two or more states, the line should follow what is termed the thalweg – the deepest part of the river channel. In the case of a non-navigable river, the line of greatest depth of the water course should be followed. The International Court of Justice used this basic proposition in 1999 to adjudicate on a disputed river boundary between Botswana and Namibia. The origin of the dispute was not about relative depth but which part of the River Chobe one should consider measuring. The two countries were arguing over which bit counted as the primary channel and both coveted a piece of land in the middle of the river. Botswana won that case. We have legal rules in place, but it remains a moot point as to whether the parties concerned have the capacity to work with them. Botswana and Namibia avoided conflict in this case.

But rivers change over time and this puts our rules under duress. The physical world is not static. The line of greatest depth in a river is not permanent. Some river systems such as the Ganges are hugely complex, especially those with extensive deltas. As anyone living and working on rivers knows, the flow and shape of a river is constantly changing. Every year, one could survey a river system and conclude that the thalweg has shifted. On-the-ground observation combined with satellite coverage means that it is now easier than ever to monitor real-time environmental change. International legal rules pre-date the satellite era and real-time environmental sensors.

Under the thalweg principle, neighbouring states should enjoy equal rights for the use of the river, including its resource potential. Any islands within the river should be owned on the basis of what side of the thalweg they lie (as Botswana would remind us), but islands in river channels can also be co-owned if the two parties are minded to share them. When a river reaches sea or ocean the UN Convention on the Law of the Sea (1982) provides a set of rules and procedures for allocating sovereignty and property resources that transform the natural borders between land and sea into highly regulated border regions nd zones, distinguishing ownership rights for the seabed and the water column based on distance from the coastline.

Historically, empires and states have found it a challenge to divide up their territories when they come into contact with terrestrial bodies of water, including rivers and lakes. Riverbanks have the ability to become objects of controversy and enmities can be enduring, with Russia and China providing a powerful example of how riverbanks and islands can be geopolitically sensitive. In the seventeenth century, an expanding Russian empire moved eastwards towards Siberia and the Pacific seaboard, and southwards towards China. As Russia grew it started to explore major river systems such as the Amur and Ussuri. In 1689 the Russians and Chinese began their first formal negotiations over where a mutual boundary between their two empires might lie. The resulting treaty established a frontier rather than a boundary line, recognising rivers, mountains and lakes as indicators of the geographical limits of both parties. As their respective fortunes altered, the Russians in the nineteenth century pushed further southwards along the River Amur. Under two new treaties called Aigun (1858) and Peking (1860), the Russians demanded a new boundary settlement. This time the frontier became a line. Taking advantage of the relative weakness of the Chinese empire, they annexed territory along the major river systems. Russian maps were swift to depict the country's sovereignty as extending all the way up to the Chinese riverbank. The rivers were no longer, according to the Russians, shared. They were under the near-total domination of Moscow.

The Amur and Ussuri rivers were considered Russian territories, and Russia was determined to control navigation, resource extraction and the occupation of any islands within the river channels. The de facto annexation of the rivers did not face any challenge from China until the 1950s, when Chairman Mao was adamant that China would no longer acquiesce to Russian opportunism. The Chinese demanded copies of the Russian maps and then began to draw their own counter maps, which rejected the idea that Chinese sovereignty only extended up to their side of the riverbank. The rivers became a geopolitical hotspot. China encouraged local communities on the River Amur to navigate along it and exploit its fishing resources, and both sides continued to argue over the meaning of the nineteenth-century treaties and their corresponding maps. On the ground, tension was high. The Soviet Union used its military forces to seize fishing boats, spray boat crews with cold water and chase Chinese civilians off river ice.

Chinese propaganda was swift to highlight the blunt force of Soviet military power against its people, and it used ongoing civilian activity to force Moscow to invest ever more resources into the river-boundary dispute. In January 1968, conflict broke out between the two countries' respective border guards, leading to the death of several Chinese civilians. In March 1969, another skirmish occurred on a frozen river island on the River Ussuri – river ice, during the winter months, gave added opportunity for the countries to amass military and civilian numbers. The conflict revealed that both sides were rigid in sticking to their mutual 'red lines' over the disputed river islands, with neither country wanting to admit defeat nor contemplate any kind of retreat. China was not going to concede that its territory ended at its side of the river but lacked local military resources to push the point. The Soviet Union did not want to concede its geographical advantage but realised if its troops touched the riverbank they would in effect be invading Chinese territory. The river islands were therefore the inevitable contact zone for the conflict.

In the 1980s, the two sides agreed, during the relative 'thaw' in relations of the Gorbachev era, to return to the Treaty of Peking and apply the thalweg principle to their mutual river borders. The deepest part of the river now constituted the border between the two countries, working on the politically convenient assumption that the deepest part would remain relatively static. The 'concession' by President Gorbachev in 1986 was significant. China was a net beneficiary as the Soviet Union in effect relinquished claims to river islands that had been under its control for the best part of 150 years. Two decades later, in 2006, the final touches were put to a new treaty that finally resolved the most contentious item of the negotiations. It was agreed that the strategically significant Bear Island would be divided between the two parties. The moral of the story is that what matters is the strategic calculations of the parties concerned and whether a river and any associated islands are worthy of potential conflict.

Even with agreements in place, so-called natural borders can continue to be contentious. On either side of the River Amur, it is still not uncommon for Chinese and Russian communities to become embroiled in skirmishes over access to the river and its resources. The river can provoke potent examples of nationalist politics, as accusations are traded that the rival community is trying to extract some kind of advantage. The Chinese talk of the Black Dragon River and not the Amur for one thing.

Yet a new cross-river bridge located at a strategic point connecting the Russian city of Blagoveshchensk and the Chinese city of Heihe was completed in November 2019. It was first mooted in 1988, and in engineering terms was very challenging because of extreme cold and water-level fluctuation due to river-ice melt. During the winter months, it was not uncommon for people and goods to travel across the frozen water via a pontoon bridge. The new bridge changed all this just in time for both cities to be hit by the coronavirus outbreak. In January 2020, the river border between China and Russia was closed because of the virus and Russian towns such as Blagoveshchensk were badly hit by the loss of Chinese trade and tourism. Chinese holiday makers were stranded in Blagoveshchensk during Chinese Lunar Year celebrations. What worries the local communities either side of the River Amur is that the virus may end up infecting Russo-Chinese cross-border cooperation in the long term.

Without ongoing Chinese investment and trade, many Russian towns and cities in Siberia and the far east of the country face an uncertain future. For all the talk of mutual friendship and understanding, the view from Moscow remains suspicious that this new bridge will enable China to consolidate its influence on the southern and eastern borderlands with Russia. Inflamed by a strong dosage of Sinophobia, many Russians are also perturbed by China's economic power in the former Soviet heartlands of Central Asia. Meanwhile, further west, President Putin had few qualms about inter-connection and mutual dependency when it came to the building of a new bridge between occupied Crimea and the rest of the Russian Federation. The new bridge over the Kerch Strait in Crimea was opened in 2018 and cost the Russians nearly $4 billion for the 19km (12-mile) long connection. The difference, of course, is the prevailing power dynamic – Russia can bully Ukraine but is dependent on China for investment and strategic cooperation.

When it comes to watery borders, the geopolitical temperature always has a way of making itself felt – under the water, along the river and seabed, and above the surface.

MANIPULATING NATURAL BORDERS

As we saw with the last example, Russia and China have found ways to argue over their river borders but also how to collaborate with one another, albeit tentatively. And while the principle of the thalweg can help to foster accord, rivers can change so radically, whether by natural means or by human geo-engineering, that 'borders' can easily become scrambled. This process can be deeply contentious. Imagine, for a moment, that a country divided by a river from its neighbour thinks the other side deliberately manipulated the course of that river for its own strategic or commercial advantage. Conflicts can and do start over this kind of action.

Some observers thought that these conflicts would be over access to drinking water, but there are other sources of potential dispute when it comes to the resource. You might not care for what a neighbour does to a shared river, for example. In November 2010, Costa Rica complained to the International Court of Justice that Nicaragua had behaved egregiously. The Costa Rican government claimed that its neighbour had deliberately interfered with their common border and illegally occupied its territory. In its complaint, it pointed to canal building and dredging along the San Juan River. The Nicaraguan government was accused of using its army engineers to alter the course and water flow of the river. Alongside this complaint was another accusing the defendant of building a road along the San Juan River and causing additional disturbance to the river's flow capacity and course.

Some five years later, after hearing a great deal of evidence and counter evidence, the International Court of Justice delivered its verdict. Costa Rican territory, the court concluded, had been violated in the northern part of what is called Isla Portillos (also known as Harbour Head Island) to the far north of the country, close to the Caribbean Sea. For Costa Rica, the area was an established ecological reserve. The court was damning of Nicaraguan behaviour. It criticised the canal-building works and noted the illegal occupation of Costa Rican territory by armed-forces personnel. Nicaragua was liable for the damage to the river system. In February 2018, the court awarded Costa Rica the rather paltry sum of $378,000 in lieu of the damage to the river and the knock-on consequences in terms of loss of environmental goods and services. Nicaragua paid up and transferred the money in early March 2018. What counted to Costa Rica, in the long-term, was not financial recompense. To be blunt, the country has no standing armed forces so a military conflict with Nicaragua (which is one of the world's smallest military powers according to the 2020 Global Firepower Index) is implausible. The imprimatur of the international court is far more valuable.

What made the incident more notable was that the dispute was inflamed by both parties claiming that they had historic evidence in their favour. The Cañas–Jerez Treaty was quoted, as was the so-called Alexander Award, named after American engineer Edward Alexander in 1897. Dispatched by President Cleveland, Alexander had been appointed to oversee a commission, which was empowered by both Costa Rica and Nicaragua, to fix and demarcate their international boundary. The work was complicated, as there was a great deal of interest from the United States at one stage in creating a trans-oceanic canal between the two countries that would enable access to the Pacific and Caribbean, but after two years, in 1899, the San Juan River was eventually established as the common border. Both countries accepted Alexander's recommendation, but his stay in Nicaragua was marred by the death of his wife, who had become ill during their time there.

Alexander's work counted for little in 2010 when Nicaragua claimed that it was Google Maps that had inadvertently encouraged them to occupy new land beyond the common border by making them think of Isla Portillos as their territory. Blaming Google Maps might seem akin to accusing the family dog of eating one's homework, but this is not the first time that search-engine providers (and the maps that they produce and circulate) have found themselves caught up in these border disputes. A professional geographer working for a large US computer company told similar stories at a borders conference in India about the difficulties of producing 'neutral' maps of South Asia in the late 1990s. I heard other examples being given at a borders conference in Israel in the early 2000s, with Palestinian geographers denouncing the fact that the Israeli military and settlement activity in the West Bank was not identified as illegal. Colleagues were, at one point, screaming at one another in Hebrew and Arabic. Eventually, the organisers got everyone to speak to one another in English, much to the relief of the international attendees.

Depicting water borders, like mountainous ones, is tricky because they can and do change. What might be termed 'facts on the ground' are not quite the same as they would be when we talk, say, of settlement activity in disputed territories. Costa Rica and Nicaragua are not alone in finding that past treaties and maps, many of which were drawn up in the nineteenth century, are out of date. Argentina and Uruguay provide another example. Their river border has long been settled, and Martín García Island in the middle of the River Plate was officially awarded to Argentina via a 1973 accord. In the intervening four decades, huge amounts of river sediment were carried downstream and out towards the Atlantic Ocean. Argentina wanted to carry out more dredging because it argued that access to its river ports was being compromised. A smaller island nearby, called Timoteo Domínguez, which had been occupied by Uruguay, became linked to Martín García by the sediment. A new land border had, in effect, been created. For the first time in their mutual histories, the two countries were no longer physically separated by the River Plate. Terraforming of this sort provides either opportunities for a spirit of cooperation to prevail or unleashes tension.

In recent times, however, the fate of the river has not been free from political controversy. The two countries have also been mired in disputes about downstream pollution. Uruguay's decision to allow the opening of a Finnish paper mill in 2010 triggered a furious reaction from Argentina, which accused Montevideo of generating a high environmental impact on their shared river system. The International Court of Justice ruled that the paper mill was not in violation of any treaties between the two countries – and there is now a second mill in Punta Pereira. This was a disappointing result for the plaintiff, Argentina.

The new land border between the two river islands could easily become a more significant source of dispute in the future: it is not beyond the realm of possibility that nationalists on either side will use the issue as fuel. Land-based occupation might follow, for instance, after one government uses satellite imagery to argue that the other has infringed or interfered with its rights. It is easy to imagine a situation where the changing course of a river or alteration in lake size and shape is picked up by such analysis. A government might then seek to take advantage of border confusion, especially where water, fish and resources such as oil and gas are potentially at stake.

As the old agreements get torn up, rivers and lakes will no longer be reliable guides. Infrastructure such as communication networks and even entire communities might inadvertently cross over old border lines. Neighbours will either have to agree on 'mobile borders', as we saw happening in the European Alps, or else they will end up locked in a never-ending game of paranoid surveillance, coupled with opportunities aplenty for provocation and even conflict.

MANAGING SHARED AQUIFERS, RIVERS AND LAKES

Because many aquifers, lakes and rivers criss-cross international borders, shared water management would seem to make intrinsic sense. In Europe, the River Danube is a good example of the river as a mobile international boundary, and over the years European states have devised mechanisms to ensure that the river is managed collectively in order to ensure safe navigation, pollution control and resource usage. The Danube River Commission (the earliest iteration dates from 1856) explicitly recognises the need for upstream and downstream states to work with one another on areas of mutual interest. In Africa, the Senegal River Basin Development Organisation (established in 1972) is a notable success story involving Guinea, Mali, Mauritania and Senegal. But out of an estimated 286 shared river basins around the world, there are only around 85 to 90 joint water-management plans in place. The norm around the world is weak or non-existent mechanisms for water cooperation.

The principal centres of global population are located in coastal areas, many of which are alongside major river deltas. These downstream areas are facing unprecedented pressures in the twenty-first century: upstream power generation, resource extraction, floodplain reduction, and infrastructure and river engineering projects that are disruptive to human and non-human communities. In South-east Asia, the Mekong River Commission, of which China is not a member, helps to manage the River Mekong that runs through a patchwork of states including Cambodia, China, Myanmar, Vietnam, Thailand and Laos. China, meanwhile, has established six dams on the upper reaches of the Mekong. More are planned, and additional mega-dam construction will place further pressures on the river's capacity to maintain downstream flow (as the transfer of sediment will be disrupted) and ecological diversity. The Mekong supports millions of people and its biodiversity is stunning. More than 1,000 migratory fish species and land fauna depend on the river system.

China wants to generate gigawatt power potential but is also mindful that part of its southern landmass has been hit by severe droughts and extreme flood events. While water extraction is a worry for downstream states, China wants to control the river's flow so that it can better prevent such floods in its own territory, even though flooding is a vital component of the river system.

Pressures on the river are only going to intensify as population growth continues. China will continue to be the leading party in the region, and its huge size and influence create disparity between it and its downstream neighbours. By 2025, it is expected that cities in and around the Chinese portion of the Mekong river system will grow by another 30 million people, and downstream states such as Vietnam worry about what China might yet do to the shared river system in the future.

As a shared resource, the power of upstream states to shape the fate of a river downstream is considerable. Countries often seek to establish confidence-building mechanisms for joint control over rivers precisely because they recognise that there are asymmetries, depending on location and terrain. Physical and political geography can push in two opposite directions: physical geography tends to emphasise flow and connection while political geography privileges control and ownership.

Rivers in Africa have often provided the most telling examples of how complicated river-related geopolitics can be. Often, post-colonial borders were not clearly defined in the immediate aftermath of independence and arrangements were weak when it came to the sharing of scarce water resources. This vagueness could often serve as a pretext for cross-border tension between states, particularly with regard to through-border rivers that flowed through two or more neighbouring countries. As we have already seen, dam-building is controversial because it impacts directly on water flow and river management. Upstream states such as Ethiopia can unleash anxieties downstream when dam construction is mooted. In the case of Lake Turkana, located in northern Kenya, the government in Nairobi was concerned that Ethiopia's plans (with Chinese financial investment) for the Gibe III dam-construction project would interfere with the River Omo. The 760km (472-mile) long river provides 90 per cent of the inflow for the lake and runs entirely through Ethiopia before reaching the northern fringe of Lake Turkana. Northern Kenya is semi-desert and the lake supports herding, small-scale agriculture and fishing communities. The lake also serves as a partial border between Ethiopia and Kenya. The vast majority of its waters falls under Kenyan jurisdiction, and Nairobi has pushed for the 130,000km^2 (50,000 square miles) of it to be recognised as a UNESCO World Heritage Site. The Ethiopian government, meanwhile, believes that the dam will boost cotton and sugar-cane production and enable surplus hydropower to be exported to neighbours.

As of 2020, Kenya is worried that the new dam, completed in 2017, will disrupt the flow of the river and Lake Turkana in the years to come, which might in turn fuel local and cross-border conflict. What makes the situation more precarious is that the region is considered high-risk when it comes to earthquakes, and the area around the river has witnessed major flooding. Despite this, the Kenyan government agreed to purchase some of the power capacity of the Gibe III dam, which provoked the ire of local community and environmental organisations. Kenya is eager to retain this energy transfer deal with Ethiopia, even though the price paid could be very high: lower water levels carry with them the danger of ecological breakdown as the lake becomes more saline, thereby reducing drinking water and fish stocks. Proponents of the dam tend to dispute the dire forecasting of environmental organisations, and the Kenyan government's official agencies such as the Water Services Regulatory Board have issued confident public predictions that the dam will have no negative consequences for the lake. However, once the dam was filled, the water level of Lake Turkana reportedly fell by 2m (6 feet), and indigenous communities in and around the lake continue to warn of further water-level loss and disruption to hundreds of thousands of animal farmers.

The Gibe III dam exemplifies a global challenge. It is estimated that there are some 45,000 dams around the world of at least 15m (49 feet) or higher. Dam building was of considerable importance from the 1940s until the 1980s, attracting foreign investment and Cold War geopolitical competition, when post-colonial states such as Kenya were eager to showcase their capacities to harness their natural environment for hydropower and wider resource exploitation. Although dam construction has not tailed off, it is now recognised that megadam projects carry with them implications for ecological and social disruption. China's investment in infrastructure projects in Africa is a case in point. The Gibe III project was partially funded by loans offered by the Industrial and Commercial Bank of China after other international investors refused to fund a project that carried with it unwelcome consequences for a part of the world credited with being home to the genesis of the human species. Kenya's attitude towards the dam could change if ecological disruption does, as many critics fear, lead to social dislocation and possible conflict within and beyond northern Kenya.

Ethiopia's physical geography not only supports river and lake systems running south of the country but also to the north. The River Nile is a case in point. One of the world's longest rivers, the Nile flows in and out of 11 countries, terminating at the point where Egypt connects to the Mediterranean. It is a truly civilisational river. Egypt depends upon it for 90 per cent of its water supply, and a disrupted Nile is an existential issue for the country. As a consequence, Sudan (through which the Nile also flows) and Egypt have developed plans for military action against Ethiopian dam-building activities. In 2010, proposals were drawn up in Cairo for an attack on new Ethiopian dam projects if they interfered with downstream river flow. Complicating things still further is the belief in Egypt that Ethiopian dam-building initiatives might be secretly supported by Israel as an attempt to keep the government in Cairo weak and compliant. Speculation about conspiratorial relationships adds further to the suspicion on all sides of the River Nile that water politics is never quite what it seems.

Through-border rivers, then, are particularly challenging and will continue to be so in the future, but some of the same pressures, such as changing shape, haunt lake management as well. A similar story can be seen across Africa in places such as lakes Nyasa and Chad. Lake Nyasa (Malawi, Mozambique and Tanzania) and Lake Chad (Nigeria, Cameroon, Niger and Chad) have more than one stakeholder. In Lake Nyasa's case, Tanzania and Malawi were involved in a dispute in 2011–12 over oil and gas exploration at the northern section of the lake, with the two sides arguing over the delimitation of the water body. In the case of Lake Chad, the four countries are concerned about lake shrinkage and the implications for farming and herding communities. As water levels drop and retreat, new land is revealed, which then attracts 'squatter' activity. Accusations abound that land is being stolen and misappropriated.

There are plenty of other examples where dam construction, water extraction and deliberate submergence of property and communities get used to engineer strategic advantage. They might not involve international boundaries in the first instance, but Turkey's ongoing plans for dam construction along the River Tigris (the South Eastern Anatolia Project) will hit resident Kurdish communities hardest. The Ilısu dam project began filling in July 2019, and international observers fear it will interfere with an archaeologically significant part of ancient Mesopotamia. Many settlements will be affected, including the historic town of Hasankeyf, which will be subject to relocation, while other settlements such as Koçtepe are going to be inundated by rising water. While this might on the surface appear to be a domestic matter for Turkey, the location of the activity reveals a problem with global heritage protection.

As the sovereign state, Turkey never requested UNESCO World Heritage status for Hasankeyf precisely because it did not want a global body interfering with its sovereign authority. As pressure mounts for governments to act sustainably, could a situation arise where UNESCO World Heritage Sites are established without the consent of relevant national governments? For Turkey, there are geopolitical and national security drivers that override any interest in prevailing ecology and heritage. Kurdish separatism, the spill-over of conflict from Syria and fears that others might be plotting against Ankara nourish a geopolitical culture that is conspiratorial and paranoid about the intentions of others. Foreign interference, however well intentioned, is not likely to be treated kindly by a state that has purposefully framed itself as a regional superpower.

RIVERS AND LAKES AS LEGAL PERSONALITIES

Anticipating that sort of UNESCO-like intervention in the future, activists are turning to legal precedent to try and secure a different future for rivers and lakes. As in the case of Costa Rica and Nicaragua, neighbouring states have been turning to the International Court of Justice for legal rulings about disputed river and lake boundaries. While the court has faced criticism about applying Western legal doctrines to non-Western states and contexts, there are other mechanisms being developed to try and seek peaceful resolutions to conflict. In Africa, the African Union established a Panel of the Wise in 2007, supplemented by Friends of the Panel of the Wise, in an explicit attempt to promote intra-African cooperation on a suite of issues affecting the continent. Conflict resolution and border disputes are two topics that fall within the mandate of the panels. In 2007, the Panel of the Wise announced that it would consider all existing land and maritime border disputes with a view to seeking resolution. This proved to be a daunting task, involving, it was thought, up to 45,000km (28,000 miles) of international boundaries. The work of the panels remains ongoing and there are at least 100 unresolved border disputes that involve rivers and lakes.

A comparatively new innovation pertinent to river and lake border disputes is the decision by courts around the world to grant water bodies *legal personalities*. In other words, courts are explicitly recognising that river systems and lakes need greater legal protection given their extraordinary ecological and cultural importance. In many cases, the river systems in question are home to indigenous communities who have had their lives disrupted by dam construction and intensifying water usage, including resource extraction and tourism. If the rights of the river are violated then there is the possibility of legal redress and compensation.

Indigenous peoples and their supporters are fighting back via the courts. For example, in Chile, activists are making the case for all rivers to be granted legal status. And they are not alone. In 2017, a New Zealand court declared that the River Whanganui was integral to Māori culture and that the river enjoyed a legal personhood. Māori have objected to resource extraction and dam construction projects. The river is represented by at least one Māori representative and there is a commission to guide future development. This follows a Colombian decision to establish a river-guardians commission for the River Atrato, which like the Whanganui flows entirely within a national territory. In the United States, the native peoples of the Yurok tribe declared in September 2019 something similar for the River Klamath in California.

By granting legal status to rivers, the activists want courts and governments to acknowledge that these bodies of water, which are endlessly replenishable thanks to rain, meltwater and tributary river systems, are not simply the property of states. Rivers are integral to indigenous and aboriginal civilisations, and they are intrinsic to eco-system health and spiritual wellbeing of communities. The 'rights for nature' movement is gaining momentum in regions and coun-tries around the world, and there are implications for how states manage their rivers and lakes, with native and indigenous peoples now sometimes sharing their management.

The future may hold the intriguing possibility of conflict in which one country establishes that a river has the same legal rights as its citi-zens, while its neighbour, which shares the river or lake system, rejects such an intervention. Would the state that recognised the legal per-sonality of the water body concerned be obligated to defend it from acts of aggression by third parties? India and Pakistan might decide to interpret any legal personalities attached to the Indus differently and disagree on its future fate. The ecological, economic, geopolitical and spiritual dimensions of a major river do not become any easier to negotiate just because more legal padding has been added to its sta-tus. Extreme water stress could just incentivise states to bypass legal mechanisms in favour of water hoarding.

As climate change intensifies, rivers and lakes are going to alter even more profoundly. Making sense of physical change is going to involve decisions that have implications for a country or community's sense of security and wellbeing. Boundary agreements will need to be increasingly attuned to sensitivities over water management. Failure to do so is likely to result in tension and possible conflict. We do have mechanisms to help us, notably the 1997 UN Convention on the Law of Non-navigational Uses of International Watercourses. But this was negotiated in a different era when we were not speaking of chaotic, non-linear and disastrous long-term environmental change. In 1997, there was some confidence that humans had sufficient agency and collective will to manage environmental issues.

Threat perceptions are also going to alter. We are used to states worrying about traffickers, extremists and illegal trespassing. In the twenty-first century, we are going to face a great deal more pressure on our river and lake systems. States are far more likely to accuse one another of inappropriate usage, poor regulation of water, excessive resource exploitation and environmental vandalism. Water levels and downstream flow are going to be ever more sensitive risk indicators for many states and communities around the world. And geographical intelligence is going to provoke and possibly mediate these disputes.

War can also produce perverse benefits to water-stressed countries. Syria is a tragic recent example. During the worst months of the civil war, which began in 2011, farming was disrupted and thus less water was taken from local river systems. In many cases, farmers fled across the border to Jordan. Satellite imagery revealed that water levels of the River Yarmouk then improved. However, as is often the case, there was a knock-on effect. In the past, Jordan, a country which has had to cope with severe water stress, expressed concerns about Syrian upstream dam construction and water usage. As irrigated cropland in southern Syria declined, the benefit to Jordan was offset by increased water usage as refugees placed more demands on the country's infrastructure. And, in the future, Jordan is likely to be ever more reliant on Israel for supplementary water from Lake Kinneret (the Sea of Galilee).

AQUIFERS AS HIDDEN BORDERS

There are some water bodies that we cannot see, namely aquifers, which can further complicate cross-border cooperation. It is estimated that there are around 600 trans-boundary aquifers around the world. Until quite recently, their size and scope lay in the realm of the mysterious. But underground mapping and geo-visualisation have contributed to the transformation of understanding and heightened interest in where water flows and gets stored within underground realms. If mining helped to spur interest in the 'vertical territory' of a state – which includes its subterranean layers – in the eighteenth and nineteenth centuries, hydrocarbons and water resources have proven powerful stimulants since then. Water in particular flows through underground spaces, so it is especially challenging to regulate. Some states, such as France and Switzerland, have had aquifer management schemes for a century and a half, while for others the concept is a comparative novelty. In the Middle East, Jordan and Saudi Arabia negotiated an agreement in 2015 for the joint management of a transborder aquifer called Al-Saq (Saudi Arabia) or Al-Disi (Jordan). While both sides had been exploiting the underwater resources of the aquifer since the 1970s, it was only then that they were able to signal some agreement on how much water should be extracted and for joint monitoring of water levels.

There are some positive signs of underground cooperation and shared water management elsewhere in the world. The Guarani Aquifer Agreement involving Argentina, Brazil, Paraguay and Uruguay is the most noteworthy. It explicitly addresses trans-boundary management, including sharing and monitoring. Signed in 2010, it took eight years to be ratified by the four parties. A commission will now be established for the express purpose of organising groundwater sharing. The importance of this aquifer cannot be overstated. Covering more than 1.2 million km^2 (463,000 square miles), it is a cavernous space with enough water to act as a global supply of fresh drinking water for hundreds of years. While the aquifer is impressive as a resource, the Guarani Aquifer Agreement needs the four parties to commit to its provisions, fund the work of the commission and engage in long-term monitoring work. UNESCO has recognised the importance of the aquifer agreement by funding their own Regional Centre for the Management of Groundwater in Uruguay. The efficacy of the agreement will, as ever, depend on the political will of the four countries, but it marks the first step to recognising the fundamental importance of groundwater boundaries in the region.

BORDERS AT SEA

Ocean borders have on the face of it been managed for a number of years by the United Nations Convention on the Law of the Sea (UNCLOS). A globally recognised framework, it was signed in 1982 and entered into force in 1994. The most important non-signatory remains the United States, and despite the endorsement of successive presidents, both Democrat and Republican, it has not been ratified by the US Senate. Although the US accepts many of the underlying principles of UNCLOS, the reticence of conservative senators to endorse a UN framework reveals some of the ongoing tensions surrounding ocean borders.

For centuries, the underlying principle informing the management of the world's seas and oceans was freedom: freedom to navigate around the world with minimum interference from others. Imperial powers built their trading networks around this freedom. More recently, global powers such as the United States have exercised their right to conduct freedom-of-navigation operations and their jealously guarded right to conduct passages that can be categorised as 'innocent' (defined by international law as ships travelling through the territorial waters of others and not engaging in spying, dumping, smuggling and military activities) or 'transit' (continuous journeying for the purpose of travelling from one sea/ocean to another). This sense of entitlement has irritated near neighbours. Canada considers its fabled Northwest Passage to be part of its 'internal waters', while the United States and others think of those northern waters as a transit passage. The difference is substantial: if waters are part of a transit passage, then third parties have far more right to pass through them without a nearby coastal state having control of that movement.

So, despite the *appearance* that historically countries were free to navigate the world's oceans as they saw fit, situations such as the one in the Northwest Passage are indicative of the fact that oceans and seas have always been locked in a series of trade-offs between coastal states and third parties. Coastal states get rights and responsibilities in their territorial waters and exclusive economic zones, but others are allowed to pass through those waters and undertake activities provided they don't interfere with relevant right holders. The idea was to prevent a free-for-all, a 'tragedy of the commons'-like situation because there were no rules to control mining, fishing, dumping, transport and the like.

The genesis of UNCLOS lies on the seabed. In the 1940s and 1950s, coastal states began to lay claim to large areas offshore from their national territories, particularly in the Pacific Ocean, given the near total absence of third parties. Up to that point, the international law of the sea had been piecemeal and at times informal. Typically, states were able to patrol and police territorial waters stretching a couple of miles from a coastline. The 1945 Truman Proclamation was a game-changer. Unilaterally, the United States declared that it enjoyed exploitative rights over the entire continental shelf and was entitled to establish its own fishing zones encompassing vast areas of neighbouring ocean. Other countries followed suit.

UNCLOS was the end result of this change in attitudes towards the world's oceans and seas. It established a framework for dividing up oceans and seas, with some 40 per cent being allocated to coastal states. The remainder was declared high seas, and Article 87 stated that:

> The high seas are open to all States, whether coastal or land-locked. Freedom of the high seas is exercised under the conditions laid down by this Convention and by other rules of international law. It comprises, *inter alia*, both for coastal and land-locked States ... No State may validly purport to subject any part of the high seas to its sovereignty.

In this framework, coastal states could claim extensive rights to what were termed exclusive economic zones, stretching some 200 nautical miles (370km) from their coastlines. Depending on the physical shape and size of the country, the exclusive economic zones could be truly enormous. Large continental states such as Canada and the United States, as well as remote islands in the middle of oceans, were granted large and lucrative exclusive economic zones. A country such as the Maldives, located in the Indian Ocean, was able to declare an exclusive economic zones of around 1 million km^2 (386,000 square miles) because of its elongated shape, made up of 1,200 coral islands and reefs.

International lawyers and diplomats such as Arvid Pardo from Malta in the late 1960s recognised the implicit dangers involved in the zoning of the world's seas and oceans zoning the world's seas and oceans. In their haste to secure maximum advantage, coastal states would focus more on resource extraction (e.g. fishing and oil/gas mining) and less on marine conservation. They would also seek to maximise their privileges at the expense of land-locked states and third parties who might wish to pass through those coastal waters, including exclusive economic zones. Indigenous peoples also expressed concern that their historic water usage would be cited by coastal states if it was advantageous to do so. But once their rights were secured, those same countries would give little time and attention to local and indigenous knowledge and usage. Pardo was instrumental in developing an idea of the deep seabed as a common heritage of mankind (CHM), a recognition that the world's remotest spaces ought to be beyond the realm of national advantage and considered a shared resource that might provide benefit for the many not the few.

Large coastal states, however, continued to focus on securing their rights over ocean and seabed. Pardo recognised that what countries such as the United States wanted to do was to use the world's physical geography to their advantage. With few immediate neighbours to the west and east of the country, the United States as a large and wealthy coastal state would, if given half the chance, engage in 'creeping sovereignty' operations. In 1967, Pardo warned his audience at the UN General Assembly that seabed mining technology in combination with Cold War geopolitical tension would usher into existence a highly militarised and exploited frontier space. The ocean's extraordinary riches would be at the mercy of the most capable and ruthless. In his view, nodules of minerals sitting on top of the ocean's seabed simply awaited appropriation. The US Navy, by the time of the

Pardo speech, had invested heavily in underwater living and submarine operations. Without restrictions being put in place, he was not confident that a 'scramble for the oceans including its seabed' could be avoided.

The speech was electrifying. Pardo's intervention helped to galvanise discussion around the management of the deep seabed and its resources. While he was not the first to suggest the potential for an international body to manage these remote areas of the ocean, the emergence of the deep seabed as a CHM had important implications for the border strategies of coastal and non-coastal states. Eager to avoid the world's oceans being bordered into 'national lakes', UNCLOS established an international seabed authority invested with powers to regulate and control underwater mining in the deep seabed. Coastal states were allowed to establish the outer limits of their continental shelves under UNCLOS rules but any territory beyond that was in effect CHM. Throughout the 1960s and 1970s, international negotiators working on draft proposals for UNCLOS were locked in conflict with one another about how to border the oceans. Developing countries in the global south were particularly sensitive to how frontier spaces of the world's oceans would be managed, while remaining attentive to protecting their own interests. Coastal states, developed and developing, wanted their sovereign interests to be maximised.

The UNCLOS negotiations in the 1970s were notable for their spirit of open participation, probably thanks to the fact that they were not left in the hands of a technical body to generate recommendations. However, the back and forth revealed that the price of consensus rested on inventing fictional understandings of geological features. In order to ensure that all coastal states received the same basic resource rights, the continental shelf was defined as being seabed extending outwards to a maximum of 200 nautical miles (370km) from the coastline. It did not matter whether it was a geological continental shelf or not. This 'coastline' was a legal invention. If coastal states want to extend those resource rights beyond 200 nautical miles from their coastline, they have to follow technical rules that relate to the underwater geology in question.

Where does the underwater border of a coastal state end? The answer (as suggested by China's actions in the South China Sea, discussed in Chapter 1) is not always straightforward. While we can point to the 200-nautical-mile marker as a good indicator, it is not definitive. UNCLOS rules governing the outer limits of the continental shelf are quixotic. If you can prove that there is an extended continental shelf extending beyond 200 nautical miles, then it is possible to make further resource claims over the seabed. This has considerable relevance in contested areas of the world's oceans. Canada, Denmark and Russia all claim that their resource rights extend all the way to the seabed of the Arctic. For the last 15 years, they have been busy mapping and surveying their respective continental shelves at great expense. All the parties concerned are hoping that they can extend their claims to a jurisdiction of 350 nautical miles (648km) from the coastline, or 100 nautical miles (185km) further at the 2,500-metre (8,200-foot) depth line. The central Arctic Ocean is around 4,000m (13,100 feet) deep at its most extreme. Using the UNCLOS rules, all three countries want to arrive at the same destination: a national flag on the bottom of the central Arctic Ocean.

Once coastal states have maximised their resource rights over the global seabed, it is the turn of the International Seabed Authority to help manage the remotest areas of the deep seabed ('the area') under the CHM principle. Any revenues generated from mining activities from 'the area' are supposed to be shared with other members of the international community. International Seabed Authority licensing is also supposed to be attentive to the ecological impact of any such mining activities.

As we look to the future, this mosaic of rules for sea and seabed activity and resource rights is going to face further pressures, with those rights being further qualified depending on whether the resource in question is mobile, immobile, living or non-living. Any living resource on a continental shelf described as 'sedentary', such as a crab, belongs to a coastal state. Although crabs move, they remain in constant contact with the seabed. These classificatory decisions matter to coastal states such as Norway, which wants to retain exclusive control over the lucrative crab trade and prevent others from 'fishing' for crab in the Barents Sea. Any fish stocks that move between a coastal state's exclusive economic zone and the high seas are subject to additional controls on what are described as 'straddling stock' management. Agencies such as the UN's Food and Agricultural *Organization* take a keen interest in fishery management, and regional fisheries management organisations are integral to spatial marine planning.

All of this sounds very orderly and processual. Many of the lines, rules and zones that inform this decision-making originated in the 1970s and 1980s. Since then, the world has moved on and fish too have moved, becoming scarce or over-harvested. Ocean warming and acidification might have driven fish stocks from their traditional areas, leaving some fishing communities and nations bereft. Inevitably tension follows when another country might be an accidental beneficiary of fish-stock migration and other 'dispossessed' parties lose interest in straddling stock management and shared conservation measures. This will place further pressure on the high seas as fishing fleets seek to exploit new fish stocks outside their traditional fisheries. All of these complicated rules cannot prevent conflict over the management of the world's seas and oceans.

Interest in seabed mining probably peaked in the 1970s, but some states such as Papua New Guinea are now leading the way in terms of new partnerships with Chinese and Western mining companies such as Nautilus Minerals. The recent history of deep-seabed mining in Papua New Guinea, however, has not been a happy one. An initiative called Solwara 1 failed in 2019 when Nautilus Minerals filed for bankruptcy. While the operational area was in an undisputed portion of the Bismarck Sea off the Papua New Guinea coastline, it proved unprofitable.

Despite this, interest in deep seabed mining has not disappeared. Remote hydrothermal vents in the so-called 'Lost City' on the seabed around the Mid-Atlantic Ridge are attracting proponents of seabed mining. Super-heated water shoots out minerals originating from the ocean's seabed. As the particles settle, they create a series of distinct mineral-rich chimney-like vents. The 'Lost City' is very remote but it has the attraction of being found in the world's high seas. Fiji, Tonga and the Cook Islands in the vast Pacific Ocean are all hoping that they can attract international investors. They believe there will be substantial subsea deposits of minerals such as cobalt. The Cook Islands' Seabed Minerals Authority announced in 2019 that it had established a 2-million-km^2 (772,000-square-mile) zone for seabed mining activities.

For now, the management of fisheries in the world's high seas are of more immediate concern but we should not lose sight altogether of the world's remote seabed. Vast areas of the world's oceans are classed as high seas, beyond the exclusive reach of any one or more coastal states. The Southern Ocean in particular is a vast high sea and interested parties have struggled to secure agreement on how to manage it. The Ross Sea Marine Protected Area is a good example of how China and New Zealand had radically different views about how to manage this remote marine environment, in terms of balancing fishing with environmental protection. New Zealand and allies such as the European Union and the United States pushed for an even larger conservation area for the Ross Sea while China, Russia and others with fishing interests wanted less stringent regulations and a nonpermanent ban. The Ross Sea agreement lasts for 35 years and then it can be revisited, and we are likely to see the arguments over conservation and exploitation rehearsed again.

Initiatives such as marine protected areas and marine spatial planning more generally are all about bordering. UNCLOS provides a legal and technical framework for establishing and managing those underwater borders. But what UNCLOS cannot do is answer other questions: will we have to reduce the size and scope of marine protected areas over time? What will the common heritage of mankind designation mean in a world facing intensifying climate change, resource pressures and an expected global population of 10 billion after 2050? Will we see island states with large exclusive economic zones finding ever more innovative ways to secure financial support or debt relief from others in return for either marine protection or access to fisheries? Will the deep seabed in due course be a source of conflict as ever more remote spaces on the earth's subterranean realm are subjected to resource-related pressures?

These pressures might not always involve resource stealing. Conflict could start more innocuously with the building and maintenance of underwater infrastructure on the high seas or deep seabed. A wealthy entrepreneur with the backing of a global power such as China, or a non-signatory of UNCLOS such as the US, might decide to invest in a new underwater world. Such plans exist. Since 2014, Japanese architects and the engineering firm Shimizu Corporation have been working on the Ocean Spiral concept project. Costing billions of dollars, the spiral city would be built sometime in the early 2030s and located at least a couple of miles underwater, where the deep seabed would be used as an energy and food source.

It is not difficult to imagine how the ongoing colonisation of the world's oceans in this way could lead to future disputes between nations. Fishing is attracting most of the attention at the moment. The seabed will be next and the UN's International Seabed Authority is discussing a new code to govern seabed mining. The so-called 'blue acceleration' encapsulates the contemporary and future pressures facing the world's oceans. Growing demand for drinking water has provoked an upsurge in desalination plants. Underwater communication cables and pipelines criss-cross the seabed and lie uneasily with other activities such as fishing and dredging. Demand for fish and minerals is increasing. By 2030, global demand for fish will exceed 150 million tons as governments seek to manage 'protein geopolitics'.

China is a ruthless exponent of techniques to manage this. Between 2017 and 2020, Chinese fishing vessels extracted an estimated $500 million of squid from North Korean waters. At least 700 ships are thought to be complicit in the illegal trade. A 2017 UN Security Council sanction against North Korea (issued because of its ballistic missile testing) prohibits the regime from selling its fishing rights. Without the detective work of an international group of academics from Australia, Korea, US and Japan we would be none the wiser about this violation. One possible explanation for the activity is that the North Korean regime has traded its fishing rights in its exclusive economic zone in return for covert payment. Another less likely possibility is that the activity is completely unauthorised. Either way, there should be no Chinese vessels fishing in North Korean waters – and when they are there it ends up displacing smaller-scale North Korean fishing activity. Unlike that of their Chinese counterparts, the North Korean fishing fleet is ageing and poorly equipped to operate in more distant waters. Forced to operate illegally in Japanese and Russian waters, so-called North Korean 'ghost ships' have ended up beached on foreign coastlines.

Finally, we have over a million square kilometres of international seabed that has been allocated to national and commercial operators. Chinese companies are world leaders in underwater mining claims and activities.

WATERY FUTURES

We know our lakes, glaciers, aquifers, seas and oceans are critical to humanity and to life on earth. We have rules in place to deal with common resources and spaces such as the world's high seas. But they were developed in a very different era from the one we face now and in the future. World population is rising. Climate change is altering the world's oceans, lakes, rivers and ice-covered areas. And if we transition to a low-carbon energy future, we will need more not less minerals to affect a global shift towards a renewable energy infrastructure, including battery storage.

It is now widely accepted that 25 per cent of the world's human population faces water stress. That means nearly 2 billion people are coming close to consuming their available water supply each year. The World Resources Institute, a research-based organisation in the United States, noted in its 2019 report that world leaders need to talk more about the consequences of water risk. The organisation produces national water-stress rankings, and the 'Extremely High

Baseline Water Stress' states are overwhelmingly located in an arc stretching from Palestine, Lebanon and Israel in the west to India, Pakistan and Turkmenistan in the east. Vast numbers of people, therefore, depend on glaciated regions, river systems, lakes and aquifers that straddle international boundaries.

We have, of course, good examples of shared management in Europe, the Americas, Africa and Asia. The most successful schemes tend to be ones in which partners are equally committed to shared international legal and political frameworks and have a history of collaboration and confidence-building measures. But those elements are not always in place, and many people doubt whether the international community is responding to the growing challenges with enough vigour. Climate change, increased economic activity and population growth all place more stress on water supplies. Floods, droughts, earthquakes, landslides and other natural disasters contaminate and compromise water infrastructure. Widespread pollution is highly detrimental to public health, and water treatment is patchy in the poorest parts of the world. Indigenous communities, even in advanced economies such as Canada, will have had experience of intermittent and unsafe water supplies. The major South African city of Cape Town faced the spectre of water exhaustion in 2018, with 'day zero' (no drinking water available) being averted by emergency measures and severe restrictions on municipal water supplies. By 2050, water stress will be commonplace for around 4 to 5 billion people, with shortages of supply commonplace.

International legal developments are responding to water stress. The Costa Rica/Nicaragua dispute revealed a willingness on the part of the International Court of Justice to award compensation for environmental damage and not just respond to a border dispute. In 2017, the Global Pact for the Environment was inaugurated with the explicit hope that a legally binding instrument would emerge that recognises there should be a universal right to an 'ecologically sound environment'. If legally binding, it would contain provisions for citizens and communities to hold their government and others to account for the impact of their actions on environments. Imagine if the citizens of cities such as Flint in Michigan and Basra in Iraq, many of whom were poisoned by dirty water, could hold their local, state and national governments to account and demand radical improvement.

This, of course, does not solve the challenge of these watery borders. Some governments might not care about a Global Pact for the Environment and might be indifferent to suffering populations. Others might regard the long-term fate of a river or lake as a profound threat to their very existence, and no amount of potential legal action would deter them from building another dam, extracting more water, taking more fish and colonising new territories revealed by the retreat of ice or the emergence of riverbeds, shorelines and islands. Shrinkage in lakes and rivers, due either to prolonged drought or excessive water extraction, only creates the scope for more land and water grabbing.

In order to achieve radical change in energy generation, as well as securing a world community that will exceed 10 billion people, we will exploit further the world's oceans, lakes, rivers and sources of freshwater such as glaciers. Will our rules developed in the 1970s and 1980s remain fit for purpose? In the spring of 2020, UN member states met again in New York to try and advance a legally binding agreement on the conservation of marine biodiversity in the world's high seas. Conserving, however, does not mean protecting. A schism exists between those who want to protect the world's high seas and a group of countries, led by China, who are looking to the seabed for minerals and food resources.

A new era of seabed grabbing and potential geopolitical disruption beckons, and the significance of border delimitation beneath the sea level will continue. Our global commons are vulnerable. And next time your internet fails, just remember – it might be due to underwater sabotage. There is no internet, as Benjamin Bratton reminds us, without an 'earth layer' – and much of that lies on the surface of the world's oceans.

A young boy sitting on a tree branch as the tide comes in with the waves beneath him. The people of Kiribati are under pressure to relocate due to sea level rise. Each year, the sea level rises by about half an inch and there are real worries that the long-term viability of the island-nation is compromised. In September 2019, Kiribati turned to China for help and Beijing has proposed large-scale dredging to reclaim land using their fleet of dredgers that built artificial islands in the South China Sea.

Chapter 4

Vanishing Borders

OUR POLITICAL MAP IS LARGELY BASED ON THE PRESUMPTION
that land and sea don't change a great deal, and that it is possible and
even desirable to divide the world via boundary lines. Claims to sovereignty and self-determination are, more often than not, bounded by
those lines. Our countries are frequently thought of as being
container-like, with governments seeking to control matters within
their own borders, as well as the movement of people in and out.
Mantras such as 'taking back control' are rooted in this belief that territory and sovereignty should be full and exclusive. But not even North
Korea manages to achieve such Olympian heights of mastery – things
have a habit of slipping in and out of a country irrespective of border
controls.

When we move offshore, this model of idealised political geography becomes even more complicated. State control of the world's

seas and oceans tapers off the further one travels away from land-forms. Coastal states don't own seas and oceans in the same way they own land. As we have seen, water borders are largely invisible, as there are no formal boundary makers at sea defining where an exclusive economic zone begins and ends. As with airspace, states can track and monitor activity within their 12-nautical-mile (22km) zones, but we don't have the same sort of border infrastructure we find on land. States are not allowed to exercise exclusive control over their waters, as allowances have to be made for vessels to travel through them and carry out activities that don't 'interfere' with another party's exclusive economic zone. Uncertainty, risk and ambiguity lurk large because it is not always very clear how to define 'interference'.

But imagine for a moment that sea-level rise meant that islands around the world disappeared. If land territory and associated borders vanish, who gets to decide on underwater resource ownership? For centuries, we developed procedures, customs and rules for a physical world with identifiable coastlines, river systems and islands. These will be inundated if sea-level rise continues as expected in the current century. On the flip side, new territory can emerge as well. Volcanic islands have appeared following eruptions, notably Surtsey to the immediate south of Iceland in 1963. No one lives on the island, and it is expected to disappear by 2100 because of the ongoing erosion of its foundation of tephra (the fragmented material produced by the eruption of a volcano). The world faces the prospect of inhabited low-lying islands in the Pacific Ocean and highly populated coastline cities and towns being inundated. It is now commonplace to speak of climate refugees, and extreme climatic events that are highly disruptive to communities around the world are likely to occur more often in the future. Even wealthy nations such as the United States have had to face the spectre of inundation, from Hurricane Katrina (2005) and its impact on the Gulf Coast to ongoing relocation efforts in the state of Alaska that have seen coastal communities adversely affected by severe winter storms. Meanwhile, 2019 was a terrible 'hurricane year' in other regions such as the Bahamas.

Vanishing borders are something we are going to have to get used to as the world is subjected to increasing levels of heat and moisture. The speed, scope and severity of climate change are pointing to a world where the sea level will be very different in the coming centuries, and many vulnerable communities worry that they will simply be obliterated by seawater. Sea-level rise is not uniform. While some island states will disappear, the surface of the sea is not flat. It is estimated that the worst affected will be Kiribati, Tuvalu and the Maldives. If the global sea level rises by around 0.8 to 1m (32 to 39 inches) by the end of the current century then it is estimated that the earth's land surface will shrink by around 17,000km² (6,600 square miles) and millions of people will be displaced.

VANISHING BORDERS AND THE ANTHROPOCENE

What happens to states that disappear? We are, of course, used to countries fragmenting. The Soviet Union ceased to exist in 1991, but the borders of that former state can and do still cause tension. The annexation of Crimea in 2014 by Russia and ongoing instability in eastern Ukraine are stark reminders of that, as was the short war between Russia and Georgia in 2008. But territorial annexation and occupation notwithstanding, the territorial footprint of those states is still largely recognisable. The territories can still be seen and are very much inhabitable.

Sea-level rise and other forms of profound environmental change pose a rather different challenge to borders. As the world recognises that our climate and environment are changing, we can no longer assume that the geography of the earth will remain largely static. Sea levels, for example, have been comparatively stable for around 6,000 years, but modelling work done by scientists around the world has resulted in some arresting conclusions. By 2030, it is estimated that around 40 per cent of urban land globally is going to experience regular flooding. The south-east coast of the United States, for example, is highly vulnerable, and more so because it is projected to experience significant population growth. If sea-level rise continues, the prospect of large-scale population movement involving millions of people seems likely. High-altitude cities such as Denver and the Midwest in general are predicted to be popular destinations for sea-level-rise migrants. Florida and the Gulf Coast, on the other hand, are at the risk of substantial inundation.

Vanishing territories and their associated borders are now considered to be a distinct feature of a proposed new climatic era: the Anthropocene. Replacing the Holocene, which marked a period of relative climatic stability lasting some 10,000 years, this new term, coined in 2000, signified a landmark break with the past. Henceforth, climate-change scientists declared that we would need to recognise humanity as a geophysical force, possessing such collective power that the earth's systems were being altered in significant fashion. Arguments continue about when the Anthropocene actually began but the message is nonetheless stark: humanity needs to be understood for what it truly is – a planetary force.

But as soon as the term gained popularity, other voices with different perspectives called into question this tendency to think of the cumulative impact of humanity as being universal. Surely it was necessary to distinguish between colonial-imperial powers, who had embraced the Industrial Revolution and exploited fossil fuels to empower their own economic and society transformation, and other parts of the world that had been exploited for raw materials. If the world's climate is changing, we need to recognise that the all-encompassing 'Anthro' (human) in Anthropocene needs to be treated with some caution. Observers such as Dipesh Chakrabarty have been vocal advocates of this point of view. Climate change is a disease of the wealthy and nearly half of the world's carbon pollution in the atmosphere belongs to the combined efforts of the United States and Europe. Africa is only responsible for about 5 per cent of the world's carbon pollution. Similarly, the term 'sea-level rise' is misleading and better thought of as sea-level change, because it will not be uniform. Put simply, larger countries are going to have more geographical opportunities to escape from excessive heat, rising water, drought, and severe cyclones and tornados.

Scientists warn that, if warming continues, ongoing ice loss in the polar regions and glaciated regions of the world is going to cause global disruption. As Afelee Pita, a representative of the Pacific Ocean island community of Tuvalu (a group of islands home to 11,000 people living on 26km²/10 square miles of land territory), warned the United Nations in 2007, the world is in the midst of a 'warming war'. Changing sea level will obliterate the lower-lying communities and territories of the world.

What, then, happens if an island is submerged by rising water? Apart from the severe human and ecological disruption, the disappearance of the island raises other troubling issues: do the waters around the previous inhabited islands become high seas? What happens to the resource rights of a previous island-state, such as access to an exclusive economic zone? A community might not only be forced to flee a flooded island but then face further loss of potential revenue through access to fishing grounds, mineral rights and the like, because it no longer has the capacity to exercise its sovereign rights.

Assessment reports from the Intergovernmental Panel on Climate Change (IPCC) have warned that sea-level change could involve rises anywhere from 50cm to 100cm (20 to 39 in), depending on how successful we are at reducing greenhouse gas emissions by the end of 2100. Climate-change scientists warn, however, that these estimates are conservative in their scope. Further ice loss from Greenland and the Antarctic ice sheet, coupled with thermal expansion of the world's oceans, might make sea-level change even more profound. Scientific studies published in 2019 suggested that as many as 180 million people could be displaced as several million square kilometres of land is inundated by rising sea levels at the end of the current century.

Vanishing borders are not only problematic for human communities but are geopolitically and legally challenging too. As the earth proves to be less stable and predictable, we are likely to discover that our borders are less durable as well. Minor adjustments to physical borders are, as we have noted, not uncommon. Sea level can and does

alter for a variety of reasons, some of which are related to glacial melting and temperature change. It can also be down to other factors,
such as earthquakes and volcanic eruptions, that are not directly
related to climate change. Our border disputes can be resolved
through negotiation, and sometimes we recognise that we cannot
resolve conditions by the establishment of buffer zones and demilitarised areas. But when borders simply vanish because entire blocks of
land are swept away or immersed by water, then so much of what we
take for granted is undermined.

Hollywood got there before us. In *Waterworld* (1995), viewers
were presented with a world sometime around the year 2500 in
which the earth's ice has long since melted. The sea level has risen
by thousands of feet and there is little to no land remaining. Surviving
communities have to make do with artificial structures (called atolls)
floating in and through an ocean world. People no longer remember
living on land, though some still dream about it. Humans are now
exclusively marine mammals. But as the movie suggests, 'water
worlds' are still dangerous, as the survivors gravitate towards the
promise of 'dry land'. The movie did not garner a great deal of positive reviews, but it did usefully raise the issue of sea-level rise and
dramatise the consequences of human communities losing access
to land.

SEA-LEVEL RISE AS BORDER THREAT

We can now point to as many as 70 countries that are going to be
affected by sea-level rise. Low-lying and smaller island states make up
most of that list, but larger countries such as China and the United
States are not going to escape the consequences of sea-level rise.

In its '2030 Agenda for Sustainable Development', the UN recognised that sea-level rise posed a major threat to many states around
the world. The international community has become increasingly
worried about sea-level rise and that anxiety is no longer confined to
just the 70 most affected countries. Our rules governing refugees will

need to be updated in an era of further displacement caused by severe weather, sea-level change and environmental degradation (as we shall see, global refugee conventions reflect the human costs of the Second World War and the Holocaust, not contemporary and future environmental emergencies). We will need to acknowledge a new kind of person or community – environmental refugees. Areas of land may simply not be capable of hosting human communities, and repeated exposure to extreme events will carry with it financial costs to host governments, including access to investment. Credit scores will inevitably suffer and, without injections of aid, there will be countries that face bankruptcy. Adding insult to injury, some of these low-lying islands have taken another financial hit with a pandemic-related collapse in the global tourism market.

The International Law Association established a new international committee in 2012 to look at sea-level rise. An earlier International Law Association Committee on Baselines warned lawyers that they were facing a radically different world to the one that had been assumed would always exist when major international frameworks, such as the United Nations Convention on the Law of the Sea, were negotiated in the 1970s. Climate change was not spoken about as a topic for international law at that time, and the world's oceans and seas were seen as bodies of water to be divided up, managed and exploited in a peaceful and cooperative manner. UNCLOS did acknowledge the spectre of sea-level rise, but it was not until the 1990s that discussion began about what would happen if the physical geographies of the earth shifted and mutated. In 2012, the Committee on Baselines concluded that sea-level rise carried with it the distinct possibility that smaller low-lying states would lose territory and thus potentially cease to be able to exercise their authority over neighbouring seas and oceans. Inundation in its entirety carried with it the existential loss of statehood, national identity, access to resources and a country's capacity to experience peace and security, and would lead to forced migration.

Following its report, the International Law Association established a follow-up body called the Committee on International Law and Sea Level Rise. The committee recognised that it would need to address the future of the law of the sea, the ramifications of territorial loss and forced migration, and the impact of sea-level rise on statehood and international security. In other words, if the earth is heading towards a more extensive watery future, then we will need to plan for a world in which some countries will see their land areas shrink or even disappear. Communities will not only become unsustainable but there is surely a fear that their territorial seas and exclusive economic zones become plundered by others.

The Alliance of Small Island States (AOSIS), created in 1990, has been active in promoting better understanding of the regional implications of climate change for small and low-lying states. It lobbies the international community and has been proactive in demanding that international law address the very real prospect of disappearing territory, population loss, environmental refugees and the danger of non-recognition of past territorial seas and exclusive economic zones. At the Climate Change Conference (COP 15) held in Copenhagen in 2009, Ian Fry, the representative from Tuvalu, came to the podium to deliver a simple message. He told his audience that 'the fate of my country rests in your hands', and implored them to commit to a radical reduction of emissions. While his plea did not fall on deaf ears, it was probably too late to save Tuvalu.

THE FUTURE OF BASELINES

The coastline, or 'baseline' in international legal terminology, is integral to assessing where the land territory of a state ends and its offshore rights to the sea and its contents begin. Drawing boundaries and establishing baselines is something that troubled past generations. In the sixteenth and seventeenth centuries, the lines of sea control were effectively decided by the gunshot rule. A nation's territorial sea was to be determined by the maximum range that a land-based cannon, located on top of a cliff, on the beach or on an offshore island, could discharge a shot. Three nautical miles (5.6km) was taken to be the de facto limit, but this relied on an assumption that the land would be a stable and consistently identifiable space. Four centuries later, international maritime law used this concept of the baseline to establish formal zoning of the world's seas and oceans. The baseline is the political and legal border of the state. When states make claims to 12 nautical miles (22km) of territorial sea, the starting point for that measurement is the low-water line of the coastline. The low-water line is not accidental; rather it allows states to make their territorial sea stretch a bit further, as opposed to if the measuring tape started at the high-water mark. The beach, in other words, is very much part of a country's national territory. It is no easy to task to measure a country's coastline, so international maritime law often operates with a simplified geographical reality because it makes it easier to establish principles and rules.

When it comes to coastlines and continental shelves, lawyers and geologists have different understandings of their physical forms and composition. Even if geologists don't approve of those legal understandings, every coastal state can and does agree on those principles. The ensuing rules allow coastal states to identify and declare territorial seas and exclusive economic zones. These delimitations then set up parameters for third parties to come through those territorial seas and exclusive economic zones. We can speak of innocent passage, transit passage, freedom of navigation and rights to do things precisely because international law establishes a mosaic of rights and responsibilities. All of this is possible because the world's oceans and seas have been measured and lines have been drawn.

The beach and the coastline, therefore, provide the geographical foundations for international maritime law, but rising sea levels threaten to undo this complex, calculative work. And coastlines are complicated geographical environments, which, as a consequence of wave action and prevailing winds, are ever-changing. The coast of any island or continent zigzags unless it has been artificially straightened by coastal engineering. We explicitly acknowledge that dynamism because we try to manage our coastal environments by building sea defences or by recognising that natural environments such as mangrove swamps, beaches, rocks and sea ice serve as vital physical buffers to inland spaces. Without those buffers, waves would directly hit areas where our homes and infrastructure are more exposed.

Coastal states have already proved to be increasingly adept at using their coastlines opportunistically. Rather than using low-water marks on beaches, low-tide elevations (such as reefs and rocks that surface as and when tides alter) have been seized upon to make claims to territorial seas. In the most egregious cases, China and others in the South China Sea have artificially created new islands and eleva-tions to support their claims to maritime control. All of which takes time and considerable effort, using in China's case a fleet of dredgers backed up by a naval and military presence. Presumably, given the importance accorded to the South China Sea, China will continue to invest to ensure that these territories are not overwhelmed by rising sea level.

We might think that what China and others are doing in the South China Sea is an abuse of legal and military power. But what happens when other states have to engage in artificial island building and fortification in order simply to endure? Reinforcement might be a survival strategy rather than a geopolitical landgrab. Our views about artificially manipulating islands and coastlines might change depend-ing on the context. Vanishing borders and inundated territories raise troubling issues for all of us regardless of where we call home. A third of the world's communities are already facing threats from sea-level rise, and no one who studies this topic thinks the number of affected communities and states is not going to increase.

MALDIVES: POSTER CHILD FOR VANISHING BORDERS

For many smaller low-lying islands around the world, the loss of terri-tory to sea-level rise is compounded further by the prospect of loss of their exclusive economic zones; depending on location, territorial shape and relative remoteness, these zones can be enormous. The fate of the Maldives has often been cited as a prime example of this. The physical geography of this low-lying archipelago, located in the Indian Ocean, is extraordinary. It is made up of more than 1,000 coral islands and sand bars in a chain-like structure of atolls that spread in a north–south direction. The atolls cover an area of some 90,000km^2 (35,000 square miles) and are composed of dead coral surrounded by a living coral reef, which is extremely sensitive to changes in water temperature and ocean acidity, and subject to damage by tropical cyclones. Much of the country is only about 1m (3 feet) above sea level.

The government organises this disparate grouping into 19 administrative divisions that encompass more sea than land. Coral atolls are highly dynamic environments, which have changed over millennia. Over time, communities on these islands have engaged in coastal engineering in an attempt to stabilise living conditions. Building sea dykes and elevating buildings are common responses to living just above the prevailing sea level.

As we have already noted, the Maldives' exclusive economic zone is huge, encompassing some 1 million km^2 (386,000 square miles). On a map the zone looks like a large rectangle, and a bit in the northeast corner comes into contact with India and Sri Lanka's respective exclusive economic zones. Fishing provides the backbone to the country's economy, including more than 65 per cent of its export commodity income, with the vast majority of that generated by tuna harvesting. Without the exclusive economic zone and tourism, the Maldives would have limited options to support its population of around 450,000 people. If sea-level change continues, it is clear that the country's atolls and other land territories will be submerged.

Inundation poses an existential risk to the Maldives, and in the last decade plans have been hatched to establish and fund a climate-change trust fund involving international partners such as the European Union and World Bank. The fund is intended to help the country prepare itself with new resilience measures such as building adaption, waste management and renewable energy generation. Previous presidents of the country such as Mohamed Nasheed were prominent in drawing attention to its plight. In 2009 he held a cabinet meeting underwater in an attempt to communicate to the world the reality of ongoing climate change: that low-lying islands and coast-lines would be overwhelmed. The meeting ended after 30 minutes with a collective communiqué calling for the world to cut its global greenhouse gas emissions. The former president also worked with other countries such as Bangladesh to highlight the fact that vulner-ability to climate change was not equally shared around the world.

The Maldives is ground zero for these debates about sea-level change and its implications for international borders and the recogni-tion of sovereign states. If the country's atolls disappeared and thus became uninhabitable, there is a distinct possibility that others would conclude there is no longer a defined territory. The 1933 Montevideo Convention sets out four criteria for what is termed a 'recognisable state'. In order to qualify, there has to be evidence of a permanent population, a defined territory, a functioning government and a capac-ity to enter into relations with other states. The loss of territory might lead some nations to refuse to recognise the inundated state and thus deny that they have the ability to enter into relations with others. Alternatively, the international community might point to other enti-ties such as the Sovereign Military Order of Malta, which has formal diplomatic relations with multiple states despite having no formal ter-ritory (its territorial presence used to be in Malta but that was lost in 1798). It has observer status at the UN and issues its own passports, stamps and currency.

What happens to islands such as the Maldives will provide impor-tant precedents for the international community and its prevailing international legal and political frameworks: no coastline, no rights to a territorial sea, no exclusive economic zone and no access to the resources therein.

THE BAY AS A VANISHING BORDER

It is not only low-lying island nations that will be affected by sea-level change, of course: coastlines and bays will be, too. Even if countries such as India and Bangladesh do not face the same existential crises as the Maldives and Tuvalu, the Bay of Bengal reveals the challenges posed by inundation and environmental change to non-island states. The Bay of Bengal is bordered by India, Bangladesh, Myanmar, Sri Lanka and Indonesia. For millennia it has hosted an array of activities, including trade, resource extraction and cultural exchange. Imperial powers took advantage of the Bay of Bengal to further their own commercial and trading interests in commodities such as tea and rubber. And for inland countries, the bay has been a vital trade route and source of commercial income through activities such as fishing. Some 500 million people live and work in the Bay of Bengal region and changing weather patterns have highlighted the scale of vulnerability now facing these littoral communities. In 2013, for example, a violent storm hit the Indian state of Odisha, forcing around 800,000 to flee from their coastal communities.

The Bay of Bengal is also a vital strategic space for coastal countries. India and Bangladesh have a recent history of conflict and tension over the bay's maritime delimitation and resource usage. Bangladesh and Myanmar have also had their own arguments over marine boundaries, which were eventually settled at a UN tribunal in 2014. What makes all of this more complicated in geopolitical terms is that there is an ongoing refugee crisis involving Rohingya (a Muslim minority community), and thousands have had to flee Myanmar to neighbouring countries such as Thailand. Environmentally, the bay is threatened by rising levels of pollution, salinisation and fish-stock management. Over the centuries, the impact of colonialism, violent monsoons and disastrous droughts has ensured that these waters have rarely been free of human and physical drama.

Rising waters and unpredictable weather are now placing new stresses on the Bay of Bengal. Coastal states worry not only about illegal migration across the bay but also about the future of marine geopolitics. Bangladesh and Myanmar are very different propositions to somewhere like the Maldives. The former has a population of 164 million, but this is predicted to rise to around 200 million by 2050, and Myanmar has a population of 56 million, which is predicted to grow to 63 million by 2050. Both are low-lying and punctuated by

extensive floodplains, and both have coastal communities that bear
the brunt of seasonal cyclones and floods. If sea-level rise continues
as expected, the living conditions of millions will be disrupted and
might lead to millions more being displaced by inundation. Both
countries are considered to be among the worst prepared when it
comes to climate-change adaption and resilience, in large part due to
poverty and the scale of population exposure.

Climate-change migration in the region is very likely and will put
considerable pressure on other states such as India and Sri Lanka to
accommodate fleeing communities. Regional cooperation is going to
be essential, and the littoral states have already initiated discussions
about how they might plan collectively for mitigation and adaption.
Progress is likely to be slow, even if there is recognition that states
such as Bangladesh are on borrowed time.

In Bangladesh, more 20 million people at present face water stress
due to salinisation, which only compounds the threat of sea-level rise.
If floodplains are poisoned by salt, they become uninhabitable even if
they are not fully inundated by seawater. While Bangladesh has
invested in storm shelters and coastal engineering, the prospect of
millions being displaced, whether in search of viable drinking water
or because of inundation, is clearly unsettling near neighbours.

At the same time, islands off the Bangladeshi coast are vanishing, lost to relentless erosion due to rising water levels. It bears
repeating that disappearing territory has geopolitical ramifications.
Even uninhabited outcrops and small islands can be the object of
disagreement. India and Bangladesh dispute the ownership of outcrops such as New Moore Island/South Talpatti (the Indian and
Bangladeshi names respectively), which disappeared in 2010. Both
sides argued about whether it was an island or low-tide elevation.
Never more than 2m (6 feet) above sea level, it witnessed the Indian
Navy plant a flag on it in 1981. India then declared that the dispute
was in effect resolved by rising sea levels. Bangladesh, on the other
hand, was reluctant to concede that the disappearance was permanent, because it worried that this might affect their shared border
more generally. UNCLOS distinguishes between islands, rocks and

low-tide elevations. Low-tide elevations and rocks cannot be used to generate maritime zones such as exclusive economic zones because they cannot support human habitation. In order to qualify as an island, the land in question must be above the high-tide mark. If more territory disappears, including offshore islands and low-tide elevations, Bangladesh fears that this will embolden India to take advantage of its dire circumstances. In July 2014, the former won an important international judgment against India regarding a disputed area of their shared sea border in the Bay of Bengal. The judgment was important because the UNCLOS tribunal used the shape of the country's coastline along the bay to come to a judgment about the delimitation of their territorial sea and exclusive economic zones. Bangladesh was awarded some 80 per cent of the disputed area, which was significant in terms of allowing the country to press ahead with resource exploration and exploitation. But this will all be moot if the country becomes ever more uninhabitable.

VANISHING COUNTRIES AND THEIR BORDERS

If, as expected, the world's oceans and seas submerge islands and low-lying coastlines, the implications for humanity, ecologies and infrastructures will be immense, and international law and geopolitics are still trying to catch up. In the ice-covered regions of the world, we have new worries that the retreat of sea ice will invite new scrambles for territorial advantage and access to resources. In low-lying environments, the spectre of disappearance takes on a difference resonance. What unites both, however, is the perception that this might invite others to take advantage of the absence of land and ice. Two issues in particular will demand ever greater attention for those most directly affected by rising waters: citizenship and international recognition.

First, what happens to a country's population if its homeland becomes uninhabitable due to extreme events? At the very least, that country will have to confront the existence of a new generation of refugees, who have had to flee due to climate change rather than war or political and economic crisis. Will it be possible to remain, say, a Maldivian citizen if one's national country is inundated? Should a larger country such as Australia or India be asked to give up some of its land territory so that the Maldivian community could potentially generate a new homeland?

It is clear that the fate of climate-displaced peoples will need to be addressed in the current century. The Maldives is one of the most densely populated countries on earth, and the population, which is also made up of significant minority populations from Nepal, Sri Lanka and Bangladesh, is forecast to rise to 550,000 by the mid-century. In the case of mass evacuation, a significant body of people will either have to be accommodated in neighbouring countries such as India and Sri Lanka or distributed elsewhere in the world.

But what happens if portions of a community decide to leave before inundation takes hold? In November 2014, a New Zealand court heard a case involving another low-lying country, Kiribati (an even more dispersed island group in the Pacific that encompasses some 3 million km^2/1.2 million square miles). The Teitiota family petitioned the New Zealand Supreme Court with a request for asylum. The family's case rested on the assertion that their home was no longer habitable, with rising sea levels forcing many families to leave for higher ground. Overcrowding neighbouring atolls caused food shortages, land conflict and worsening living conditions, including contaminated drinking water, and the family therefore claimed they were environmental refugees. The court rejected their case in 2015, citing their failure to meet the benchmarks set out in the 1951 Convention Relating to the Status of Refugees, with the judge arguing that the family could not claim that they were in fear of persecution. If the case had succeeded, it was feared by many commentators that New Zealand would face multiple requests from other Pacific Ocean island citizens.

The case revealed that the 1951 convention did not have climate-change refugees in mind when it was negotiated. The traumatic experiences of the Second World War and the Holocaust loomed large at the time of its genesis. The focus of the convention was, therefore, on someone who lives in fear of persecution and/or physical danger. The convention's definition of a refugee – as someone fleeing persecution and violence and who has crossed an international border to escape that source of danger – does not sit easily with a broader view of a refugee as someone who escapes from home in order to seek refuge or protection. If the convention doesn't change, the international community will in all likelihood have to come up with other mechanisms to address climate-change refugees. Unlike economic migrants, they would not have a home country to which they could be returned, and our categories for dealing with refugees and migrants would no longer be applicable.

The very idea of a climate-change refugee is also controversial in some quarters. After Hurricane Katrina hit New Orleans and the Gulf Coast in August 2005, there was widespread flooding of parts of New Orleans. Surges of seawater burst past levees and inundated entire neighbourhoods. The Lower Ninth Ward of the city was devastated by water. At least 1,800 people perished in New Orleans and elsewhere along the affected coastline, and hundreds of thousands were internally displaced. The cost of the clean-up ran into billions of dollars and President George W. Bush found himself in the middle of a controversy about the response of the federal government before and after the hurricane. African-American communities were disproportionately affected by the displacement and many were unhappy to be categorised as 'refugees' in case it implied they might be second-class citizens or, worse, foreign residents. While the costs of Katrina and other hurricanes such as Sandy and Harvey have been considerable, the displacement has been internal to the United States. The flood waters eventually subsided but many residents of the Lower Ninth Ward never returned.

The second question relates to international recognition. In particular, climate change poses challenging legal questions for low-lying island states. If you don't have a recognisable and inhabitable land territory, do you lose your formal representation in international bodies such as the UN or the South Asian Association for Regional Cooperation (SAARC)? As already touched upon when discussing the prospects for the Maldives, can submerged countries still make claim to their exclusive economic zones if their land territories are no longer capable of supporting human communities? International maritime law distinguishes between rocks and islands, and posits that only the latter are capable of supporting human habitation. If the Maldives no longer existed, would the international community 'freeze-frame' the exclusive economic zone that did once exist and commit to helping the community exploit and manage that area? The obvious alternative is that this part of the ocean is reassigned as high seas with a different model for fisheries management in the region being adopted.

The loss of an exclusive economic zone would be disastrous to the community and, as the political leaders of other low-lying islands have warned, the world needs to address these issues now before inundation and the flow of climate-change refugees generate more tension and crisis. For the international community it would probably be possible to recognise the legal existence of a country (i.e. by maintaining its presence as a UN member state, distinct telephone dialling code and even a historic exclusive economic zone) while acknowledging that its physical existence is compromised. What that does not resolve, however, is what to do with a raft of displaced peoples that cannot possibly return to their home territory. While long-term refugees exist already, this is not because countries such as Afghanistan have disappeared. Thus host communities will need to adjust to the fact that long-term migration crises affecting many parts of the world are likely to become the new norm.

The potential disappearance of countries such as the Maldives and Kiribati is stimulating some interesting new initiatives such as Migration with Dignity. Supported by Australia and New Zealand, the plan allows for Kiribati citizens to travel to those two countries to gain new skills and employment experience, the rationale being that if and when Kiribati becomes uninhabitable, it will have a population that is composed of skilled migrants who are less likely to be seen as a burden to a host country. In 2014, Kiribati also purchased a parcel of land in Fiji, which might allow the refugees an opportunity to regroup and rebuild, albeit one limited to about 20km^2 (8 square miles) for a current population of around 120,000. Fiji itself has also had to deal with extreme weather and a rising sea level, and has invested heavily in making adjustments to infrastructure and even community distribution. Since 2014, a number of Fijian villages have moved further inland or contemplated new locations. What makes some of this possible is population size. The numbers of people affected is not insignificant but it is not of the scale that might yet affect more populous areas of the world such as the Bay of Bengal.

It is clear that those countries facing inundation are having to think of alternative strategies. Kiribati is the first low-lying country to buy foreign land, but this approach is not without its risks, as the state that has agreed to sell the parcels of land might demand that these enclaves are formally incorporated into their national territories on the grounds of national security considerations in the future. The Maldives considered something similar in 2009 but did not go ahead with any purchase. Instead, it has discussed building upwards on the atolls – in other words, using stilts to elevate and extend community life. There are, of course, examples of overwater bungalows in the islands, many of which are luxury hotels and villas designed for well-heeled foreigners. The challenge is to build not just for resorts but for indigenous residents facing sea-level rise.

We might also need to recognise that abandonment brings opportunities for other well-funded and financed states. The South China Sea provides a model of a possible future for reefs, atolls and low-lying elevations. China and others might decide to capitalise on abandonment and use fleets of dredgers to rebuild inundated land territory. One country's misfortune is another country's opportunity. Inundated territory offers third parties two basic options: either offer to help the country in need of elevated housing and infrastructure or simply occupy where that land territory once was and start to reclaim it for themselves. While a humanitarian intervention might end up leading to a third party using land reclamation to achieve military or strategic advantage. It is worth bearing in mind that the Maldives is heavily indebted to China after giving sovereign guarantees totalling around

$3 billion. Chinese money has paid for a new highway and bridge connecting the national airport to the capital city Malé. There has also been investment in an artificial island called Hulhumalé. Opposition politicians in the Maldives have accused China of using foreign direct investment to deliberately weaken the national government and use debt as a technique to subjugate weaker nations.

FUTURE BORDER SOLUTIONS?

The spectre of vanishing borders might be mitigated by direct action and support from others. States tend to dislike geographical vacuums. Fleeing citizens from low-lying states such as Kiribati might find themselves in new relationships, such as a federation with another host state, or they might establish a government in exile (similar to the Tibetan Government in Exile in India) hosted in a third-party state. A sympathetic third party might undertake to protect the interests of the submerged party. The international community might give additional funding to the most vulnerable states to enable extensive engineering projects designed to elevate essential infrastructure and community support. Artificial additions to islands are likely to become increasingly prominent.

It is not unusual for countries to invest heavily in artificial engineering to ensure that their coastlines are not inundated and can maintain communities. The Netherlands, for instance, has invested significant sums in coastal engineering and dykes to ensure that the country's future is as secure as possible, and the South China Sea provides another illustrative example of countries pushing resources towards artificial islands. Japan has invested in Okinotorishima (Douglas Reef) in order to ensure that its southernmost 'island' is inhabited. Artificiality in this context is being used to preserve sovereignty and ensure maritime rights, and the more extensive projects have been carried out by wealthier states. In the case of those low-lying states with huge exclusive economic zones in the Indian and Pacific oceans, it is questionable whether powerful, even predatory, fishing nations such as China, Russia and Korea would respect the maritime zones of disappearing island states.

What we can say with some confidence is that disappearing island states and climate-change refugees are going to demand increasing attention from the international community, with natural disasters and ongoing climate change creating new drivers for internal and international displacement. The 1951 convention on the status of refugees could be updated to define 'persecution' as including severe environmental state-change. Or perhaps the world's largest producers of greenhouse gases might be seen as indirectly 'persecuting' more vulnerable communities in the world. Currently, there is no international legal recognition of the category 'climate-change refugee' because 'receiving states' are likely to be concerned about how to manage either temporary or permanent relocation. The matter is complicated by such questions as how one might recognise the scale and intensity of 'disappearance', what the right of 'return' should be and whether a third party could insist a refugee community return to their original territory if it re-emerged from the sea.

Vanishing borders are going to be a reality for low-lying states around the world and there will be coastal communities also at risk of inundation. The risk factors vary, as do the immediate and long-term consequences. International legal frameworks designed in the 1970s and 1980s seem out of kilter with the current conditions. The future will place further pressures on assumptions we might have once made about a world where the distinction between land and sea was relatively stable. Earlier interventions such as the Montevideo Convention (1933) told us that a state had to have a defined territory. Being recognised as a defined territory matters and when countries become submerged, challenges of the first order emerge.

Vanishing and drowning territories have the capacity to generate border conflicts of the future. When a territory disappears, it throws up a host of unedifying possibilities. Most of those states facing existential ruin are small and low-lying countries such as the Marshall Islands, which could easily fall victim to great-power competitiveness between China and the United States, including over commercial fishing. Illegal fishing, often fuelled by long-distance fishing fleets, is an uncomfortable fact of life around the world – even when island states are not yet inundated. The Marshall Islands are plagued by illegal fishing by East Asian fishing operators hunting for lucrative tuna. It is inherently unjust that the most vulnerable to theft of resources are the least culpable when it comes to climate change.

The view from the North Korean Side: North Korean Soldiers guard the border between South and North marked by a short concrete wall at the Joint Security Area in Panmunjom, DMZ. The JSA is also known as the Truce Village and is the only area of the DMZ where it is possible for North and South Korean military personnel to stand face to face. It is possible to visit the JSA as a tourist.

Chapter 5

No Man's Land

HAVE YOU EVER WONDERED WHAT HAPPENS IN THOSE SPACES WHERE no one really exercises a great deal of control? Our maps tend to present us with a picture of a world in which every bit of the earth's surface is under the control of one state or another. Look more closely and the picture becomes less clear. In Europe, for example, our maps cannot keep up with territorial ambiguities. All along EU borders, migrants huddle in a series of roving no man's lands where European neighbours cannot decide whether to repel, to facilitate transit or to accommodate. The border ends up being fuzzy rather than clear-cut and border guards on either side of the line end up creating grey zones where it is not clear where one country ends and another begins. Most of our maps don't even mark up the world's largest no man's lands, namely the high seas.

As we have seen, two-thirds of the world's oceans are beyond the jurisdiction of any one country or countries, and until quite recently this legal no man's land was accepted as part of the balance to be struck between coastal states and third parties. Nowadays, we care a great deal more about the fate of the high seas because of technological advancements that have made fishing, genetic resource harvesting, seabed mining and hydrocarbon extraction more intensive. Governments around the world are being asked to consider further the cumulative environmental impact of navigation, and the safety and resilience of underwater critical infrastructure. Sharing half the planet is never going to be straightforward, and there are powerful incentives to ensure that there is no change to the international legal status of high seas as no man's land.

Back on dry land, we have examples of territories being either abandoned (simply left free of any kind of governance) or carefully enclosed and subject to 'special rules' precisely because neighbours and third parties cannot agree on ownership, regulation and security. In some cases, these areas are so volatile that they require the near-permanent presence of the UN or a more limited intervention by international peacekeepers to ensure that peace and stability are preserved. One example would be a strip of land between Kuwait and Iraq. A UN peacekeeping force (the UN Iraq–Kuwait Observation Mission, UNIKOM) was established for the purpose of monitoring this demilitarised zone stretching some 190km (120 miles) and about 15km (9 miles) wide. Established in April 1991, in the aftermath of Saddam Hussein's defeat by a US-led coalition, it was designed to ensure that Iraq's invasion of Kuwait was reversed permanently. Iraqi forces were prevented from gathering at the shared border with Kuwait, and the UN force was authorised in 1993 to take any military action necessary to ensure that there was no unauthorised activity in the buffer zone. The work of the mission was formally dissolved in 2003, in the aftermath of the overthrow of Saddam Hussein's regime. The buffer zone ceased to exist as a consequence of the normalisation of relations.

Sometimes these no man's lands can become places for naked opportunism, free from the watchful gaze of authorities. Between the fourteenth and seventeenth centuries, raiding and rustling cattle was endemic in the Anglo-Scottish borderlands. In between hills and moorlands, and criss-crossing rivers, marauding parties on either side of the border pillaged with impunity. If there was justice, it was the rough sort. Families from either side of the border would plot and carry out raiding parties, and victims would then be forced to endure considerable losses or hatch a revenge operation. What made all of this possible was that the area between the English and Scottish borders was not policed or patrolled by any crown-appointed sovereignty. The rivers and hills of the border country were zones of exception. It was not until the union of the English and Scottish crowns in the early seventeenth century that greater effort was made by James I of England/VI of Scotland to regulate this cross-border raiding. King James renamed the borderlands the 'Middle Shires' and established a commission designed to bring this no man's land under sovereign control. By the early 1620s, the worst excesses were largely tamed.

The history of cattle raiding and the activities of what were called border reivers (Middle English for 'raiders') is a reminder that no man's lands have been with us for centuries. In English history, during medieval times, the ownership of land beyond city walls was ambiguous. This mosaic of competing sovereign interests could be quite modest, however, possibly involving a field or common. In some cases, you might have a strip of land between two towns, or even church parishes, that remained unclaimed, and where in the absence of a figure of authority opportunists could thrive. In these circumstances, rival towns might find new ways to take over unclaimed land, such as establishing cemeteries and grazing grounds.

For many people, the term no man's land conjures up the pock-marked battlefields of the First World War. There have been many tales of deserters on both sides living underground and eking out a precarious existence in the no man's lands of those European battlefields. Lying beyond straightforward control by states, no man's lands, therefore, reveal the capacity for people, animals and landscapes to adapt to unusual circumstances. In the most unlikely environments, there are examples of creatures making abandoned and deeply contested spaces their homes. In October 2019, pigs were the cause of a security alert in the Korean Demilitarised Zone (DMZ). African swine fever had been spreading across Asia, and the South Korean authorities expressed concern that diseased boars were travelling from North Korea across the DMZ into the South. South Korea informed its northern counterparts that pigs spotted in the DMZ were likely to be shot as a precautionary measure. In February 2020, South Korea was given special permission to enter the DMZ and carry out a health survey of the wild pig population. It concerned the South Korean authorities that North Korea might not worry too greatly if more infected animals travelled through the DMZ and on to South Korean territory.

No man's lands are of interest to us because they reveal the cracks and gaps of international politics. They vary in size and scope. We have high seas, demilitarised zones, buffer strips, neutral zones and impromptu areas around the world where extraordinary circumstances prevail. On the one hand, we have had examples of migrants being trapped between the international borders and, on the other, examples of remote and densely forested areas acting as places beyond the effective control of particular state authorities. The Kenyan government has been battling for years a network of Al-Shabaab terrorists hiding in the Boni Forest, which sits on the Kenyan–Somali border. Kenyan troops have struggled to 'flush out' their foe and local Kenyan villagers are afraid to enter the forested areas. An unwelcome no man's land continues to exist. Whatever their provenance, there will always be examples of how those with political and military interests deliberately manipulate borders and create exceptional regimes for their activities.

No man's lands vary in genesis, size, scope and longevity. They also vary in terms of how recognised their borders are – buffer zones monitored by UN forces tend to be measured in terms of length and width while the exact extent of a territory within which rebels and terrorists are hiding is harder to pin down. During the First World War, the size and scope of the operational space known as no man's land varied depending on the terrain, the firepower of the rival armies and battlefield tactics. The amorphous quality of the area in question was long lasting. In some parts of France, the battlefield was so scarred by unexploded ordnance and toxic legacies of gas attacks that the authorities had to create a new border or zone called the *Zone Rouge*. The areas in question were judged to be so unsafe that entire villages and their immediate surroundings, including heavily contaminated soils, were declared out of bounds. The French authorities planted trees and hoped that over time the areas might detoxify. And while some villages and areas around Verdun have been declared safe, other areas are so toxic that humans will never be allowed to return. British historian Christina Holstein, author of *Walking Verdun: A Guide to the Battlefield* (2009), told *National Geographic* in 2014 that the French authorities 'reckon that they have 300 years' work ahead of them before they have cleared the whole battlefield, and they never will'.

A no man's land, therefore, can be generated by lingering danger. During the Second World War, the UK government under Winston Churchill approved a biological warfare test on Gruinard Island in the Scottish Highlands. Anthrax was released by British scientists so that they could better understand the destructive capabilities of the disease. The island was so contaminated that it was declared out of bounds for at least half a century. After spending millions of pounds in a clean-up operation, the island was officially reopened in April 1990. Famously, the island was repurchased by the original owner's heir for the agreed sale price of £500.

Environmental disasters and public health emergencies can be the trigger for the creation of accidental no man's lands, whereby states might feel pressurised to establish a cordon sanitaire around an affected area. A tragic example is Ukraine and Belarus in the aftermath of the April 1986 Chernobyl nuclear disaster. Plant reactor No. 4 blew up after a capability test revealed shocking weaknesses.

A fire lasting some ten days followed, which allowed a nuclear cloud to develop and float across European borders, with near-neighbour Belarus the worse affected. In the aftermath of the fire, the Soviet authorities entombed the devastated plant reactor No. 4 in a concrete sarcophagus, which collapsed in 2013 and required further remedial attention. Several hundred tons of radioactive material are believed to be trapped under the concrete blanket, and the 'new safe confinement' completed in 2017 is designed to prevent the material from escaping and poisoning others. Chernobyl remains a public health emergency, with analysts warning that its soil, water and air remains unsafe for human habitation.

Shortly after the disaster, the Soviet authorities evacuated the immediate area and established an exclusion zone totalling some 2,600km^2 (1,000 square miles). An area approximately the size of the US state of Rhode Island was effectively sealed off and abandoned by first the Soviet Union and later Ukraine. The relevant authorities established a border regime and instigated a patrolling system, and radiation levels are routinely monitored. Meanwhile, the site has become a dumping ground for Ukraine's nuclear power stations' spent fuel rods.

At the time of the accident, everyone in the area was evacuated. However, what transpired later was something no one expected. Former residents, especially a small community of older women, returned to their homes. There might only be around 100 'self-settlers' but their presence reveals a determination not to give up their homes willingly. In her award-winning documentary, *The Babushkas of Chernobyl* (2015), Holly Morris showed how this community was undeterred by radiation legacies and content to defy the exclusion order. The Ukrainian authorities have chosen to tolerate their presence, probably calculating that it would be better to have some of their citizens living there just in case other parties were tempted to settle more permanently. In other words, they did not want the area abandoned entirely, and allow visiting researchers and border guards to continue their collective work. Wildlife has also proven to be resilient, with a remarkable diversity of plants and animals being recorded by motion-activated cameras and drone footage.

No man's lands can also lead to opportunism on behalf of host governments. If Ukraine has tried to seal the exclusion zone, near neighbour Belarus has pursued a different strategy. The Belarusian leadership has proposed that migrants currently living in the country's cities and towns be relocated to the south of the country, which was worst affected by the 1986 disaster. In the past, some of the country was a prohibited zone, but the former no man's land has now been reclassified as a space for new opportunity, reversing abandonment in favour of re-habitation. Revealingly, the relocation plan was created for migrant communities who have always been considered by the long-standing Belarusian president to be unwelcome in his country.

If war and environmental disaster can create a no man's land (or several), then border architecture can do so, too. The construction of the Berlin Wall in 1961 created a fortified and divided city. A so-called 'death zone' between the two divided communities was established in which anyone attempting to flee to West Berlin was likely to be shot by East German border guards. Wild rabbit colonies were the unintended beneficiaries of this barrier to human mobility. Further south, all along the Iron Curtain, wildlife was able to flourish as electrified fences, barbed wire and security patrols provided a brutally effective barrier to those seeking to cross into the West. Remarkably, there is evidence that deer populations either side of the fortified German–Czech border have inculcated into 'herd memory' the prior existence of those artificial barriers.

One of the most notable no man's lands is the Demilitarised Zone (DMZ) of the Korean peninsula. Established after the armistice of the Korean War in 1953, the DMZ is 250km (around 155 miles) long and only about 4m (13 feet) wide, although there is a buffer zone as well which is 4km (2½ miles) wide. Only two populated villages remain within the DMZ. Elsewhere the DMZ is empty of human presence. Landmines, fortified fences and lethal security patrolling are a powerful deterrent for people on both sides of the divide but, again, it has unexpectedly become a nature reserve.

For those countries living with a no man's land, demilitarised zone or green line, there is the dilemma of how to treat that bordered space.

They can be temporary, semi-permanent and permanent. The Berlin Wall zone remind us that these divisions and exclusions can end quickly and unexpectedly, the wild rabbits having their world turned upside down in November 1989 with the fall of Soviet communism. Elsewhere, the South Korean government acts as if the DMZ is a temporary blip. While it acknowledges that the nuclear-armed North Korean forces might one day cross the DMZ and invade, it has not given up on the idea of a peaceful resolution. Unwilling to accept the de facto legitimacy of North Korea, South Korea invests in a bureaucratic architecture in the event of reunification. For the last 70 years, South Korean officials have been appointed by Seoul to be governors of five provinces that lie in North Korea, even though none of the present governors has ever been to the areas for which they are supposedly responsible. These appointees are members of the Committee for the Five Northern Provinces. There are a further 100 city mayors and nearly 1,000 civil servants attached to the committee, ready at the drop of a hat to serve their northern compatriots if given the chance. They are modestly salaried positions, costing South Korean taxpayers around £5 million per year. The committee is banned from making direct contact with North Korea but does do what it can to keep abreast of 'their' northern provinces. For this purpose, therefore, the DMZ is imagined to be changeable rather than permanent.

Beyond this, the Korean DMZ has a complex geopolitical history. Apart from the zone itself, there is also a military demarcation line, at which each side maintains their own liaison offices and conference facilities. South Korea established a Peace House at Panmunjom, where the armistice of 1953 was negotiated. The Peace House is located in the Joint Security Area (used for diplomatic meetings involving North and South Korea in the DMZ region), which is tightly controlled with strict rules in terms of how many troops can enter the 3,200m^2 (35,000-square-foot) zone at any one time. In between the landmines (which number in their millions in the DMZ) and security towers, there is not one but many no man's lands. Depending on where you are there are different rules of engagement in terms of how and when troops and diplomats can enter. At the same time, the DMZ has become a popular tourist destination for visitors around the world. The tourists are allowed to enter what is termed the Civilian Control Zone, adjacent to the DMZ. The scale and scope of access and mobility vary, depending on who you are. In 2018, over 100,000 visitors came from South Korea and around 30,000 visited from the North.

Each side used to broadcast propaganda across the DMZ, including K-Pop, leader speeches and defector interviews, the last of which were designed to encourage further defection from North Korean border communities. What is less well known is that the DMZ had an underground dimension that undermined the exclusionary nature of the surface. Unbeknown to South Korea, North Korean military engineers had constructed a network of tunnels under the DMZ. The so-called Tunnels of Aggression provided a chilling vision of what North Korea might be capable of. The discovery of the tunnels was in large part due to the testimony of defectors, who told their South Korean hosts that North Korea had ordered them to be constructed in the early 1970s. A surprise underground explosion in 1978 led to the accidental discovery of the exact location of one of those incomplete North Korean tunnels. The idea was that the secret tunnels would enable the North to move troops quickly below the DMZ and avoid the landmines and security architecture manned by South Korean and US troops. In the end, four cross-border tunnels were discovered by 1990, including one that was dubbed the Third Tunnel of Aggression. This tunnel terminated only 50km (32 miles) from Seoul, the South Korean capital, and was found to be over 60m (200 feet) below the surface. What is not so clear is whether there are any other North Korean tunnels that have not yet been found and whether the US or South Korea might have covertly constructed their own tunnels northwards.

In December 2019, it was announced that Taesung Freedom Village was getting 5G connectivity courtesy of the telecommunications provider KT Corp. What makes the case unusual is that this village of nearly 200 people is located within the DMZ. The men living in the village are the only ones automatically excluded from South Korean compulsory military service, and all 46 households receive special incentives from the government in Seoul to remain in situ.

Having high-speed and robust connectivity is vital in a place where there are strict living and working conditions. There are no hospitals, department stores, gyms or supermarkets. Their nearest neighbour is the North Korean Kijŏngdong 'peace village'. There is no direct communication between the two villages in the DMZ. Taesung residents wishing to go to their rice fields must be accompanied by South Korean soldiers. More positively, children enjoy high levels of personal contact with their teachers, and, as a consequence, the small school with 35 pupils includes students from a South Korean village called Munsan. Parents of non-DMZ children are keen to cross the de facto border and access a school that has 21 teachers for only 35 children.

Despite the small numbers and tough restrictions, both the North and South Korean governments want their villages to remain in place. The residents, though, can never truly relax. Surveillance is ubiquitous, and there are troops everywhere, including from the US-led UN Command. At the very worst moments of inter-Korean tension, there have been incidences of kidnapping by North Korean forces and rapid evacuation to special underground shelters. And each village had to endure the propaganda blasting out over the DMZ until it was stopped in late 2018.

The Korean DMZ endures and provides a telling example of what happens when borders appear frozen in the aftermath of an armistice. Yet as the discovery of the four underground tunnels revealed, the ground beneath the no man's land was still capable of accommodating plenty of intrigue. In the meantime, wild boars come and go and, in the fictional South Korean television drama, *Crash Landing on You* (2019–20), there is a storyline of a paragliding young woman crashing into the DMZ. The unfortunate pilot not only makes it back safely to South Korea but cultivates a romantic relationship with a North Korean military officer. It has been a huge hit in South Korea and, fictionally at least, suggests that the DMZ might not be quite as fixed as it has been for seven decades. Love without borders.

For now, back in the real world, it is a stubbornly real no man's land.

CHALLENGING NO MAN'S LANDS

Beyond fictional television drama, the world's no man's lands are under threat. The most obvious areas of concern are the largest examples. Described as global commons, the world's oceans, atmosphere and polar regions, especially Antarctica, are areas that lie beyond the jurisdiction of any one state. They are legally established no man's lands and, as Pope Francis noted in 2015, there is an urgent need to find 'an agreement on systems of governance for the whole range of so-called "global commons"'. As our cumulative impact on the earth's biomes continues, the common pool resources such as forests, fish stocks and oceans risk being degraded further if there is not widespread agreement on what constitutes sustainable usage. This means that there have to be restrictions on the sovereign rights of states.

In the case of Antarctica, the 1959 Antarctic Treaty has created a governance regime that reconciles the sovereignty claims of the seven claimant states (the largest being Australia, with a 42 per cent stake in the continent) with those that don't accept any claims to polar territory. Science and international cooperation are often heralded as integral to the success and endurance of the treaty. All parties, and there are now over 50 signatories, recognise that the governance of the Antarctic requires compromise.

The 1959 treaty declared that the polar continent should be nuclear-free, demilitarised and dominated by a spirit of collaboration and goodwill. Science was at the heart of its governance regime. China, India and Brazil did not sign the treaty until the 1980s. By that stage the rules of the Antarctic club were largely set, and the parties concerned were beginning to tackle tricky resource-related questions such as fishing and mineral rights. The Soviet Union (and now Russia) and the United States reserve the right to make their own claims in the future. China may well make its own claim, too.

The fate of Antarctica's ocean offers some important insights into what is at stake. On the face of it we have a long-established convention for the regulation of Southern Ocean fishing. It has been in force since 1980. However, over time, it has become clear that the regulation of fisheries divides the Antarctic parties. China, Australia, the US and Russia have often found themselves in opposition to one another, as they argue over how to manage the fisheries of the Southern Ocean. The 1980 Convention on the Conservation of Antarctic Marine Living Resources sets out the rules and structures for polar fishing and conservation. The balance between the two is often hard to strike. Fishing nations accuse conservationists of being too eager to push for restraints and bans while the conservationist-minded states accuse fishing nations of being obstructive.

It is going to be interesting to watch how those different visions for Antarctica hang together. China is often viewed with great suspicion by others, including Australia. Beijing is building a fifth permanent Antarctic station, has invested in a new icebreaker vessel (*Snow Dragon 2*), and is developing inland polar infrastructure designed to improve access and power projection across the continent. As mentioned in Chapter 3, China is also the most vocal critic, alongside Russia, of the Ross Sea Marine Protected Area and tends to be suspicious of attempts to restrict fishing in the name of marine conservation. Chinese polar tourism is buoyant and at some stage in the 2020s may well exceed the dominant presence of US citizens in Antarctica. In the future, hotels, ports and landing facilities could place fresh pressures on the governance of Antarctica. As the Antarctic Peninsula continues to warm, it is not inconceivable that larger and more permanent human habitation will follow. China is developing a new generation of distant-water fishing vessels capable of operating in polar waters. Already numbering some 2,000 boats, the so-called Deep Blue fishing fleet will be capable of fishing continuously for months at a time. By 2030, China is expected to account for nearly 40 per cent of the world's fish consumption, and its regional waters are already close to exhaustion. It is not hard to imagine why relatively unexploited areas such as the Southern Ocean are so attractive to a country that has to feed well over 1 billion people, with prior experience of African swine fever decimating its domestic pig population. Food security is and will remain of fundamental importance to Beijing.

Another former no man's land that is experiencing the challenge of increasing exploitation is Svalbard, located almost 1,000km (600 miles) away from the North Pole. Formerly called Spitsbergen, the islands were a resource hotspot for centuries, with the Netherlands, Great Britain and other nations vying for marine resources such as whaling, walrus hunting and fishing. The 1920 Spitsbergen Treaty, ratified in 1925, put in place a new legal framework for a location where there were no clear-cut answers to ownership. The treaty stipulated that Norway was the exclusive owner of Svalbard. In order to placate potential counter claimants and existing parties busily extracting the area's other resources, such as coal, the treaty noted that signatories would enjoy access rights equal to those of their Norwegian counterparts. Scotland, for example, was an active participant in coal extraction in the early part of the twentieth century, with companies such as the Scottish Spitsbergen Syndicate notable in its promotion of the possible UK annexation of the islands prior to the treaty. Other mining companies such as the Arctic Coal Company lobbied the governments of their respective states, including the US. The original signatories included Norway, Denmark, the Netherlands, the US, the UK, Russia, Sweden, Norway, Italy and Japan. Since it came into force, additional signatories have joined the treaty, including North Korea in 2016, taking the total to 46.

A hundred years after they originated, the terms of the treaty are having to bend to keep up with a very different operational environment. The careful balancing act between respecting Norwegian sovereignty while allowing equal access is under pressure on several fronts. First, and foremost, international legal developments affecting the sea have placed a new spin on a treaty that made no reference to exclusive economic zones and extended territorial seas. Are the waters around Svalbard Norwegian? Other parties inevitably contest Norway's right to border those waters, and disputes have arisen over resources such as snow crab, with the Norwegians winning a notable legal victory in February 2019 regarding their exclusive rights over the seabed around Svalbard. The ruling carries with it further implications for oil and gas mining in the future. Coal mining is in serious decline and Norway is worried that if it no longer mines coal then Russia might take it as a sign of weakness, and thus further strengthen Moscow's desired grip on the archipelago. Russia has been mining coal on Svalbard since 1913 and the settlement of Barentsburg continues to support a Russian-speaking community.

There is no shortage of media commentary about a possible Russian takeover and others speculate about China's presence on the island as well. For now, Norwegian and American observers tend to look carefully at large-scale military wargames and exercises such as the Tsentr-2019 drills, which were partially based in the Russian Arctic, as possible practice runs for any future annexation plan. The prospect of 'little green men' (as Russian special forces operating in Crimea were termed) entering and occupying Svalbard, which is formally demilitarised under the terms of the 1920 treaty, feels more plausible to some because of the experience of Crimea in 2014, when Russian forces annexed the territory. Despite the imposition of sanctions, Russia is not going to return Crimea to Ukraine. And in October 2019, it was alleged by Norwegian media sources that Russian special forces were spotted on Svalbard. So questions will inevitably be asked about whether Russia and its strategic partner China might have designs on this unique no man's land – a Norwegian territory governed by a treaty that guarantees equal resource rights to the signatories.

Even scientific exploration carried out in Svalbard in special settlements such as Ny-Ålesund has become more tense in recent years, with other parties accusing Norway of trying to control their research infrastructures and places of investigation. One complaint is that the Norwegian authorities use their 'concerns' over cumulative and new environmental impact to restrict the activities of others, which seems somewhat hypocritical when you consider the long history of Norwegian coal mining on the main island.

There are, therefore, a number of signs at both poles that the treaties governing these remote places might be subject to fresh pressures in the future as nations seek to extend their territorial and resource interests in the regions. Fishing is the most obvious area of interest, and Svalbard remains strategically valuable as a gateway to the High Arctic and a port for shipping routes that might well grow in significance in the latter part of the twenty-first century if sea ice continues to diminish, as scientists predict, in the Arctic Ocean.

If China in the Antarctic and Russia in Svalbard were to further assert their rights, it is possible that those treaty arrangements could become redundant, with new borders and zones of occupation established. Would NATO parties invoke Article 5 and come to the assistance of Norway if it faced a military-like occupation of Svalbard by either Chinese or Russian forces? The answer to that question is clouded in uncertainty but what is clear is that the no man's lands of the Arctic and Antarctic could become future flashpoints and possibly battlefields. It might start over a fishing-related dispute around the waters of Svalbard or it could be a clash involving rival military training exercises in the High North.

HIGH SEAS AS ENDANGERED NO MAN'S LANDS

As we have seen, the UN Convention on the Law of the Sea enables coastal states to border our oceans and seas, and it also makes provision for the largest no man's lands on the planet, the high seas, which cannot be claimed and enclosed by any one state or states. But borders are still relevant when it comes to the high seas, particularly because the latter start where exclusive economic zones end. There are a number of rules and treaties that govern their use, including one that will address marine biodiversity from 2020 onwards, but the world's high seas face new dangers in the twenty-first century. Fishing and seabed mining are the two activities that threaten to undermine the ecological resilience of these regions. The scale of the challenge is daunting.

The world's fishing industry is operating at dangerously unsustainable levels. The UN's Food and Agriculture Organization estimates that over 30 per cent of fish populations are exploited at unsustainable levels and 60 per cent are at their sustainable limit. High-seas fishing has become increasingly attractive as nearer coastal waters have been exploited, sometimes to the point of collapse. The Food and Agriculture Organization estimate that there might only be 7 per cent of world fish stocks that are 'under-fished'. High-seas fishing is expensive due to the huge distances from ports and major centres of population, but fuel subsidies by countries such as China encourage ever more fishing outside coastal waters. Other major players include Spain, South Korea and Japan, but China is currently responsible for 20 per cent of high-seas fishing and this figure will grow in the twenty-first century.

The World Trade Organization could impose a ban on fuel subsidies in the near future, but this might only encourage other forms of behaviour that do little to protect the marine ecology of the high seas. Its proposals might end up being 'watered down' as the fishing nations of Africa and Europe, along with large fishing companies, lobby hard to propose 'exemptions' if they can prove their activities are not detrimental. China is championing so-called 'green-box' exemptions, which shifts the burden onto the fishing industry to prove that they are not doing any harm to the marine ecologies of the high seas.

The debate over fishing subsidies captures the difficulties and opportunities posed by no man's lands. As areas beyond national sovereignty, they demand international agreement. Discussions about bringing fishing subsidies to an end started as long ago as 1999, and scientists and advocacy groups have been warning for some time of the need to take action. But, as we have seen, the world's high-seas fishing grounds are not the only cause for concern: at the bottom of the ocean lies the deep seabed, another no man's land beyond the sovereign reach of coastal states. The deep seabed matters because of its significance to marine biodiversity. Deep-sea ecosystems are no longer thought of as being remote and lacking in marine life. Thanks to underwater exploration, marine features such as hydrothermal vents are now recognised as being hotspots of biological diversity.

Deepwater ecosystems are attracting increasing interest from states and corporations, some of which affect underwater environments under the sovereign control of an individual coastal state.

During the Cold War, however, seabed research was driven by military objectives. Both the US and Soviet militaries wanted to acquire ever greater intelligence on ocean floors and underwater environments in order to better understand resource potential and spy on the movement of strategic adversaries. Scientists worked with military sponsors and funders to develop exploratory programmes.

In 1974, a US expedition led by the *Hughes Glomar Explorer* was sent to the Pacific Ocean. Superficially, the expedition was designed to explore the seabed for mineral resources. In reality, the expedition was a cover story for a secret CIA operation called Project Azorian, intended to locate a sunken Soviet submarine, the *K-129*. Lost somewhere north of Hawaii, the Soviets had failed to locate their lost submarine themselves. The US believed, via their underwater surveillance network, that they knew where the stricken vessel was located. Lying on the seabed in the high seas of the Pacific Ocean, the submarine was considered 'fair game'. The US ship, sponsored by the billionaire Howard Hughes, was fitted with special equipment designed to help recover any remains of the *K-129*, which lay some 5km (3 miles) underwater. Throughout the operation, Soviet ships monitored the Americans' progress. For all the secret preparation and huge investment (running into hundreds of millions of dollars), only the front section of the submarine was recovered, the rest shearing off when it was lifted from the seabed. A year later the cover story was broken.

Five decades on, deep-sea mining is formally on the agenda of states and businesses, generating some interesting new partnerships. As we noted, a Canadian company called Nautilus Minerals has been working with Papua New Guinea to develop the resource potential of hydrothermal vents off the country's coastline. Seabed mining is attracting ever more interest around the world. Moving further offshore, the UK government has teamed with up with the US defence contractor Lockheed Martin to investigate the possibility of mining polymetallic nodules in the Pacific Ocean. It is worth remembering that when it comes to the seabed in the world's high seas, the UN-established International Seabed Authority, based in Kingston, Jamaica, is playing its part in supporting the deep-seabed mining industry.

The deep seabed has long been imagined to be a treasure chest of minerals simply awaiting extraction. For the world's high seas, beyond the control of coastal states, the International Seabed Authority issues licences for seabed mining exploration. The licences, sponsored by national governments in cooperation with commercial organisations, can cover enormous areas of any of the world's oceans. The UK–Lockheed Martin joint venture in the Pacific Ocean covers some 130,000km^2 (50,000 square miles) of seabed. Under their subsidiary trade name, UK Seabed Resources, Lockheed Martin aims to extract iron ore, copper and rare-earth minerals such as scandium and cerium. The latter are used in low-carbon technologies. While such mining has not yet proven economically viable, companies such as Lockheed Martin are confident that the latest generation of underwater autonomous technologies (developed for the industry) will play their part in making underwater mining profitable in the future. Lockheed Marin is not alone in preparing for this new industry by describing it as 'seabed harvesting' rather than 'mining'.

China is yet again leading the way. Working with two Chinese companies, Beijing holds three of the 29 exploration licences issued thus far by the International Seabed Authority. The US, meanwhile, cannot be formally involved in the management regime because of its non-ratification of UNCLOS. For anyone mining seabed resources in the high seas, the terms and conditions of UNCLOS stipulate that some of the commercial value of those minerals must be shared with the international community. The royalties are a small proportion of any revenue generation and have been seen as a 'tax' rather than a revenue-sharing scheme, designed in part to recognise that the world's high seas and seabed are of importance to all states, including landlocked ones. American opponents to UNCLOS have seized upon this requirement to justify their opposition to ratification.

China, the UK, India, Russia and others view the seabed as a legitimate resource that belongs to the international community. They regard seabed mining as an emerging industry that might support the transition to a low-carbon future. The world will continue to require metals and minerals, and advocates of seabed mining claim that as terrestrial mining becomes unsustainable, attention must turn to underwater prospects. Environmental advocacy groups such as Greenpeace, on the other hand, are deeply concerned about the ecological impact of such mining activities. The International Seabed Authority has not so far refused a licence request, even in areas that have been evaluated as having high biological diversity and richness. The so-called 'Lost City' in the Mid-Atlantic Ridge is a case in point. This is a zone of hydrothermal vents and in 2018 the authority awarded a licence to the Polish government for a 10,000km^2 (3,900-square-mile) mining zone.

Investment in underwater technologies also offers a clue as to the growing interest in deep-seabed mining. India, for example, holds four of the current 29 licences and is a major investor. The deep seabed is undoubtedly going to be a geopolitical hotspot in the future and the International Seabed Authority will face greater pressures. For environmentalists, such as the oceanographer Sylvia Earle, who has been a vocal critic of deep-seabed mining, the industry is incompatible with an environment that is poorly mapped and understood. Deep-sea sediments will inevitably be disturbed by mining operations at a time when we have a limited understanding of how the deep ocean helps to regulate earth systems.

The world's areas beyond national jurisdiction are integral to global geopolitics, and the no man's lands that are the high seas are in the crosshairs of competing interests. Currently, UN-level negotiations are addressing biological diversity in areas beyond national jurisdiction, with stricter controls being contemplated on how the world's high seas and seabed are used by states and companies. Negotiations for a UN agreement on the 'conservation and sustainable use of marine biodiversity of areas beyond national jurisdiction' are also going to be crucial to shaping the future of the world's largest no man's lands. Protecting marine biodiversity is a huge undertaking, and a fourth meeting in March–April 2020 (postponed because of the COVID-19 pandemic) was intended to address the means and mechanisms necessary for the protection of marine biodiversity. Further delays seem inevitable in convening any major international conferences. The imperative to act remains as over 60% of the world's oceans are considered to be international waters. The problem facing advocates of marine biodiversity protection is that the work of the UN's International Seabed Authority is ongoing. So seabed mining and marine biodiversity protection will have to co-exist with one another in the world's high seas.

While much attention has been focused on fisheries and the mineral and the genetic resources of the seabed, the biggest struggle may be to get resource-hungry parties to recognise the far greater value of things to which we barely give a second thought, such as phytoplankton. These remarkable organisms store vast amounts of carbon and thus help to facilitate conditions for life itself in the high seas and territorial waters. The vast majority live in the high seas and their ecological service to humanity is second to none. They supply 50 per cent of the world's oxygen and make life on earth possible.

Its advocates hope that the prospective UN marine biodiversity agreement will help us to safeguard the future of our planet. The omens are not good. By 2050 it is estimated that high-seas fishing will be severely stressed, and emerging areas such as the central Arctic Ocean, created due to retreating sea ice, may or may not allow new commercial fisheries, depending on what regulatory structure follows the 2018 Agreement to Prevent Unregulated High Seas Fisheries in the Central Arctic Ocean. The agreement did not seek to ban such a development, instead establishing a moratorium period of 16 years on the introduction of commercial high-seas fisheries in the region. Notably, China wanted a moratorium for only four years, while others were pushing for over 30.

Meanwhile, the Southern Ocean will face ever greater pressures, including in the Ross Sea Marine Protected Area, the existence of which might not be renewed or extended. Much of the world's high seas should, ideally, be classified as marine protected areas. This might enable fish stocks to recover, assuming that the world's oceans are not already radically transformed by acidification and pollution.

The UN faces an uphill struggle to secure a long-term consensus about how to manage the world's high seas. Conservationists tell us that around 30 per cent of the world's oceans need to be under marine protection arrangements and that we need to achieve this by 2030. Whether that is possible in a world where food and resource security needs are going to increase is questionable. Conflict in the world's high seas cannot be ruled out.

NO MAN'S LANDS BY DESIGN

Two types of no man's lands are likely to gain greater prominence in the future. The first is impromptu. And the second is by design. Both will generate a new generation of border wars.

One of the effects of the increasing number of migration crises is that wider mobility injustice is revealed around the world. Rich people want to enjoy unfettered movement but don't want poor and desperate people to have the same privilege. In late 2019, a group of Central American migrants, most of them poor and vulnerable, found themselves trapped between the river borders of two countries, neither of which wanted them. On one side of the riverbank was Mexico, with the Mexican National Guard deployed to prevent people from wading across the River Suchiate; on the other side, Guatemala. This standoff was spontaneous, and it was the migrants themselves who spoke of a no man's land (*tierra de nadie*) between the opposing riverbanks.

For all the hype surrounding the promise of digital technologies and virtual walls, the reality is stark for border towns and zones in southern states of the US such as Arizona and Texas. Along the Rio Grande, which constitutes some of the natural border between the US and Mexico, there is a mosaic of unintended no man's lands between the riverbank and security fencing. Farmers and other inhabitants have found their properties divided into separate zones, with demands that they open and close security gates. Local opinion is divided between those who have aided and abetted migrants and those who demand a greater border-security presence. These no man's lands have been created purposefully by the US authorities – security fencing cannot be built on riverbanks because the foundations are not secure enough, so secondary perimeters are created inland.

As border security has intensified, migrants have been forced to seek out new opportunities to cross over. In the midst of President Trump's desire to expand the border wall across the southern borderlands, there has also been a corresponding spike in legal action contesting his presidential authority. The residents of Laredo in Texas have complained that any border-wall expansion would not only cut through the city and interfere with the Rio Grande's ecological services, it would also create yet more no man's lands where the wall would restrict access to indigenous territory and further complicate local, state and national borders. Residents worry that their land would be out of bounds unless, for example, border guards were willing to grant them access to it. In effect, land would be stranded beyond the wall. Border guards might deny them access, citing national security concerns as an explanation.

In small towns in Texas such as Uvalde, located some 110km (70 miles) from the border town of Del Rio, newspapers have published stories about community struggles to accommodate migrants from the south. Both Uvalde and Laredo have been identified as being located on a major smuggling route for illegal migrants. Local officials have complained that federal and state-level authorities have been slow to act, leaving smaller towns such as Uvalde with the task of bussing migrants to large cities such as San Antonio. Intriguingly, newspaper reports have described parts of Uvalde as no man's lands; for example, public areas such as car parks where migrants are released when migrant holding facilities reach their capacity. Along major highways and railways, local communities and their political leaders have complained of state retreat – areas where state power has been pushed out, in effect abandoning space that it does not possess the necessary resources to regulate (or declines to invest in accordingly). It has long been recognised that drug cartels and people traffickers benefit from border infrastructures being either under-funded or simply overwhelmed by sheer migrant numbers. Any no man's lands, however deliberate or impromptu, are usually considered to be business opportunities for criminal organisations.

The migrant crisis that affected Europe from 2015 onwards also revealed the spontaneous creation of a network of no man's lands. European media carried stories of how railway stations, highways and even underpasses came to be occupied by migrant communities. Local police forces were then said to be reluctant to intervene. Humanitarian organisations often assumed a crucial role in the aftermath of this apparent retreat of the state, providing essential medical and food supplies to vulnerable migrants. Throughout the summer and autumn of 2015, news organisations reported the existence of a series of rolling no man's lands along the borders of Croatia and Serbia. When those borders were closed for periods of time, the migrants were trapped. States absolved themselves of responsibility for the fate of people claiming asylum and refugee status, in turn provoking uncomfortable reminders of how Jewish communities fared throughout Central and Eastern Europe; stripped of citizenship, expelled from one country and blocked from entering other countries. The border, for Jewish communities in the 1930s and 1940s, became a zone of ensnarement, with disastrous consequences.

Around the world, an archipelago of impromptu mobile no man's lands will be formed as the world population continues to expand, shift and move. Depending on the scale and impact of global climate change, displacement estimates vary wildly from 200 million people to up to 1 billion people by 2050. Alongside that we have the other no man's lands – the ones that make human and other life possible. The uncertainty in all of this is huge because it depends on the scale and pace of climate change and the capacity of states to mitigate and adapt. We cannot assume that there will not be more civil wars and natural disasters, including pandemics, allied with food and energy resource shortages. The balance between conservation and exploitation will vary depending in part on how robust international conventions are for the global commons. The future of humanity will be decided by how we govern these extraordinary spaces, and our collective capacity to hold irresponsible states and corporations to account.

The second type of no man's land of tomorrow is deliberate and designed. States and other interested parties might want to create a no man's land, or see an existing one endure, because it gives them scope to operate within a purposeful 'grey zone'. Here, the focus might be on the individual calculations of political leaderships, and the claims they make about the future security of their states. Governing in an era of political and ecological change could bring to the fore geopolitical opportunism and naked ambition in the name of regime survival.

The deliberately cultivated no man's lands will act as sites and zones for military adventurism, resource profiteering and political scheming. In December 2019, President Recep Erdoğan of Turkey spoke publicly about islands and inlets in the Aegean Sea that were disputed with Greece. Notably the uninhabited Kardak/Imia islets have been a source of tension between the countries since the mid-1990s. The presidential statement noted that 'The owner of both the Aegean and the Mediterranean are all of the countries which have coastline with these seas. As the country with the longest coast, we are determined to continue the struggle with all of our resources in protecting our rights there.' What makes the islets noteworthy is their location: the Greek–Turkish maritime border runs across them. Third-party maps simply draw a circle around them and don't apportion ownership. This is a no man's land that Turkey might decide it needs to occupy in order to secure its coastal borders more fully.

China's artificial island building in the South China Sea (for Vietnam the preferred term is East Sea) is an audacious attempt to re-engineer geography away from non-ownership into something more clear-cut – reclamation, occupation and long-term inhabitation. As we have seen, small geographical features such as shoals and reefs get occupied and turned into fully functional habitable islands. A fleet of dredgers is put to work and then there is a concerted attempt to invest in naval facilities and defence. The Chinese Navy wants to deny access to resources to regional neighbours and disrupt the navigation rights of others, especially the US Navy. Termed sea denial, this is a deliberate strategic calculation by

Chinese military planners. The plan appears to be to establish a ring of anti-ballistic missile systems capable of striking enemy ships hundreds of miles offshore, the ultimate goal being to transform the South China Sea, the Taiwan Strait and other areas of the Indian and Pacific oceans into safe operating spaces for the Chinese military and commercial shipping fleets. China's relationship with near neighbours could, US military analysts fear, further extend this ring of anti-ship missile defence. All of which might force the hand of the US Navy to invest further in submarine patrolling and freedom-of-navigation operations in the South China Sea.

In the meantime, in the midst of the pandemic China quietly continued its administrative enclosure of the South China Sea. In April 2020, the Ministry of Civil Affairs announced that Sansha 'city' had acquired two new districts, Nansha and Xisha. The latter are the Chinese names for Spratly and Paracel Islands respectively, and Sansha is not a city but a maritime region encompassing 2 million km^2 (1.2 million square miles) of water. While others such as Vietnam and Malaysia will issue their diplomatic protests, China will continue to press on with its plan to claim 'historic waters' while funding more activity in deep-sea mining and energy extraction via methane hydrates (so-called 'flammable ice' found in the seabed). As economic belts tighten, China will be eager to defray the costs of occupying and defending the South China Sea with news about a resource bonanza.

This will encourage smaller regional competitors, such as Vietnam, to turn to larger partners including Russia, India and Japan to pursue their own energy and mining projects in the South China Sea/East Sea. Depending on the scale of the economic downturn after the pandemic, China might even have its ambitions to turn this no man's land into an exclusively Chinese sea.

THE FUTURE OF NO MAN'S LANDS

No man's lands come in all shapes and sizes. They can be small, time-specific and impromptu on the one hand and simply vast in the case of Antarctica and the world's high seas on the other. And everything in between. But all of them show the very real difficulties of reconciling two fundamental tensions that have become ever more manifest and urgent in our modern world.

The first tension involves the management of the movement of people in a highly unequal world. Along the borderlands of the wealthiest parts of the planet, Europe and North America, we have pop-up no man's lands. Along the riverbank, inside the buffer zone and even in shared infrastructure such as bridges and public transport people find themselves trapped between two jurisdictions. As migrants on the shared border between Turkey and Greece discovered in February and March 2020, you end up being pawns in a game of geopolitics that spans multiple countries and continents.

Second, no man's lands such as Antarctica and the high seas bring into sharp relief something that we have tried to manage for decades. How do we adjudicate between the needs of an international system of sovereign states and the highly integrated natural systems that make life on earth possible? Imposing rigid political and legal boundaries on oceans and seas will always sit awkwardly with environments that are composed of highly mobile species such as fish, whales and birds. They face acute challenges such as pollution and ocean acidification, which do not respect national boundaries. Proposals for a UN agreement on marine biodiversity in what are termed areas beyond national jurisdiction will reveal quite how widespread a collective sense of purpose to avoid further degradation of the global commons is.

However, there might be other possibilities of conflict that reside elsewhere. What happens to biologically diverse regions within the sovereign borders of states? In the summer of 2019, there was a very public spat between the Brazilian and French presidents over fires in the Amazon basin. President Emmanuel Macron accused his Brazilian counterpart Jair Bolsonaro of political inaction in the face of deliberate fire-related clearances for the sake of resource exploitation and commercial farming. Macron insisted that Bolsonaro did not have an absolute right to treat the Amazon as if it was not of vital importance to the rest of the global community. In other words, the biodiversity of the region trumped any claim to exclusive sovereignty on the part of Brazil. Bolsonaro was furious about the intervention but it is conceivable that the global community might decide to 'convert' biomes into no man's lands. The international rulebook could be torn up in the name of planetary emergency, and foreign intervention justified on the basis of the right to protect very significant environments such as rainforests, coral reefs and mangrove swamps.

The Western Sahara (formerly Spanish Sahara) is a deeply disputed territory. Military woman from the Arab Democratic Republic Saharawi (ADRW) waiting for the beginning of manoeuvres in the fourth military region in Mehaires, Western Sahara. The ADRW is actively resisting Moroccan occupation and is a recognised member of the African Union. The UN recognises Western Sahara as a Non-Self-Governing Territory and has worked with the parties for over 30 years to try and find a solution to the conflict.

Chapter 6

Unrecognised Borders

THERE ARE PLENTY OF REASONS WHY BORDERS MIGHT BE UNRECOGNISED or even ignored. In international law, *recognition* means the location of an international border being acknowledged as having legal status. So, for example, if we say that the US–Canada border is internationally recognised it means that other parties acknowledge the right of both parties to impose border regulations, impose customs checks, and carry out security and surveillance activities.

In areas of the world where borders have been the object of dispute, countries might one day be able to sign a mutual agreement recognising an official border. They might secure a UN resolution expressing wider international support for a particular border. Failing that, parties might secure agreement for a border to be based on the shared reality of an armistice or ceasefire line. Until such recognition is secured, however, the border line can often be a source of tension and frustration. For example, Russia and Estonia have not been able to finalise their land and maritime boundaries, with each side accusing the other of bad faith. For the smaller state, Estonia, any lack of recognition inevitably brings with it a degree of anxiety about the long-term intentions of the larger neighbour. Recognition is not just a bilateral matter. In December 2019, Prime Minister Boris Johnson flew out to Estonia to serve Christmas lunch to UK troops stationed in the country. Their expressed purpose is to help protect Estonia's national border as well as the EU/NATO's eastern front.

Recognition might, therefore, encompass international *acceptance* as well as something specific such as an international border. For many citizens in the most privileged parts of the world, this border recognition dilemma might not even register. It can be taken for granted. Annual surveys about passport power usually reveal a group of countries from Europe, North America and the Middle East, and others such as Singapore, at the top of the rankings. Passport holders from Finland can travel to 170 countries either visa free or by securing visas on arrival. There is an implicit high level of recognition and trust. By way of contrast, an Afghan passport holder will need to seek visas for the vast majority of countries around the world. As Tom Hanks's character, Viktor Navorski from the fictional country of Krakozhia, discovered in the film *The Terminal* (2004), the loss of official recognition of his country carried with it dire consequences for his right to move out of an administrative no man's land. Viktor ends up being trapped in JFK airport in New York.

A lack of general international recognition matters. In international law, it is integral to how states, or other non-state entities such as the European Union, conduct themselves. Recognition is a legal and political matter.

The membership of the United Nations is defined in the UN Charter as being open to all 'peace-loving states' capable of honouring the obligations of the Charter. In order to join you have to be recognised as a 'peace-loving state' by the existing membership. Unusually, the Holy See (Vatican), a non-state entity, was granted permanent observer state status in April 1964. The Holy See can participate in

UN debates but cannot vote. It chose not to apply for full membership. Switzerland applied to be a permanent non-member state between 1948 and 2002. It became a full member in March 2002 after a referendum in which the country voted in favour. While the vote was decisive, critics were concerned for the country's policy of neutrality. The rules on recognition can be bent depending on circumstances.

More controversially, the fates of Palestine and Taiwan reveal why international recognition matters in its own right and beyond. Without recognition as a legitimate diplomatic and political entity, securing any sort of agreement on borders is hard and sometimes impossible. Palestine was eventually recognised as a non-member observer state by the UN in 2012. Then, in 2019, Palestine was elected chair of the UN Group of 77 (G77) in a move that was criticised and voted against by Australia, Israel and the United States. The G77 was created in 1964 and is now a coalition of over 130 countries (there were 77 in 1964), with the explicit purpose of strengthening the collective presence of recently decolonised countries, predominantly in Africa and Asia. Being elected to chair the G77 was important because it gave greater credibility to the desire on the part of the Palestinian Authority to establish an independent state in the West Bank and Gaza Strip, with East Jerusalem as the site of its national capital. Despite a greater role in the UN, Palestine's position was undermined by President Trump's decision to move the US Embassy to Jerusalem, which only added further fuel to a delicate situation. In December 2017, he announced that the US would now recognise Jerusalem as Israel's capital city. In a stroke, he reversed previous US policy spanning many decades. But Israel's occupation of the West Bank and East Jerusalem is not recognised internationally. The UN General Assembly, over the last five to seven years, has also used votes to upgrade Palestine's status in the New York-based organisation.

Taiwan's fate is even more challenging, given that China considers the island to be a rogue province. As a result of the Chinese Civil War, which ended in 1949, the government of the Republic of China fled to Taiwan, while mainland China and other territories became the People's Republic of China. The Republic of China (i.e. Taiwan) was an original member of the UN, but the People's Republic of China, which maintains that Taiwan should be regarded as one of its territories, only acquired China's permanent seat at the UN in 1971, when it replaced Taiwan. Eight years later, the United States finally recognised the People's Republic of China as a UN member state. Since then, the People's Republic of China has blocked any attempt by Taiwan to regain any membership of the UN, including as an observer state, and the status of the island remains controversial.

In July 2019, Taiwanese President Tsai Ing-wen told UN permanent representatives in New York, at a reception at Taiwan's de facto embassy, that Taiwan would continue to press for membership. As Taiwan is not recognised as an independent state, its 'embassy' in New York is officially called the Taipei Economic and Cultural Office. The president used the reception to express her gratitude to the representatives of the small number of countries such as Paraguay and Saint Vincent that recognise Taiwan. In what appears to be a deliberate strategy, the political leadership of Taiwan uses diplomatic tours in the Caribbean as an opportunity to travel via Washington. The decision in 2019 by the United States to approve an arms sale agreement with Taipei worth $2 billion, involving over 100 tanks and Stinger missiles, has added zest to these visits. Since Trump became president in January 2017, Taiwan has been the recipient of several notable deals involving training, armaments and torpedoes. The total value of the four deals between 2017 and 2019 exceeded $4 billion.

Securing military assistance is not inconsequential. To achieve widespread international recognition, however, is going to be a tall order for Taiwan and Palestine. China is not going to recognise the Republic of China as an independent entity, and Israel and the United States are likely to be resistant to acknowledging Palestine. In December 2018, Australia also recognised West Jerusalem as Israel's capital, but not East Jerusalem, and it will not move its embassy to the city until a peace settlement has been secured. What all this reveals is the deep-rooted desire of Australia to cultivate goodwill with the United States and its strategic ally, Israel. Such is the economic, political and military power of China and the United States, smaller states and even 'middle powers' such as Australia and Canada will think carefully before expressing any support for either Palestine or Taiwan. The world can be a very lonely place when the international community withholds recognition.

Unrecognised borders have been endemic at certain times and places. The collapse of the Soviet Union and Yugoslavia in the late 1980s and early 1990s, for example, led to the rapid creation and establishment of a host of new states, and decisions had to be taken quickly about the recognition of new borders. This process varied from relatively painless in the case of Slovenia in 1991 to tense and violent in the case of Bosnia-Herzegovina, which was subsequently wracked by a bloody civil war costing the lives of tens of thousands. Bosnia remains a de facto split country. Kosovo's uncertain existence is illuminating as well. A 2008 referendum revealed a majority of the population were in favour of independence from Serbia, with a Serbian minority voting against it. After the result, Kosovo went ahead and declared independence. A ruling from the International Court of Justice in 2010 confirmed that the declaration was consistent with international law, and Kosovo has been recognised by over 100 countries, but not Serbia and its close ally Russia. China has also refused to acknowledge its independence. Kosovo is not likely to become a member of the UN because of Russian opposition, but Serbia's bid to join the European Union is likely to pivot on its acceptance of Kosovo's independence. As of 2020, a UN peacekeeping operation remains in place to ensure that Belgrade and Pristina do not comes to blows.

UNRECOGNISED STATES AND UNSETTLING BORDERS

There are a number of unrecognised states around the world. The no man's land that divides the island of Cyprus finds expression along the barricaded streets and abandoned buildings of Nicosia as well as the Buffer Zone that snakes across the island's hills and plains. As we have already seen, the Republic of Cyprus shares the island with the

UK's so-called sovereign base areas and an unrecognised northern neighbour, the Turkish Republic of Northern Cyprus (TRNC). Turkey is the only country to acknowledge the legal and political existence of the TRNC. The Turkish lira is the only recognised currency, and any visitor wishing to enter the Turkish sector must undergo a formal passport/ID inspection at the 'border'. The genesis of the TRNC lies in the aftermath of the division of the island following the 1974 invasion by Turkish forces. Even after a ceasefire was secured, the island and the capital Nicosia remain divided. A UN peacekeeping force continues to ensure that the line of control remains a distinct and demilitarised barrier between the Greek- and Turkish-speaking communities.

When Cyprus joined the European Union in 2004, there was an underlying hope that the disputed island might in time become reunified. The unrecognised yet de facto border would simply disappear from the map. By allowing the Republic of Cyprus to join the EU, Greece dropped its opposition to EU expansion in eastern and central Europe, and some EU officials in Brussels hoped that this might give fresh impetus to reunification. But a proposal, via a referendum for a settlement of the disputed status of the island, failed to secure sufficient support from the Greek Cypriot community, and Cyprus joined the EU as a divided member state. The unrecognised TRNC was excluded from EU membership and Turkish political elites have waxed and waned about whether they believe the TRNC should pursue independence or continue to seek reunification. The population of TRNC is estimated to be around 300,000 people, while the Republic of Cyprus's national population is just over 1 million.

The island's future status is complicated still further by the enduring presence of what are the UK's sovereign base areas and so-called retained sites scattered around Cyprus. This is a legacy of the 1960 Treaty of Guarantee in which the UK, Turkey and Greece agreed to guarantee the territorial integrity and security of Cyprus. When Turkish forces invaded in 1974, they cited the treaty as justification, arguing that they were intervening to protect the status of the Turkish-speaking communities on the bi-communal island. Since 1974, the island's political geography has been characterised by a complex array of borders separating the TRNC, the sovereign base areas, the Republic of Cyprus and the UN Buffer Zone. Road signs inform the visitor of where and when one border is ending and another beginning, and watch towers, minefields and barbed-wire fencing are noticeable on the Turkish side of the border.

The continued non-recognition of TRNC has ramifications for the island's division as well. In July 2019, President Erdoğan spoke of his willingness to re-enact the '1974 invasion' if he thought Turkish-speaking peoples were in peril. Echoing the sentiments of President Putin, who has also spoken about the need to defend Russian-speaking peoples wherever they are located, the presidential statement was issued on the forty-fifth anniversary of the Turkish deployment. Framed as a humanitarian intervention rather than 'invasion', Turkey's stern words coincided with the latest spat over the status of Cyprus, which was more concerned with offshore matters than onshore. At stake are oil and gas resources in the Eastern Mediterranean, with Turkey, Greece and the Republic of Cyprus disagreeing about who should be allowed to develop and exploit these potential resources.

After initial discoveries off the Israeli coastline, a giant gas field called Aphrodite was discovered to the south of Cyprus in 2011; it has an estimated value of $10 billion accrued over 15 years of development. The find, however, did not stimulate an outburst of love and goodwill between Turkey and Cyprus. The Republic of Cyprus was understandably eager to develop the field with international partners including Shell and worked to agree a development and production plan. The recovered gas would then be exported to neighbouring Egypt. An enriched Republic of Cyprus would, it is feared by Turkey, embolden the Greek Cypriot community to isolate the TRNC from the East Mediterranean Gas Forum, which includes the Republic of Cyprus, Israel and Egypt. Turkey did not join the organisation because it does not want to offer any recognition to the maritime borders it shares with the Republic of Cyprus.

At present, oil and gas exploration in the disputed Eastern Mediterranean revolves around recognised and unrecognised borders, mixed up with revanchist projects. While Turkey does not want to recognise the Republic of Cyprus's maritime borders for fear of enabling further energy deals, the Republic of Cyprus and the rest of the world do not recognise TRNC and thus any claims this entity might have to maritime sovereign rights. At the same time, Greece and the Republic of Cyprus don't want to recognise the right of the TRNC to be a beneficiary of the gas revenues, as to do so would not only imply a recognition of the TRNC as a legal and political entity but would also establish a recognised border. The Republic of Cyprus's position holds that any revenue from oil and gas drilling will be shared in the aftermath of a peace deal on the future of the island. But by offering to sell gas to energy-hungry Egypt, the Republic of Cyprus – working with international partners including American, Israeli and Dutch companies – is using hydrocarbon diplomacy to shore up regional support. Turkey, in the meantime, has been active in its determination to protect the interests of the TRNC by sending warships and drilling ships to the disputed area.

The maritime area in question is not inconsiderable. The exclusive economic zones of Turkey and the Republic of Cyprus already overlap and will be difficult to reconcile because of the de facto division of the island. The unrecognised TRNC, supported by Turkey, believes that it is also entitled to an exclusive economic zone. Greece and the Republic of Cyprus have demanded that the EU threaten Turkey with sanctions, and Turkey has relented on the issue for now. But the problem is fundamental because any disagreement over land ownership carries with it implications for the identification of territorial seas and exclusive economic zones. Recognition carries with it immense implications for resource ownership and exploitation.

The EU has also had a tense relationship with Turkey over the migrant crisis from 2015 onwards, amplified further by the weakening of its commitment to advance Turkey's membership of the EU. Notwithstanding the cooling off regarding EU accession, Brussels continues to allocate so-called pre-accession funds to Ankara. In recent years, these funds have been cut because of Turkey's poor human rights records, but the EU will be reluctant to stop the flow of money altogether because of the pivotal position of Turkey in the Eastern Mediterranean and the Middle East. Despite the continued payments, by siding with Greece and the Republic of Cyprus, the EU has ruled out any possibility that it could be straightforwardly involved in any reunification process.

Matters are complicated further by Turkey turning to Russia for arms sales and moving away from its traditional NATO ally, the US, following a worsening in the US–Turkey relationship as tensions have increased about how to respond to Kurdish communities not just within Turkey but also in Iraq and Syria. Kurdish struggles for self-determination reveal the border anxieties embedded in Turkish geo-political culture. Although the US supported Kurdish aspirations in Iraq through the creation of the Kurdistan Regional Government in northern Iraq, by withdrawing US troops from northern Syria the Trump administration has greenlit a potential new border deal between Turkey and the regime in Syria.

Some observers fear that President Erdoğan might double down on a more aggressive geopolitical strategy, which seeks not only to appropriate a territorial corridor as a 'security buffer' in northern Syria but also make a play for Cyprus and even smaller Greek islands. Economic sanctions against Turkey in retaliation for any occupation of parts of northern Syria might unleash reverberations across the region. Adding further complexity to this tension over who owns what in the Eastern Mediterranean is the involvement of US and Israeli oil and gas production companies. Israel has also been a long-term Turkish ally, with Turkey being the first Muslim-majority country to recognise Israel. China is also a geo-economic player, with links to the Libyan oil industry and investment in debt-ridden Turkey. Another thing to watch is Turkey facilitating Chinese maritime access to the Eastern Mediterranean as part of a debt-relief and trade access deal.

The UK sovereign base areas are yet another complicating factor for the situation in Cyprus. The two areas – Akrotiri and Dhekelia – are home to British and Cypriot communities, with about 10,000 native Cypriots living there, and they are partially coastal. British

Forces Cyprus is responsible for the control of those areas and the other retained sites on the island. The UK claims a territorial sea off the sovereign base areas (some 3 nautical miles/5.6km from the coastline) as it is integral to their defence but thus far has not claimed an exclusive economic zone (which would be seen as provocative by the Republic of Cyprus, Greece and Turkey).

Brexit has added extra significance to these territorial entities. The sovereign base areas are not part of the European Union – they are UK overseas territories that apply and implement some EU legislation. The Akrotiri area borders the Republic of Cyprus (ROC), while Dhekelia borders the TRNC. In any post-Brexit agreement with the Republic of Cyprus, it is highly likely that the UK government would wish to retain the sovereign base areas, as they have functioned as important intelligence-gathering centres for the UK and NATO. In any new agreement with the UK, the ROC might push for the return of the sovereign base areas or at the very least wish to re-secure the rights to the territorial seas adjacent to the bases. The future of the territorial sea might actually be more valuable to the Republic of Cyprus than the land territory. Given uncertainty over the intentions of Turkey (and its relationship with China and Russia), a UK military presence might be considered desirable by the Republic of Cyprus.

Cyprus's situation is a complicated territorial dispute featuring multiple parties. While the focus is often on trans-border crime and local incidents along the green line, the real story is offshore. Oil and gas exploitation, worsening relations between NATO partners Turkey and the United States, and a tense relationship between Turkey and the European Union (which Greece and the ROC are members of) could increase conflict in the future.

The nightmare geopolitical scenario for the ROC is that Turkey becomes a close ally of China and Russia at the same time as the United States turns its back on the NATO alliance. In 2019, Turkey aligned itself with Libya as they signed security and energy-related agreements with one another. The threat of further European Union sanctions might also provoke Ankara to be ever more belligerent in and around the land border and disruptive of any attempts by the ROC to exploit its maritime resources. Any peace deal, let alone the reunification of Cyprus, therefore seems a remote prospect. In the meantime, Turkey might just yet seize other tiny Greek islands such as Kastellorizo, which because of its proximity to the Turkish coastline, interferes with Turkey's continental shelf and exclusive economic zone in the Aegean Sea and Eastern Mediterranean.

President Erdoğan might well assume, in the coming years, that NATO wouldn't risk a war with Greece and Turkey over some of the smaller Greek islands (rather than, for example, the largest island Rhodes) lying closest to the southern Turkish coastline. As any government in Athens appreciates, Turkey is the second largest standing military force in NATO and continues to host US forces at the Incirlik Air Base (since 1955) in the south-east corner of the country. What would any seizure achieve? It might be used as a bargaining chip to persuade Greece not to interfere with Turkey's plans to actively exploit a large swathe of seabed in the Eastern Mediterranean in close co-operation with Libya. Greek islands such as Crete and Rhodes get sidelined in a Turkish-Libyan grand design to dominate offshore oil and gas exploitation and fishing rights. Redrawing borders, exploiting the seabed, 'carving up' sea and the occupation of small islands is a daunting prospect for the Eastern Mediterranean.

ANTARCTICA AS UNRECOGNISED BORDER

While we considered Antarctica as a no man's land, it also has the dubious distinction of having a great many unrecognised borders. We could even claim that the largest area of the world affected by unrecognised borders is the polar continent.

Since 1908, claims have been pressed on Antarctica by seven countries: Argentina, Chile, Norway, France, New Zealand, Australia and the UK. The first to make a claim on the polar territory was the UK and the largest claimant remains Australia. While the two South American countries, Argentina and Chile, argue that their polar territories are natural extensions of their mainland republics, the European and Australasian claimants make reference to their previous episodes of exploration, discovery, exploitation and continuous human occupation for the purpose of conducting science. While it might be tempting to think of the Antarctic as a cold, windy, dry and remote sort of place (and it possesses all of those qualities), it has been and continues to be imagined as an extraordinary resource frontier. Captain James Cook might have had his doubts about the value of Antarctica when he encountered monstrous icebergs and seas in the eighteenth century but others did not.

After humans reached the Antarctic in the 1820s, the northern Antarctic Peninsula region and outlying islands such as South Georgia in particular were meccas for sealers and whalers. Cook's reports were filled with accounts of seas containing marine mammals. Seal pelts and whale and seal oil were global industries. Hundreds of thousands of seals were killed in the 1820s and 1830s and fur pelts exported to North America and Europe, where it was a popular material for clothing and hats. The Chinese port of Canton (now Guangzhou) was a major supplier for the Chinese market. Sealers hunted intensively during the summer season and then abandoned their camps during the long, dark winter months. At the same time, whalers established stations along the polar coastline designed to facilitate the slaughter and processing of whales. Whale oil was used for heating and only started to be replaced in the late nineteenth century by other fuels such as kerosene. Whale oil was also found to be integral to the manufacture of explosives, and it was later transformed into an ingredient in margarine. Norway and the UK in particular helped to establish a commercial whaling industry in northern Antarctica, which endured until the early 1960s.

When the UK pressed the first territorial claim to Antarctica in 1908 it did so for resource-related reasons. It was eager to regulate the whaling and sealing industries, and help profit from them further by insisting that the Norwegians respect the regulatory authority of London. In the subsequent three decades, the six other countries pressed their own territorial claims to various parts of the continent, and by 1943 there was only one unclaimed sector, an enormous area in the Pacific Ocean. The unclaimed sector was in the remotest and most inaccessible part of the continent and the UK hoped that a friendly power such as the US might eventually decide to formally claim that part of the region.

Using a sector-like approach, Antarctica is divided into slices, although in the case of the Peninsula, the UK, Argentina and Chile have counterclaims for the same territorial area. Significantly, the United States and the then Soviet Union declined to recognise any claim and announced that they reserved the right to make their own claims at a later date. Apart from the European and Australasian claimants mutually recognising their claims, none of those slices are recognised as legitimate by anyone else.

As the prospect of the Second World War loomed ever larger, the world faced a problem with Antarctica, which only a handful of countries were interested in addressing. Germany had an active record of polar exploration, and the UK feared that Nazi Germany might press its own claim on the continent, although at that point it was barely mapped and more often understood as being two or more large islands. Norway was encouraged by the UK to claim the empty territory between the British and Australian claims in the early 1930s, and it did so in January 1939. By the time Germany invaded Poland in the autumn of 1939, imperial and territorial rivalries in the Antarctic were well established and rival parties strove to map, survey, explore and exploit polar territory onshore and offshore. Things were in danger of spiralling out of control; expeditions were launched by multiple parties, including the United States, which dispatched a naval flotilla in the late 1940s to assert its strategic presence in the region.

Under a unique arrangement, the 1959 Antarctic Treaty, the polar continent and surrounding ocean were declared a zone of peace and goodwill. Following on from the cooperative spirit of the 1957–8 International Geophysical Year, the 12 treaty parties sought to use science and international cooperation to address the knotty issue of ownership of Antarctica. By signing the treaty, all the parties accepted that the territorial claims made by the seven claimants would be held in suspension. No signatory to the treaty had to accept their legitimacy. In the midst of the Cold War, the United States in particular recognised that Antarctica was in danger of becoming another area of discord, but not before it had speculated about using the continent as a nuclear-testing ground and hotspot for resource extraction. The Antarctic Treaty insisted that all parties be committed to demilitarisation and denuclearisation. Minerals, on the other hand, were not mentioned in the text.

Over the intervening six decades, the Antarctic Treaty parties have grown from 12 to over 50. Notably in the 1980s and 1990s, the treaty was signed by countries such as Brazil, India and China, the global south having been largely excluded from the original negotiations in the late 1950s. In order for the disputed ownership of territory and unrecognised borders not to become disruptive, over time the parties found ways to negotiate over resources, especially fishing. Mineral resources were the subject of intense debate in the 1980s, but the signatories later adopted a Protocol on Environmental Protection, which bans all forms of mining and mineral exploitation. Instead, there has been growth of other industries such as biological prospecting and tourism. The latter seeks to take advantage of Antarctica's biological and aesthetic value, while commercial fishing has found a relatively under-exploited frontier in the Southern Ocean.

What can we expect in the future? In answering that question most commentators have looked to China, an active participant in the region. As a non-claimant, it uses the governance mechanisms of the Antarctic Treaty to promote its interests. A good example was its proposal to create a 'specially managed area' designation around Kunlun, its research station on Dome Argus, the highest point on the Antarctic ice sheet. China saw this as an opportunity to use environmental stewardship as a mechanism to establish its own boundaries on the polar ice, demonstrating what a country can in theory do with a research station. Akin to an 'island' in a large expanse of ice, the station would become the focal point around which a special conservation area would be established. The Chinese proposal involved around 20,000km^2 (7,700 square miles) being subject to special environmental management and monitoring, but it was not well received by other parties, who believed China was using the specially managed area to cement its own sovereign authority, despite the fact that no other party operated in and around Dome Argus due to its remoteness.

China has also been the most resistant country to plans to extend marine protected areas, and, along with Russia, it was a reluctant party to the Ross Sea Marine Protected Area agreement in 2017. Chinese opposition was rooted in concern that marine protection and spatial planning were being used by claimant states such as New Zealand as a proxy for their own sovereignty – which is exactly what others accused China of doing around Dome Argus. China might also block future marine protected area proposals because it fears that conservation is being used to prevent it from fishing in the Southern Ocean. As the Antarctic Treaty works on the basis of consensus, all parties will need to be careful how they treat China.

The Ross Sea Marine Protected Area only brought to the fore simmering tensions. Proposed by the United States and New Zealand, it highlighted two very different views of Antarctica: one that regards Antarctica as an underdeveloped resource frontier and another that wishes to enhance and strengthen environmental conservation.

Australia in particular is worried about China's intentions. While Canberra has sought to work with China in terms of supporting Beijing's polar logistics operations via Tasmania, Australian governments have spoken of their concern about China's future behaviour. As the largest claimant state, Australia appears to be the most vulnerable to China's growing scientific, tourist and logistical presence on the continent.

Unrecognised borders in Antarctica arguably made the 1959 Antarctic Treaty and the associated governance regime possible. The treaty parties agreed to work with sovereign uncertainty. The seven claimant states did not have to relinquish their sectoral claims to Antarctica, but they also had to accept that their claims, including borders, were not going to be recognised by the wider international community. As a consequence, there are few activities onshore and offshore that don't have the potential for dispute. With no recognition of sovereignty and borders, environmental management, fisheries conservation, tourism planning and scientific operations all carry with them implications for how the global community secures agreement over its future usage.

ILLEGAL OCCUPATION AND UNRECOGNISED BORDERS

Formerly called Spanish Sahara, Western Sahara is a disputed territory of some 260,000km² (100,000 square miles), approximately the size of Great Britain, although the population of the region numbers around 560,000 people rather than the more than 60 million in the UK. It is largely desert and is one of the most sparsely occupied places in the world. The former Spanish colony was annexed by Morocco in 1975 after the fall of General Franco led to a power vacuum. Morocco and Mauritania sought to capitalise on the uncertainty and advanced their presence in the area. While Mauritania later withdrew as an occupying power, Morocco did not. Since that point, Morocco has been locked in conflict with the indigenous population (Saharawi) of Western Sahara. Led by the Polisario Front, the Western Saharan community has been campaigning for the creation of a Saharan Arab Democratic Republic (SADR). The SADR government established itself in exile just over the border in Algeria, and a long insurgency against Moroccan occupation ensued in the 1970s and 1980s. Formally speaking, the SADR has been recognised by around 80 states – Germany and Sweden, for example, have acknowledged the SADR in different forums – and it was admitted to the Organisation of African Unity in 1982. However, the United States, Russia, China and the European Union as a whole do not recognise it.

In the early 1990s, a UN-brokered truce was premised on a commitment to hold a referendum to determine whether Western Sahara should become independent. The referendum has not taken place and in the meantime the disputed territory has been split into two portions separated by a buffer zone: a Moroccan-controlled western section with access to fishing and phosphate, and an eastern area controlled by the Polisario Front. In sharp contrast to the EU reaction to the Russian invasion and annexation of Crimea, European Union states have been reluctant to push the referendum issue because of their concerns about souring their relationship with Morocco, which is integral to EU strategies for trans-Mediterranean migration and drug control. In particular, the two former colonial powers in Morocco, Spain and France, have been reluctant to criticise the North African country. Spain has a significant economic and strategic relationship with Morocco, with many Moroccans working in Spain's agricultural and service sector. Spain also has two enclaves in North Africa, Ceuta and Melilla, which border Morocco. As a consequence of this geographical proximity and economic entanglement, Spain has lobbied the EU to provide money for border-patrol investment with Morocco.

If there has been a challenge to the recognition of the Moroccan occupation it has come directly from legal channels such as the European Court of Justice. The court ruled in December 2016 that an EU–Moroccan agreement over agriculture could not extend to the disputed territory of Western Sahara. Rather than accept the decision unreservedly, the EU engaged in some furious diplomacy designed to mitigate any damage to its relationship with Morocco, and the EU was noticeably reluctant to engage with the representatives of the people of Western Sahara. In another ruling in February 2018, the court concluded that the EU–Moroccan Fisheries Agreement could not apply to the waters off Western Sahara. The court in effect followed the UN ruling that Western Sahara is not integral to Morocco but is rather, in UN terminology, a non-self-governing territory, illegally occupied by the government in Rabat. The UN is clear on this point: Morocco is not recognised as the rightful occupier of Western Sahara.

Shortly after the second European Court of Justice ruling, Morocco and the EU reaffirmed the importance of their strategic partnership and rarely mentioned the troubled status of Western Sahara. Migration, fisheries and common security (including anti-terrorism) continue to be the touchstones for this partnership, and the land border between Spain and Morocco created by the Ceuta and Melilla enclaves is also a major concern for both parties. The EU is worried that if migrants broke past Spanish security infrastructure, they could claim refugee status because those Spanish enclaves are within the EU. The price of Morocco's support is the EU's non-recognition of Western Sahara.

As other non-self-governing territories around the world will recognise, the price paid can be a high one as powerful neighbouring states either continue to occupy territory illegally or third parties such as the European Union ignore the legitimate representatives and governments of those territories in favour of strategically important neighbours such as Morocco. Since 1963 the UN has listed Western Sahara as a territory that has yet to be decolonised. The prospects for the disputed territory are not good. Morocco's plan for autonomy, first mooted in 2008, does not commit Rabat to holding a referendum on the future of the disputed territory. Instead, Morocco has used the interregnum to build a coalition of support for its position. Countries such as Peru have sent delegations and issued public expressions of support for Morocco. In order to legitimise its presence in Western Sahara, Morocco also chooses it words carefully, speaking about the 'population' rather than 'people' and emphasising 'interests' rather than 'wishes'. And the word 'consultation' is routinely used when referring to Western Saharan claims for independence, rather than Morocco actively securing a democratic mandate or the consent of the Western Saharan peoples.

The ongoing impasse in Western Sahara amounts to the non-recognition of a community illegally occupied by a third party by a regional organisation and its member states who champion the rule of international law. But the stakes are high for the EU, eager as it is to regulate illegal migration from North Africa, and economic levers have been deployed to purchase the support of countries such as Morocco. Not only has the EU established a lucrative trading partnership with the country, but it also offers financial support to the

Moroccan fishing industry. Some of that money is being used to create infrastructure such as port facilities in Western Sahara. In other words, it is being used to consolidate the illegal Moroccan occupation.

Shamed by its de facto acceptance of the illegal occupation by Morocco, the European Parliament voted to extend preferential tariffs to Western Sahara in 2019. They now match those enjoyed by Morocco. The European Court of Justice rulings and public campaigning in favour of independence for Western Sahara in effect forced the European Commission to agree a new trade agreement with Morocco that acknowledges when products originate from Western Sahara and not a southern 'Morocco'. A European Parliamentary resolution also declared that the EU should support the Western Saharan people and their autonomous economic development while a political solution was being sought. But this should be taken with a pinch of salt. In June 2019, the EU and Morocco agreed a new partnership agreement for 'shared prosperity' and the EU praised Rabat for its handling of the dispute with the people of Western Sahara. Earlier in the year, a new sustainable fisheries partnership was approved. In short, the EU has gestured towards the Western Sahara's political situation without compromising its relationship with Morocco.

Longer term, the EU–Morocco relationship could be undone by tensions within Morocco and how Rabat deals with migrants who choose to stay in the country rather than make the perilous journey to EU states such as Spain. The latter approved a special grant to Morocco worth €30 million for the expressed purpose of discouraging illegal migrant activity. The Spanish government has also used public funds to purchase equipment such as drones for its Moroccan counterpart. Spain's territories in the Canary Islands, enclaves in North Africa and southern border with the Mediterranean make it a complex geographical region to patrol and regulate.

The fate of Western Sahara reveals a broader truth about the geopolitics of recognition. In February 2020, Japan reiterated its support for the territorial integrity of Morocco and thus the non-recognition of Western Sahara as an independent entity. Japan made a decision to prioritise its trading relationship with Morocco over other considerations. Japan is a major investor in the country's renewable energy sector and car industry. Recognising Western Sahara means alienating Morocco permanently and poisoning relationships with Rabat's allies. Even the UN does not appear to know quite what to do. The post of UN special envoy for the Western Sahara has been vacant from May 2019 onwards. Part of the problem facing any appointee is that they have to be both acceptable to the parties affected as well as willing to take on a mandate that is one of the world's toughest to address.

UNRECOGNISED FUTURES

This all brings us to Crimea and a string of other Russian protectorates, which provide ample evidence of why the unrecognised border will continue to matter in the future. In February and March 2014, Russia illegally annexed Crimea and overran Ukrainian security forces. While the EU and United States have declared their support for Ukraine's territorial integrity and internationally recognised borders, Russia remains de facto in control of Crimea. Since 2014, Russia has militarised the disputed territory and shown every indication that it will not respect the unhindered and free passage of Ukrainian vessels through the Kerch Strait to and from the Azov Sea. In 2018, Ukraine and Russia clashed over this access to the Kerch Strait, a body of water that acts as a chokepoint between the smaller Azov Sea and the larger Black Sea. Ukraine retaliated by holding a Russian tanker, which it believed had been used to block Ukrainian ships operating in the disputed waters around Crimea. Russia is still holding up to 24 Ukrainian sailors following the 2018 incident. Russia is determined to disrupt Ukrainian port and maritime activity, and while sanctions were imposed on Moscow there is little evidence that Russia will ever leave Crimea.

Meanwhile, in Georgia there are two breakaway regions with a Russian majority: Abkhazia and South Ossetia. Recognised by Russia as independent in 2008, after a short war involving Georgia, these enclaves are only recognised by three other countries in the world. The government of Georgia is not one of them. Yet the border between Georgia and Abkhazia has now taken on a formal quality, as this breakaway province in effect falls under the protective orbit of the Russian Federation.

The very existence of Abkhazia allows for some strange things to happen. A small group of around 400 North Korean guest workers continue to be employed there. Accommodated in a former Soviet-era holiday resort, they are helping to build infrastructure for the main town of Sukhumi. Their continued presence violates UN sanctions that demand the expulsion of North Korean guest workers. Abkhazia as a largely unrecognised entity is not a UN member and thus not subject to UN resolutions per se. Russia is happy to tolerate their presence because it provides some leverage when it comes to strategic relationships with North Korea and East Asia. There are thousands of guest workers in Russia and their remittances are crucial to regime survival in North Korea. More generally, North Korean workers play a vital role across a Russia that is experiencing long-term population decline, especially in the far east.

Breakaway republics and protectorates provide strategic options for the Russian Federation. Money can be funnelled through them and into them. The Russian rouble is the de facto currency. People can be kept there too. Sanctions can be bypassed. At the same time, these unrecognised borders are secure because of the proximity to the Russian war machine, and Russia has agreed to underwrite the modernisation of military forces in Abkhazia. Meanwhile, Abkhazia can build a degree of international recognition by participating in and hosting, for example, sporting events for unrecognised states. Abkhazia plays football against teams from other unrecognised states such as Kurdistan, the Turkish Republic of Northern Cyprus and South Ossetia. They even have their own football authority, the Confederation of Independent Football

Associations (CONIFA), and Abkhazia hosted and won the CONIFA World Football Cup in 2016.

Georgia has few options when it comes to the long-term occupation of its former territories. Russia has been adamant that if Georgia does become, as it wishes, a NATO member country, it would accept that membership only if the collective security provisions applied to just the territory administered by the government of Tbilisi. The separatist territories of Abkhazia and South Ossetia would be, in effect, outside the NATO security umbrella. The price of NATO membership, as dictated by Russia, would therefore be to recognise those unrecognised borders.

Unrecognised borders will continue to punctuate the global political landscape and test prevailing legal and political regimes. As we have noted, the Antarctic continent and surrounding ocean are shot through with unresolved and unrecognised borders, and the treaty system designed in the 1950s to manage disputed ownership may or may not endure, depending on the preservation of consensus on non-mineral and possibly even mineral exploitation. There are and will continue to be disputes over fishing rights in the Southern Ocean, as rival states argue about whether to push harder on resource exploitation or demand ever greater environmental conservation. The situation will become more fraught in the future.

Meanwhile, the continuing non-recognition of the Turkish Republic of Northern Cyprus has enabled the long-standing presence of Turkish military assets. At present, some 30,000 troops are stationed in the TRNC, and the Turkish government has spoken publicly about building a new naval base. Given the strategic uncertainty in the wider region, Turkey will be in no mood to compromise on Cyprus while its attention is turned to managing its shared border with Syria, and while it is mindful of extracting maximum advantage from its fraught relationship with the United States and the European Union. Maintaining a working relationship with Russia is also likely to be useful to President Erdoğan's plans to keep Turkey as a regional superpower.

Finally, for those living in the midst of unrecognised borders they provide a ragbag of consequences. Georgia will have to accept that parts of its national territory are no longer under its control, while others profit from their annexation. In other parts of the world, community life might never recover from past histories of conflict and non-recognition. In the late 1960s, the people of Biafra attempted to create their own republic in south-east Nigeria and establish their own distinct territory. The legacy of the civil war was horrific, with at least 100,000 deaths due to conflict and many times more than that due to starvation, disease and hardship. The final death toll was over 2 million people and the Republic of Biafra was crushed in 1970. Fifty years later, it is not hard to find people demanding a so-called Biafrexit referendum, asking communities in the south-east whether they still wish to be part of Nigeria.

Travel is harder if a de facto state such as the TRNC is not recognised internationally. Infrastructure and resource projects may be delayed or never completed because third parties might be reluctant to participate in areas that are subject to dispute. Or else suppliers don't get paid at all. Conflict can occur over a range of matters, especially if the formal structures of international legal life don't apply. Alternatively, oppressed peoples might not get the support they think they deserve because third parties are concerned about the consequences for their relationship with neighbouring states. Some countries such as Western Sahara and Somaliland may never secure independence and internationally recognised borders because others don't want to jeopardise their relationships with countries such as Morocco and Somalia.

The difference between the recognised and unrecognised border can be a fine one and depends ultimately on the reaction of others. Recognition is ultimately always a political process. But it is never divorced from a gamut of other considerations from the commercial to the geostrategic. And bear in mind the following example as a simple illustration that recognition is a process, not a fixed outcome. Ever since Kosovo declared its independence from Serbia in February

2008, Belgrade has committed itself to getting Kosovo's recognition reversed. It has lobbied other countries and boasted in March 2020 that it had encouraged at least 18 countries to reverse their previous declaration of recognition of independence. Relations with the EU suffered after Kosovo imposed a 100 per cent tariff on Serbian goods in response to the Serbian campaign to undermine its international recognition. This sort of conflict, and associated activist campaigns, will be a potent source of future unrest.

Airports have been pioneers of smart border technologies. Haikou Meilan International Airport in Hainan Province of China was opened in 1999. It has become a hotspot for smart border technologies and 5G communication networking. The airport is experimenting with new technologies, including passenger identification systems, automated border control systems, biometric systems, highly automated baggage reclaim systems. It has been described as all part of the 'smart-travel-service' system.

Chapter 7

Smart Borders

Travellers to international airports, ports and approved crossing points are only too familiar with border paraphernalia: the passport checks, the security inspections and near-constant surveillance in semi-enclosed transit spaces; the national flags, the signage warning of an approaching border and the queues. As air travel increases, there is greater interest in putting new technologies to work. Many readers will have experienced first-hand the self-service kiosks (entry/exit system devices) in airports around the world. Passengers are now doing more and more borderwork themselves, for the airlines, the airports and the border management authorities.

However, we encounter the border way before we reach those self-service kiosks. As anyone who checks in online for a flight can testify, airlines ask for advanced passport information (API) to be logged into their booking system. It helps airlines process their passengers more efficiently, while responding to demands by governments around the world to be able to monitor more closely international passenger travel. Self-service kiosks are promoted to passengers as aiding and abetting a 'better airport-security experience' – shorter queues, instructions available in multiple languages and more accessible to those who have mobility challenges.

The annual Passenger Terminal Expo is a good place to discover what is coming next in terms of biometric verification, baggage scanning, virtual security agents and self-service border control systems. The 2019 Expo attracted over 7,000 attendees and scores of commercial operators exhibited and promoted their products. The airport of the future is likely to have many more touchpoints for passengers to present their biometric data in order to progress through security gates and aircraft boarding. The usage of facial recognition technology is increasingly widespread. Images of passengers are taken and then matched against images of persons on 'watch-lists', but what is not clear is how that data may be used by airport and security authorities. Between 2017 and 2020, US airport authorities were responsible for generating at least 20 million images of passengers and it remains unclear as to what legal redress citizens and third parties have to combat excessive or malicious usage of such facial data. Activists and legal organisations in the US and UK have created interactive maps, which log the latest airports, cities and law-enforcement agencies to deploy facial recognition technologies. In 2020, the American Civil Liberties Union began legal action against the US Department of Homeland Security, accusing the latter of indiscriminate surveillance and lack of proper accountability.

Smart borders make sense for businesses like the global travel industry. When they work as planned, the experience for 'trusted' and vetted passengers should not be too bothersome. Airlines are involved in facial recognition trials and boast that they can load and unload large passenger planes more quickly than ever before. There still might be queues to negotiate but the airport and airline authorities have every incentive to ensure that the process is as smooth as possible, because that means that passengers are more likely to continue to travel and spend money in airport environments. London Heathrow welcomed over 80 million passengers in 2018, served over 200 destinations and handled 1.7 million tonnes of cargo. As any visitor to London Heathrow would notice, EU and European Economic Area (EEA) citizens have the added bonus of e-passport facilities. Since leaving the European Union in January 2020, some non-EU/EEA citizens can use the e-passport gates but only if they hail from one of the 'trusted' nations of Australia, Canada, Japan, New Zealand, Singapore, South Korea and the United States. For other citizens, it might be possible to register with what is termed the registered traveller scheme, which allows passengers to avoid the longer non-EU passport queues on arrival at a UK airport.

For those who work in the smart border industry, new technologies are championed as enabling friction-free and secure mobility regimes. However, the claims made for the benefits of the smart border need to be counterbalanced with the costs and implications of 'smartness'. Following the 11 September 2001 attacks, the United States and others faced a dilemma about borders. Some borders could be shut for a while but the United States decided to reopen its own after several days. Decisions were then taken by the George W. Bush administration about how it might be possible to enable trusted individuals and cargo or trade to continue to move across borders while filtering out the dangerous and undesirable. It was the catalyst for what we will term the smart border revolution because it coincided with legislative change such as the Patriot Act, which enabled law-enforcement agencies and federal government to access phone records of citizens. What has followed is a ramping up of surveillance technologies to the point that civil rights campaigners often note that what was once used in the fight against terrorism has now been domesticated. State police in the United States use facial recognition technology, phone tracking and automated licence readers to track the movements of citizens.

The surveillance of people, services and goods goes hand in hand with contemporary capitalism. Global industry is predicated on highly integrated supply chains and mobility regimes that authorise and regulate the flow of goods, technology and people. Regional organisations such as the European Union champion internal mobility within partner countries. They want to see more usage of what they term the smart border package, which calls for ever more biometric data sharing and monitoring of third-party nationals. Travellers expect to glide through airports and consumers expect to be able to order goods and services from around the world. Meanwhile, the inter-governmental organisation, the World Customs Organization, promotes the harmonisation of border controls and customs knowledge-sharing. All of which is good news for companies eager to sell new technologies designed to respond to the threat of cyberattacks and hybrid warfare. Smart border technologies will be integral to how airports, land crossings and seaports process increasing passenger and cargo numbers, while there will be more investment in algorithmic processes to anticipate suspicious behaviour and weed out unwanted travellers.

Smart border technology does not, however, make border conflict or outright attacks by adversaries any less likely. In an era of cyberattacks, fake news and drone attacks, third parties including terrorists can strike anywhere in the world. A drone attack wreaked havoc on the Saudi Aramco facility in September 2019, leading to substantial disruption to the supply of goods and a crash in share price. In areas of high military tension and border conflict, there will be a push to invest more in areas such as autonomous technologies, biometrics, remote weapon stations, anti-drone technologies, predictive analytics, and maritime and aerial surveillance. Military security intersects with the management of civilian air travel through smart border technologies.

THE SMART BORDER

A working definition of a smart border is one that uses information and communication technologies to ease, extend and intensify border controls. The information and communications technology component of smart borders often involves biometric and information-sharing capacities and systems. Airports have been hotspots for smart border innovation and rollout. The US Visitor and Immigrant Status Indicator Technology (US-VISIT) programme was introduced in 2004, designed to match passenger fingerprint and image data to visitors and their passport/visa. Every passenger entering the US on a visa-waiver scheme has to submit to biometric measures at their port of entry. President Trump has demanded that all US airports are able to use facial recognition technologies by 2021, in order to ensure that all passengers are processed within a 'biometric entry/exit system'. Hundreds of millions of passengers every year will need to be accounted for via this facial recognition technology. What is less clear is how this facial recognition data will be stored and used by others.

The underlying drivers for smart borders are a mixture of the geopolitical and the technological. In the wake of the War on Terror, states have intensified their investment in surveillance capabilities and extended their usage of 'big data' analysis. Biometric analysis, image processing and facial recognition technologies depend not only on supportive IT infrastructures but also processing power. Huge amounts of data have to be stored, processed and evaluated, all of which takes investment and resourcing. Geopolitically, countries and regional organisations such as the US and the EU have invested in these areas because of commitments to address either terrorism or migration crises. Whether it is the southern border of the United States or the European Union's borders with neighbours, there has been a stated eagerness to reinforce security, both physical and electronic.

The collection and processing of data and knowledge generation are in keeping with a shift towards what has been termed knowledge-intensive forms of governance. The turn towards 'smartness' gathered further momentum after the 2008 financial crisis. Attention turned to how states and governments could be entrepreneurial and use data generation in new, more profitable manners. What this means for borders is that they are asked to work in two ways.

First, they act as traditional markers of national territorial limits. The boundary lines that distinguish the United States and Mexico, and Turkey and the European Union continue to matter in terms of basic security, resource development and migration control. Militaries will continue to operate on the basis that those lines and boundaries are highly significant in terms of domain control. Second, borders are also regarded as opportunities to collect and harvest data. The electronic border, which is a great deal more expansive that the traditional land or sea border, is more continuum than line. The border can follow an object or person of interest many miles away from any formal border line. These two understandings of the border are complementary: border guards can work hand in hand with other entities that are busy collecting and processing biometric data many miles away from those borderlands.

For all the fanfare, the smart border is really an update of something that has been preoccupying border security officials and national governments for some time: namely better situational awareness and stronger control of unwanted or unreported mobility. In an ideal world, the smart border would also eliminate the 'grunt work' of the border security agencies and, more importantly, act to deter and even anticipate unwanted border crossers even before they board a plane, ship or train. The downsides remain unchanged: data analysis is fraught with challenges, including the danger of false positives (for example, errors in data reporting leading to incorrect action against an innocent party – sometimes simply because they have a similar surname to another person of interest) and the perennial and ever-growing demands of managing mountains of surveillance and biometric data. Communities, either living close to the border or simply identified as of interest on the basis of ethnicity, religion and citizenship, are left with concerns that their civil liberties are being violated in the name of national security.

SMART BORDERS AND BORDER WALLS

In and around the US–Mexico borderlands, we find plenty of evidence of the smart border being targeted towards migrants and asylum seekers. Prior to his election victory in November 2016, President

Trump made border security an integral part of his campaign pledge. Building a 'beautiful wall' was part of a package of measures designed to make Americans feel more secure, especially to the south of the country. Although the president has often focused on physical walls and barriers, border-security planning has also been more expansive and invasive. In the midst of a border crisis, the administration's Department of Homeland Security launched a pilot programme designed to collect DNA from would-be asylum seekers. Intended to target what were described as 'fraudulent families', the Department of Homeland Security intervention deliberately used the testing regime (described as voluntary) to check whether the DNA samples matched individuals purporting to be family members. Fact-checking the claims made by families claiming asylum remains a key plank of border management. Smart technologies are envisaged as the ultimate truth-seekers. People can lie about their family origins and citizenship, but they can't lie about their DNA. Armed with this knowledge, the intervention was designed to stop opportunistic coupling by adults using 'their children' to mitigate detention conditions. While this might be seen as a deterrent to illegal trafficking, it can also be used and abused. If you don't hand over DNA samples, you run the risk that your claim for asylum will not be entertained by the United States.

What worries civil liberties organisations is that the smart border becomes a pretext for ever greater intervention in the lives of others, including US citizens. The reach and scope of the Customs and Border Protection (CBP) agency (under the supervision of the Department of Homeland Security) do not end at the border line with Canada and Mexico. There is a series of zones of potential interdiction and intervention. Within 40km (25 miles) of the border with Mexico, CBP operatives enjoy what has been described as limited immunity. Agents can patrol on private lands and ranchers have described finding surveillance paraphernalia on their properties, sometimes more than 40km from the land border. The reach of the CBP can extend even further. As touched upon previously, up to 160km (100 miles) inland from every border and coastline of the

United States, agents can set up checkpoints and detain suspects on the basis of 'probable cause'. Some 200 million Americans live within this extended border perimeter. Hawaii and Florida fall entirely within the scope and reach of the CBP.

Three recent developments provide insights into the future of the smart border and its capacity to stretch ever further into the lives of citizens and non-citizens alike. First, the CBP is using aerial drones to patrol border and coastal areas of the United States. A US Government Accountability Office report from 2014 revealed that drone surveillance also extended beyond 100 miles, which raises concerns about privacy and administrative overreach. 'Border communities' could be under near-constant surveillance as local police and the CBP use facial recognition technologies, licence-plate-reading cameras and drone surveillance. Second, the CBP has used this 'border zone' to stop private cars and public buses in the interior of the United States to check on the immigration status of passengers. Cities such as Chicago and Philadelphia are just as likely to be targeted as 'border cities' such as San Diego and Miami. Substantial parts of the interior of the United States have become a vast dragnet and activist groups such as the Electronic Frontier Foundation, an international non-profit digital rights group, produce regular updates of the CBP's surveillance activities and its operational scope. Checking buses and cars may not seem indicative of the smart border but it is enabled by the operational reach of the CBP and the technologies that are used to monitor the movement of 'suspicious' individuals and cargo. Finally, and most egregiously, in 2017 CBP purchased access to a licence plate database owned and operated by a private company. This means, in effect, the CBP has had even wider data access to the movement of cars on US highways, without having to seek legal permissions to exploit it.

As indicated, much of this owes its origins to the immediate post-9/11 environment. With border and homeland security at a premium, the George W. Bush administration ordered investment (with congressional approval) in new smart border technologies. Plans were developed for 'virtual fences' along the US–Mexico border. In 2007, Boeing was commissioned by the Department of Homeland Security to test what was called Project 28, a network of mobile sensor towers, ground-based sensors, smart communication devices and mobile surveillance patrolling. The aim of Project 28, which was part of a wider Secure Border Initiative, was to generate a 'Common Operating Picture', which would eventually be erected all along the US–Mexico borderlands.

The project was eventually cancelled in 2011 after a $1 billion investment. It was found to be too expensive and not sufficiently flexible to the diverse physical geographies of the borderlands. The land border, stretching some 3,200km (2,000 miles), incorporates a large river environment, huge deserts, mountain chains and extensive coastal stretches. Tumbleweed and animals produced difficulties when it came to the detection of what might be thought of as suspicious objects; extreme weather was found to damage sensory towers and interfere with camera functionality; radar stations proved prone to breakdown; and operators at the command centre were overwhelmed by data generation. Remote and unattended infrastructure brought with it the spectre of vandalism as well. And as the Secure Border Initiative was rolled out, migrants were choosing ever more precarious journeys across remoter parts of the southern borderlands. Inevitably, this led to a heightened death toll as those migrant parties tried to evade the sensory capacities of the initiative.

Fast-forward a decade, and smart border technologies and infrastructure are integral to President Trump's walling manifesto. Surveillance technologies have moved on from the earlier experiments in the smart border. Wars in Iraq and Afghanistan allowed for new drone and other surveillance technologies to be tested elsewhere, often in remote, mountainous environments. The investment of the Trump regime in these improved technologies coincides with a growing confidence among US tech companies that the 'virtual border' is possible. Anduril Industries has been busy championing its 'Lattice' system, which promises the user the capacity to detect and distinguish cars from tumbleweed and/or human beings. Using cameras, infrared sensors and LIDAR (Light Detection and Ranging – a technique that uses light pulses to measure variable distances) the collected data is then processed by analysts back in the command centre using AI. The company used ranches on the Texas–Mexico border-land in 2018 to test the technology and was then touting the fact that its detection system contributed to a series of arrests of suspected illegal migrants.

Other tech experts have expressed their doubts about the effectiveness of the smart or virtual border. But it is not hard to imagine why it might appeal to some governments. From the Atlantic to the Pacific Ocean, the 'smart wall' of the sort that has been imagined would involve a network of drones and sensor technologies designed to supplement the border-patrol and law-enforcement communities. This idea of the smart wall has attracted bipartisan support because its 'smartness' lies in the fact that its physical footprint would be less than a large fortress wall. Cross-border communities and properties, it is argued, would be less directly affected. It also promises to be potentially cheaper and more flexible in reach than physical barriers (and the Mexican government shows no sign that it will pay for any physical investment in border walls). Critics of the 'smart wall' initiative, on the other hand, note that these surveillance technologies raise privacy and data sharing issues, with surveillance regimes falling disproportionately on border cities and communities. Algorithms can reveal racial and other forms of profiling as drone surveillance fails to distinguish between migrant and non-migrant. Facial recognition might be used to target minority communities. Licence-plate-reading technologies could be used to monitor anyone, not just search for undocumented migrants. Drone flying is, according to the CBP, only used within 40km (25 miles) of the US–Mexico border but it could legally deploy drones up to 100km (60 miles) from the land and sea borders of the United States. In 2019, the CBP confirmed it would be placing further orders for smaller and cheaper drones because they can typically fly for several hours and over shorter distances compared to the larger drones favoured in war environments. It also thought it would deflect criticism for simply importing the same drone technologies used on overseas battlefields.

In other jurisdictions such as Hong Kong, biometric techniques have been used in new smart identity cards. From 2018, the Hong

Kong Identity Card has been issued to young adults and anyone who has lost or damaged their earlier identity card. The exercise was ostensibly designed to tackle illegal migration and employment, but civil rights groups objected that the measures will eventually impact all Hong Kong citizens, because everyone will need a identity card to demonstrate that they are legal residents, and will thus be forced to submit to further biometric data profiling. The card is necessary for residents to access public services, including health and education, which will ensure that compliance is going to be ever more complete.

PROFITING FROM THE SMART BORDER

Within the European Union, the Schengen Agreement of 1985 was heralded as a brave new political world composed of free travel in a borderless zone. Dispensing with border controls, the plan was for EU citizens to live and work freely across the EU and for foreign visitors to apply for a Schengen visa, which would allow them access to all the participatory countries, including most EU countries and near neighbours such as Norway and Switzerland. In 2016, in response to what was described as the European migrant crisis, seven countries including Austria and France reintroduced border checks, and as they did so they created new opportunities for commercial and political stakeholders to profit.

In a hard-hitting report on 'border wars' in 2018, Mark Akkerman explored the beneficiaries of border-security investment and the implications that will follow from the EU's shift away from the Schengen principles. The European Commission has plans to invest in an enhanced European Border and Coast Guard Agency (developed from its existing FRONTEX agency), with plans for operational staff to be expanded to 10,000 by 2027. Supplementing the new agency will be a network of border surveillance and monitoring called EUROSUR, which is designed to link the situational awareness capacities of all Schengen members. The EU has also been working closely with third parties such as Turkey and North African states, including Libya, to help control the flow of migrants and refugees heading towards European states.

As the EU invests more in border security and monitoring, it is expected that the border-security industry is going to become increasingly valuable in areas such as defence spending, information and communication technologies, and employment of border-security personnel. It is estimated that the EU bloc will spend at least €20 billion in the next seven years as its enhanced border agency seeks to attract those 10,000 employees (from a current level of around 700) and extend its situational awareness and capabilities. The EU's plan is to work with third parties to deter migrants and refugees, but there is a clear trend towards more aggressive border policing and security regardless. The 2019 European Border and Coast Guard Day annual conference gives a good indication of the direction of traffic. At the conference, held close to the Poland–Ukraine border, speakers were invited to think about how digital/smart border technologies could be used to assist the work of EU border guards charged with protecting the vast southern and eastern borderlands, a topic that Polish television had already tackled via its fictional drama *The Border* (2014), which dramatised the work of Polish border-security guards, working in cold and remote mountainous terrain, attempting to stem illegal migration and smuggling from Ukraine.

The EU is going to introduce a new entry/exit system in 2021. This will involve biometric border control, the widespread introduction of e-gates and what are described as biometric self-service kiosks. The entry/exit system is targeted at what are termed third-party nationals (including UK citizens post EU departure) who will be required to register their biometric data at the border of Schengen countries. On arrival at an airport, station or seaport, visitors will be expected to use self-service kiosks only after pre-registering their data. The biometric data captured by those kiosks will then be stored alongside other data such as facial recognition. Biometric and facial image capture is compulsory. Investment in entry/exit-system compliant technologies and facilities is going to involve hundreds of millions of euros, and the European Commission has already warned that there will still need to be considerable border-guard surveillance given the possibility of fingerprint and facial image manipulation.

European data companies are going to be some of the beneficiaries of this turn towards digital bordering. Meanwhile, it is likely that the EU and the United States as leaders in smart border technologies are going to be locked into further demands for visitor information. Not content with facial and biometric data, travellers to the United States will also have to reveal their relevant social media accounts.

Since 2014, US officials have been able, if they wish, to screen social media postings. Those demands to investigate social media behaviour are in part rooted in domestic terrorism such as the 2015 San Bernardino shootings in California. The Federal Bureau of Investigation requested Apple's assistance to access the cell phones of the perpetrators, revealing an awkward tension between the privacy of the customer versus the pressing needs of national law enforcement. Law-enforcement officials argued that access to personal social media accounts and telephone history would yield vital clues on the motivation of perpetrators and their possible support networks.

In waging an undeclared war against illegal migrants, terrorists and irregular persons, smart border technologies and investment show little sign of abating. It is not hard to see who might profit from this turn towards the 'smart border'. Populist leaders and nationalist governments will champion investment in the smart border as a way of deterring further illegal and unreported migrants and those they might imagine to be potential terrorists. In the US–Mexico borderlands, the ramping up of surveillance, detention and border patrolling is heavily impacting those with whom it comes into contact. In July 2019, a Guatemalan mother named Yazmin Juarez gave harrowing testimony to a congressional committee about how her baby daughter died after she was released from a detention centre in southern Texas. In 2020, the distraught mother began legal action against the US Immigration and Customs Enforcement agency for a failure to provide adequate medical care for her daughter, who was afflicted by a serious respiratory infection. Her testimony also revealed that the living and sanitary conditions in the detention centres were dire, especially for children. Human rights organisations have warned repeatedly that the detention centres operated by the agency are inhumane and cruel. Representatives of the House of Representatives' Committee on Oversight and Reform were visibly upset while listening to the distraught mother. Smart border infrastructure will cost more lives, but the humanitarian crisis that it generates is unlikely to deter political leaders elected on manifestos promising stronger walls and better border protection.

HACKING THE SMART BORDER

Smart borders capture data – big data. As we've seen, biometric data such as fingerprint and eye-retina information are already routinely collected by border-enforcement agencies around the world, and land-based smart border crossings involve the mass photographing of passengers and their vehicles. The US–Mexico border, for example, typically involves hundreds of thousands of unique crossings every week. In June 2019, it was reported that a CBP contractor's database containing images of travellers and licence-plate data had been breached. According to reports, the contractor gained access to licence-plate scans and images of travellers after copying them onto its own data-storage networks. The named contractor did so without the authorisation of the CBP and an estimated 100,000 people were affected by the data breach.

Even if border-enforcement agencies follow legal guidance, the large-scale nature of data collection still carries with it risks that centralised databases might be used in ways not intended by those who implemented the original measures. As others have discovered, human error and oversight allow plenty of opportunities for hacking. As this data breach demonstrates, contractors to government agencies add another layer of vulnerability to the smart border operation. The loss of data could have been worse given it was mainly just photos of drivers and corresponding licence plates of their cars. However, the case does raise the possibility that this basic information might allow the determined hacker to begin to get hold of additional personal information, such as the registered address of the vehicle and driving-licence details.

The CBP data breach also opens up a vista that is more sinister. As agencies such as the CBP continue to gather ever more personal data, we face the possibility of hostile third parties hacking biometric and other personal information databases. Smart border infrastructure collects a vast amount of personal data about individuals and their vehicles, and most of those people are likely to be either citizens or legitimate travellers. But biometric data collection is not without its potential flaws. Facial masks might be used routinely to confuse such technologies, and personal data is always going to be valuable to criminals and others seeking to profiteer. Investment will therefore continue in AI technologies, with a particular focus on ensuring that fingerprints and faces cannot be faked successfully.

And the stakes may be high: rather than licence-plate data or other personal information being stolen, it is perfectly possible to imagine sensitive aerial surveillance data being hacked as well. In 2015, news outlets in India carried a story detailing a suspected Chinese-backed hacking operation against government departments and universities in India. The target of the hackers was sensitive information pertaining to ongoing border disputes in the north. Around 70 institutions in India were thought to have been targeted. This is not the first time the Indian authorities have been assailed by such a digital assault. In 2012, it was revealed that thousands of email accounts of government and military personnel had been breached.

Keeping the smart border secure is a major challenge, and the fallout from the June 2019 incident involving leaked licence-plate data is a reminder of how easily information security can be compromised. Law-enforcement data can be stolen, drones can be repurposed and sensor systems shut down. The smart border reveals only too well the competing priorities of states, citizens and commercial actors. US companies such as Google and Amazon are integral partners for the federal government, including on smart border technologies. Citizens and employees might well turn their back on these companies as misgivings arise about the scale and extent of their surveillance activities and their collaboration with governments. No individual, however, appears to be immune. Remarkably, in March 2019 it was revealed that Saudi intelligence agencies were intent on hacking Jeff Bezos's personal phone. Remarkably, in March 2019, it was revealed that Saudi intelligence agencies had hacked Jeff Bezos's personal phone sometime in April 2018. While it is not clear what intelligence officials learnt from the hack itself, it was enabled by malware embedded in a series of WhatsApp messages between Bezos and the Crown Prince of Saudi Arabia, Mohammed bin Salman. The Saudi authorities were unhappy with Bezos, as the owner of the Washington Post, for allowing the Saudi dissident Jamal Khashoggi to write critical newspaper columns of the Saudi Royal Family. In October 2018, Khashoggi was murdered while attending the Saudi consulate in Istanbul.

What starts at the border rarely stays there. Poor software and unencrypted communication systems provide ample opportunities for others to carry out damaging hacks. Companies are often only too happy for us to use insecure devices if they can better target advertising and services at us. Hostile parties can do the same, potentially stealing enormous personal and group data archives or hacking smart border technologies.

If conflicts of the future do not involve the hacking of smart border technologies, foreign hackers might instead focus on critical infrastructure and energy suppliers such as Saudi Aramco, which was hit by a massive hack in 2012. We should not assume that an investment in smart border technologies straightforwardly contributes to national security. Indeed, across the Middle East, there have been lots of other examples of hacks and cyberattacks. In 2017, Qatar accused hackers in the United Arab Emirates of disrupting the digital operation of the Qatar News Agency. The UAE denied sponsoring the attack. It came at a time when other countries were boycotting Qatar because of its alleged support of terrorist groups, funding of Al Jazeera and support for Iran. As a reaction to the boycott, which included airspace closure, Qatar invested more in smart border technologies, food self-sufficiency and military equipment.

All of which demonstrates that smart border technologies are not a magic bullet. Contributing to a better travelling experience in a busy commercial airport might be one thing, but the issues get a great deal more complicated when geopolitical turmoil is the norm. In parts of the world where borders are continually disputed, we have examples of countries investing in what India has termed the Comprehensive Integrated Border Management System. On closer inspection, what we learn is that another government is pledging to spend more money on ground sensors, smart fencing, electronic intelligence gathering and surveillance along the Indo-Bangladeshi and Indo-Pakistani borders. The aim is to disrupt the 'menace of illegal activities' including cross-border terrorism. Meanwhile, Pakistan has vowed to escalate its security patrols and investment in its own 'smart fencing'. A smart-technological-border security arms race will inevitably follow.

BREXIT AND THE QUEST FOR THE SMART BORDER

Despite the challenges, the quest for a watertight and hyper-efficient smart border remains undiminished. The drama created by Brexit revealed the desire among some for technical solutions to border management. After the referendum in June 2016 on the UK's future relationship with the EU, the mechanisms for departure had to be considered. Although not widely discussed during the referendum campaign, the relationship between Northern Ireland and the EU-member state the Republic of Ireland demanded careful attention. How should the border between the two countries be managed in a post-EU world? Both communities either side of the border were acutely concerned that the confidence-building work of the 1998 Good Friday Peace Agreement should not be undermined by the referendum result, which was narrowly in favour of leaving the EU. No one in the island of Ireland wanted the return of a 'hard border' and the violence of previous decades.

For those charged with planning the UK's departure from the EU, the smart border was seized upon as a potential solution. Was it possible to design and implement a new border regime that would avoid hard-border checks on people and commercial traffic? Could such a regime avoid any militarisation of the border as an EU and non-EU member state managed their relationships with one another? For some, the Norwegian–Swedish border provided inspiration, with a non-EU and EU member state using a 'trusted trader' scheme (the Authorised Economic Operator) to ensure that cross-border business communities could work with one another as smoothly as possible. The idea was to keep physical checks of people and their vehicles as minimal as possible. But it was admitted that the Authorised Economic Operator scheme placed an administrative and cost burden on operators and that members of the scheme had to agree to the inspection of their facilities in order to deter smuggling and tax evasion.

How both parties can ensure that the border with Northern Ireland does not limit or constrain the free movement of people, trade and services has proven to be a controversial question for the Irish government. In 2018, there was no shortage of claims that the Norwegian–Swedish example could be updated to produce a Smart Border 2.0, which could take into account the sensitive nature of the Irish borderlands by using further tracking measures, such as unique consignment numbers for goods, data sharing between the two governments and pre-custom clearance away from the border.

The Irish government, however, expressed concerns throughout the Brexit process that the border could attract unwanted investment in physical infrastructure and staffed border posts. Debates raged over what was described as a 'backstop', a guarantee that cross-border trade would remain as free as possible in the event of the UK leaving the EU without some kind of regulatory alignment over their shared border. For the Republic of Ireland, the economic stakes were high. The UK is the country's third most important export partner, and the UK is its largest source of imports. While the wider EU and the United States are more important overall, the UK–Ireland trading relationship is therefore significant.

Geopolitically, a friction-free border is a world away from the 1970s and 1980s, when the British Army was busy patrolling the borderlands and monitoring movement from a network of security watchtowers.

The confidence-and-supply agreement between Northern Ireland's Democratic Unionist Party and former Conservative Prime Minister Theresa May, following a hung parliament after the 2017 UK general election, complicated matters further. For the Democratic Unionists, regulatory alignment with the Republic of Ireland could be construed as Northern Ireland in effect remaining in the EU, while the rest of the UK, in the absence of a land border with the EU, would have a different relationship, a situation that would be intolerable to the staunchly unionist party. Even if, for example, technical solutions could be found to ensure that the border arrangements between Northern Ireland and the Republic of Ireland were as smooth as possible, there would always be limits to what any smart border could do. Public appetite for a smart border solution has been low on the island of Ireland, and there are no smart border solutions anywhere in the world in which there are not some physical checks at the border and beyond.

The EU was clear in its negotiations with the UK government that the backstop was designed to safeguard the Republic of Ireland in the event the UK failed to come to a customs agreement with the EU after departure. For leave voters in the UK, the backstop was resented because they feared that the UK would remain entangled with the EU trading bloc. As of 2020, debate continues as to what the UK's future relationship with the EU, including the island of Ireland, will be, although it is difficult to see how the two governments in London and Dublin can avoid some kind of border solution involving pre-clearance for trade and services while largely leaving the border unmanned for civilian traffic.

The 1998 Good Friday Agreement, negotiated at a time when no one imagined the UK might leave the EU, is pivotal to Irish concerns. The role of the United States, rather than the European Union, was crucial during this period – if anything, the EU was part of the taken-for-granted geopolitical landscape. But politics in the region is even more complicated following the UK general election in 2019, as the Democratic Unionists now occupies only a minority position in Northern Ireland. Because the people of the province voted to remain in the EU in June 2016, one possible outcome of Brexit could be to turn public opinion in favour of integration with the Republic of Ireland. Smart border solutions, therefore, might not only prove to be unworkable, they might also generate outcomes that political leaders in London did not imagine at the time of the referendum. Any interference with the largely open border, which 30,000 people are estimated to cross every day, may not turn out to be very smart after all.

The question of the Irish border in a post-Brexit future serves as a good reminder that there are always limits to technical solutions. Licence-plate reading does not get around the violent geopolitical histories of the Irish borderlands. And smart border technologies are not just directed towards trade and services. They are also intensely personal. If trusted trader schemes work in places such as Norway and Sweden, they do so because there is no recent history of conflict and strife between the two countries. The exchange of electronic information, personal data, risk assessments and the like depends upon high levels of political trust. The 1998 Good Friday Agreement was integral to confidence-building across the island of Ireland, and to undermine it could lead to an unwelcome return to violence.

SMART BORDERS OF THE FUTURE

As the world's borderlands remind us, smart border technologies are being developed for a diversity of reasons: deterring drug-cartel activity, illegal immigration and cross-border terrorism above and below the border. Investment in new smart border and fencing technologies is also part and parcel of the sort of technological and military arms races that have so often characterised relationships between bitter neighbours and rivals such as India and Pakistan.

In the United States, the smart border has enabled further domestication. The border continues to retreat further and further away from airports and international boundaries. Agencies are now given permission to move ever further inwards in their surveillance activities. The immigration policies under President Trump have involved ever greater coordination between the US armed forces and an over-stretched border patrol. It appears to be becoming more commonplace to invoke exceptional measures in the face of a declared 'national emergency', and there is no reason to think that there won't be more investment in manned surveillance and smart border technologies such as the latest generation of thermal-imaging equipment, which boasts ever-greater capacity to penetrate poor visibility and inclement weather.

It is possibly not only illegal migrants but businesses and citizens who will continue to be caught up in this smart border revolution. As travellers, we conduct our own pre-departure checks. We have to register more information to government databases in order to secure trusted trader or traveller status. Going forward, there is going to be more inter-state information-sharing about all of us, which inevitably raises issues about privacy and data security. Biometric systems using iris recognition, fingerprints and facial recognition are going to be commonplace in airports and border crossings.

The consequences for those who are targeted by smart borders are very real and extend far beyond the airport. Universities, employers and private renters in the UK, for example, have discovered that you can be asked to perform the role of unpaid border guards – by being asked to check and process personal data. Generating false and misleading information will remain a big business for those seeking to circumvent border controls. Hackers, including foreign governments, have added incentive to try and breach ever more mountains of data being collected in border environments. Hacking the smart border is going to be part of the next generation of conflicts, some of which will appeal to mischief-making states as well as terrorist groups.

Smart borders don't remove borders in the traditional sense, they simply repurpose them. In an era of pandemic, the travelling public are in all likelihood going to face more of this: thermal pre-scanning, immunity passport checks, stringent health assessment and quarantine requirements (as discussed further in Chapter 9). However, the smart border of the future will also be one that is able to allow 'trusted travellers' to verify their identities and health status through their mobile phones, while enabling tracking applications to enact biosurveillance at, within and beyond the border zone.

Astronaut James Irwin (1930-1991) gives a salute on the Moon. Irwin was the pilot of the Lunar Module during the Apollo 15 mission in 1971. The Outer Space Treaty of 1967 declared that the exploration and user of outer space should be carried out peacefully and was signed by the United States, United Kingdom and Soviet Union. Article II of the Treaty declared that 'Outer space, including the moon and other celestial bodies, is not subject to national appropriation by claim of sovereignty, by means of use or occupation, or by any other means'. 110 countries are party to the 1967 Treaty including China and India.

Chapter 8

Out of This World

IN JULY 1969, THE APOLLO 11 SPACE MISSION LANDED TWO ASTRONAUTS on the surface of the moon. It was a momentous occasion. While Jules Verne imagined a moon landing in his novel *From the Earth to the Moon* (1865), it took around $26 billion dollars of investment, a fatal accident with Apollo 1, and vast technical experimentation to make it possible for two men (the third remained piloting the command module in orbit around the moon) to make it all the way to the lunar surface. The honour of being first out of the landing module *Eagle* belonged to test pilot and aeronautical engineer Neil Armstrong. As he left the module and descended to the ground, he was heard to utter the famous words, 'That's one small step for man, one giant leap for mankind.' What Armstrong did not claim was equally important. He did not claim that the step was being taken by an American man, and he did not claim the moon for the United States because two

years earlier the United States and the Soviet Union agreed to prohibit the appropriation of celestial bodies. And the universalist spirit
implied by Armstrong mirrored that of President Nixon, who in
January 1969 told his audience that the Apollo programme was
empowered by a desire to explore 'new worlds together' rather than a
quest to 'conquer' new worlds, and turn outer space into a new colonial frontier.

But this being a time of Cold War competition, it was perfectly
possible to say one thing and do another. Every Apollo mission carried
with it a Lunar Flag Assembly kit, which was designed to allow an
astronaut to assemble an aluminium tube and attach a nylon flag of
the Stars and Stripes. The flag was around 1m by 1.5m (40 inches by
60 inches). Stored in a capsule close to the descent ladder, the kit was
designed to be protected from the extreme heat generated by the
rocket motors and exhaust gases. One of the most iconic images taken
by Neil Armstrong is of Buzz Aldrin saluting the American flag on 21
July 1969 with the *Eagle* module in the background.

In the months and weeks leading up to the mission, the wonderfully
named Committee on Symbolic Activities for the First Lunar Landing
considered the options available to the astronauts. While the United
Nations flag might have been more in-keeping with the suggestion that
the Americans were acting on behalf of 'mankind', the time and money
invested in the Apollo programme meant that the Nixon administration
did not want to squander a moment of national triumph. Many people at
NASA were still smarting that some years earlier the Soviets had successfully launched the world's first artificial satellite, Sputnik, in October
1957, and later in September 1959 crash-landed a probe, Luna 2 (with a
Soviet flag on board), for the first time on the moon's surface.

In the Cold War heyday of the astronaut and cosmonaut, space
was largely the preserve of the United States and the Soviet Union.
Satellites were large and built to last, and space programmes were
veiled by secrecy. Fifty years later, the 'new space' era is radically different. We have far greater involvement from the commercial sector
and there are many more states involved, in some form or another,
with space. Satellites now come in all shapes and sizes, and launch

costs are so much lower than they were in the 1960s and 1970s. There is far greater scope nowadays to buy satellite components 'off the shelf', and the private sector has responded accordingly. Commercial satellites are integral to broadband connectivity and earth observation. Good money can be earned by those who operate low-earth-orbit satellites and sell their imagery of earth. As the number of satellites being launched into orbit has expanded, we have also witnessed a corresponding rise in attacks on space-based infrastructure including cyber-hacking, data spoofing and radio jamming.

With heightened interest and investment comes the prospect of either grand designs for space colonisation or worries about the weaponisation of space. Humans have found ways to scheme and fight over every conceivable earthbound geographical feature and landscape — floodplains, mountains, rivers, seabed and valleys — and outer space might not be any different. Mapping remains integral to modern colonisation and settlement. It is worth remembering that there is far more high-resolution mapping of the moon and Mars than of the earth's seafloor, because it is technologically easier to accomplish. What you do with that information is up to you. While some, such as BBC presenter Patrick Moore, marvelled at 'the sky at night', others such as German-American scientist Wernher von Braun warmed to the idea of using outer space to exercise planetary dominance.

Space is now a far more complex operational environment than in the Clarke-von Braun era. But what von Braun speculated about has not diminished in importance. The drive for space security remains an imperative. Norway, for example, will be investing further in satellites in 2022 as part of its plan to make its communications coverage over Arctic territories more resilient to mischief-making. Russia's repeated willingness to deploy radio jamming (interference with data transmission and reception) and spoofing (false data generation) is a fact of strategic life. Russia dislikes Norway's predilection for hosting NATO training exercises and radio jamming is a way of registering its displeasure, with obvious implications for the safety of everyone there.

Elsewhere a nightmarish world involving attack satellites, cyber-hacking, electromagnetic pulses, laser weapons and the next generation of missile defence is no longer the creative fodder of a 1970s James Bond movie. This time it is the US, Russia and China that are leading the pack. The US Defense Intelligence Agency thinks that China and Russia will develop further space-based weapon systems. President Trump turned to his Space Force in 2018 in the hope of ensuring American superiority in outer space. The late Dr von Braun would have surely approved of such a thing.

Now, however, it's time to look to the heavens for potential clues to what might yet happen.

FLOATING WITH THE FINAL FRONTIER

As Apollo 11 was preparing for the moon landing, the fictional USS *Enterprise* led by Captain Kirk was busy trekking across outer space. The American crew of the USS *Enterprise* and their odyssey into 'strange new worlds' made compelling viewing for many of us. Launched in September 1966 on NBC, *Star Trek* coincided with the negotiation of the path-breaking 1967 Outer Space Treaty, which was the product of US–Soviet joint leadership. The UN Committee on the Peaceful Uses of Outer Space (established earlier in 1958) has the task of ensuring that the purpose and spirit of the Outer Space Treaty is respected – an easier job back in the late 1960s and 1970s.

Article II of the 1967 treaty declares: 'Outer space, including the Moon and other celestial bodies, is not subject to national appropriation by claim of sovereignty, by means of use or occupation, or by any other means.' Thus, astronauts and cosmonauts could plant their flags on the moon's surface but that did not translate into property rights. The treaty is notable for its articulation of rules and restraints. Space exploration and the accompanying technology were in their infancy and so was space geopolitics. There were few space-faring nations, with space-launching capabilities resting squarely in the hands of two states, the United States and the Soviet Union.

Nowadays, the space community is a great deal more diverse and the public appetite for rules and restraints a bit more frayed. Small states such as the Grand Duchy of Luxembourg are making plans for a profitable future in space. A leader in the space communications industry, with two of the largest satellite operating companies, Luxembourg is planning for mining in the final frontier. It has established a Space Resources Initiative, created a national space budget and reached out to private-sector companies in order to plan for the execution and regulation of space mining. The Grand Duchy and Planetary Resources (which ceased operating in 2018) had at one stage an equity-sharing relationship and both parties were confident that the sector would attract ever greater interest. In 2017, Luxembourg followed in the footsteps of the United States by adopting a legal framework that recognises the right of companies based in the Grand Duchy to harvest space resources provided they are consistent with international law.

Our future in outer space is being made in an array of places, from Luxembourg to the large space powers such as China, Russia and the United States. Private companies are also highly significant, with Planet Labs in California being a notable example of ambition and capacity. Their objective is to use their Triple-CubeSat mini-satellites in order to provide continuous observation data of earth. With over 350 satellites, their Twitter account shares stunning images taken from space on a daily basis. Either way, there is no danger of anyone losing interest in space, it is simply integral to our lives on earth. Large and small states alike are eyeing the moon and outer space, and eager to turn science fiction (just think of television series such as *Space: 1999* and films such as *Outland*, 1981) into opportunity and profit. There is plenty of speculation about extracting helium-3 from the surface of the moon – helium-3 has been talked about as a core fuel in the pursuit of a new generation of fusion reactors. It is now commonplace for some to regard the moon as yet another resource to be exploited, with no shortage of opportunities to exploit solar energy as well.

Outer space will generate its own border quandaries and controversies. Space colonisation and exploitation inevitably asks the same questions of control and management as it does for other remote and uninhabited spaces such as the ocean floors. Everett Dolman, a professor at the US Air Force Air Command and Staff College, warned his readers in the 1990s that space geopolitics demanded greater attention, including power projection, resource exploitation and denying access to others. In 2019, NATO acknowledged that outer space was an operational domain for the security organisation, joining land, sea, air and cyber. President Macron of France had earlier described space as a 'true national security issue' and warned of 'new zones of confrontation'. As President Trump told his Rose Garden audience in August 2019, 'It's a big deal' because outer space will be 'the next war-fighting domain. And I think that's pretty obvious to everybody.'

But is it? What President Trump gave less time to was a counter-history of space-based cooperation, which existed even during the Cold War era. In the 1980s, at the height of antagonism and threats of mutually assured destruction, 45 participants including the two superpowers established the international Cospas-Sarsat programme, a search and rescue initiative aided and abetted by satellites. A shared network of satellites helps to monitor the earth and co-ordinate rescue missions. This was supplemented by the 2000 International Charter for 'Space and Major Disasters', which encourages parties to share relevant space-based information for the purpose of disaster relief. All of which continues, despite worries about a new era of space competition and rivalries. Extreme environments like outer space have a way of teasing out the very best of humanity, as well as the worst.

'CONGESTED, CONTESTED AND COMPETITIVE'

The UN reported in 2013 that space was in danger of becoming ever more 'congested, contested and competitive'. The UN's conclusion rested on several straightforward observations. Congestion in space is an issue. There are over 2,500 satellites currently in operation and this number is only set to grow. The Union of Concerned Scientists, a science advocacy organisation based in the United States, maintains a database of such things and the US is listed as the largest satellite operator, followed by China. Defunct satellites and dangerous outer space junk only add to this sense of congestion, especially if older satellites are not removed from their orbit.

A major change from the days of early space exploration is the role of ultra-wealthy visionaries. Elon Musk's SpaceX has permits to deploy up to 12,000 satellites in a bold bid to create a 'Starlink', with the aim of delivering high-speed access to the internet for billions around the world. The figure has risen to 30,000, and in May 2019 the first 60 Starlink satellites were launched into space. At the time of writing, the number of satellites in orbit was around 480. Musk's plan involves launching most of his satellites at lower altitudes, which he hopes will avoid the problem of space debris and outer space junk. But his plans are indicative of outer space becoming more *congested*.

In January 2020, space-monitoring stations revealed evidence that two defunct satellites nearly collided with one another – which in itself is not a new phenomenon. What was noteworthy, however, was how these 'near-misses' serve as opportunities for commercial companies to showcase their situational awareness. In this case, one satellite weighed in at over 1,000kg (2,200 pounds) and the other was smaller at around 85kg (187 pounds). Seasoned observers used the incident to highlight the very real potential to generate more space debris with corresponding dangers of further collision (the so-called Kessler Syndrome) with space-based infrastructure that is active rather than defunct. SpaceX plans to fill our skies with more artificial objects and they are not the only ones – Amazon (Jeff Bezos and his Blue Origin) and Virgin Galactic (Richard Branson) have their own grand designs.

Ever since the launch of Sputnik in 1957, space has been *contested*, caught up in national rivalries and races. The Apollo missions were driven by Cold War geopolitical enmities. Scientific investment for universities and public bodies followed. The US civilian agency NASA (founded in 1958) has been the recipient of around $650 billion of federal funding so far in its limetime. The United States is now worried that their dominant position in outer space can no longer be taken for granted. The US Secretary of Defense, Mark Esper, spoke in January 2020 of, 'Maintaining American dominance in that domain is now the mission of the United States Space Force [which reports to the US Air Force].'

Popular culture had been quick to pursue the creative opportunities afforded here. Netflix recently launched the series *Space Force*, which pokes fun at both President Trump and his plans for American space dominance in the 2020s. But it also uses humour to raise an important point. The new 'space race' brings with it some inherent dangers. The show explores Chinese opportunism on the moon, with a memorable scene of a Chinese space buggy knocking over the Apollo 11 American flag – proving that even one of the world's largest settler colonisers back on earth can have the tables turned on them. What provokes American anger in the show initially is the declaration by the Chinese that a large surface of the moon is a site of scientific interest and others should avoid landing in and/or entering this bordered zone. Space Force suspects the Chinese of using the cloak of 'science' to land-grab the moon. Season 2 will, no doubt, explore further how the US and Chinese astronauts manage to adapt to life in the Sea of Tranquillity.

Space is also a highly *competitive* field. As well as the major space-faring nations such as the United States, Russia, China, India and newer actors such as Israel, there are a number of non-state interests. From Elon Musk's SpaceX and Richard Branson's Virgin Galactic plans in sub-orbital space to remote sensing and telecommunication companies such as Maxar Technologies and Google respectively, space is home to big business. Finally, there are regional entities such as the European Space Agency (established in 1975), which help to ensure that many other states are represented in outer space matters as well, managing remote sensing and earth observation, and maintaining its own spaceport in French Guiana.

The competitive spirit at work here comes in part from a recognition that our global communications networks depend on an archipelago of satellites that enable us to watch television, use the internet and mobile phones, navigate safely in our cars, planes and ships, and obtain strategic information on the state of the earth's climate and biomes. Our global economies and societies depend on those communication and intelligence networks: fishing, banking, search and rescue, food production and disaster relief are all beneficiaries. Questions of national identity politics and regional superpower status are also at play: for example, it sits well with the Modi government that India is a space superpower and Europeans can take pleasure in the fact that they have their own space agency even though its spaceport is located in a remnant of the French empire.

Treaties that were designed at the start of the 'space age' are going to face new challenges aplenty as space travel, resource ambition and defence technology continue to evolve. If nature abhors a vacuum, so too do humans, and what is termed 'soft law' (for example statements of principles, codes of conduct, frameworks, UN General Assembly resolutions) has emerged to fill the gap. When space law was first developed in the 1960s, however, private companies and non-governmental entities were not recognised as capable of 'doing space'. An advantage of using 'soft law' is that you seek to create norms of behaviour that could apply to states and non-states alike – as legally-binding treaties can only have state signatories.

Space tourism, space transportation and longer-term space colonisation were thought to be the preserve of a few space-faring nations. The relevant treaties refer to outer space and celestial bodies lying beyond national appropriation. These space treaties do not ban private companies from operating in space (most states and space lawyers would concur that private companies are prohibited from space mining) and they don't stop private individuals from imagining themselves as a future president of the moon or Mars. Suggestible individuals can, if they so wish, purchase 'rights' to meteorites and stars. In 2019, for example, private US-based firms such as Moon Express and Shackleton Energy were working on vague-sounding plans to extract lunar water for the purpose of facilitating the long-term colonisation of the moon. All of which nourishes speculation that the moon and more likely Mars might one day be subjected to rival colonies with their own areas of operation.

PEACEFUL USAGE OF SPACE

In 1958, the ad hoc UN Committee on the Peaceful Uses of Outer
Space was established in order to consider what the implications of
human entry into space would be, not only for the management of
outer space but also for our earthbound relationships. Within a year it
went from ad hoc to permanent, and a UN Office for Outer Space
Affairs opened in the Austrian city of Vienna in December 1958. Its
current director is the distinguished Italian astrophysicist Simonetta
Di Pippo. In 1960, the International Institute of Space Law was created as an independent non-governmental organisation (funded by
national and individual members) designed to encourage the development of space law. Both the UN committee and the institute are
going to have to grapple with what 'peaceful uses of outer space' means
in the 2020s and beyond.

For now, the 1967 Outer Space Treaty is still the linchpin of
space law. Under the terms of the treaty, space is free to explore,
sovereignty claims are banned, nuclear weapons and other weapons of mass destruction are prohibited, and individual nations are
responsible for their space objects and space-bound nationals. A
year later, the international community established the Agreement
on the Rescue of Astronauts, followed by a Liability Convention in
1972 and a Registration Convention in 1974. Progress faltered with
the 1979 Moon Treaty (the Agreement Governing the Activities of
States on the Moon and Other Celestial Bodies), as only a select
number of states chose ratification. The UN Committee on the
Peaceful Uses of Outer Space also continues to discuss outer space
and encourage member states to work collaboratively with one
another.

The Outer Space Treaty, which has more than 100 signatories,
created a benchmark for outer space behaviour. But things can and do
change. President Xi has been clear that China is going to be the most
advanced space-faring nation. By 2045 it wants to project the country's interests to the moon and beyond. But China is not alone in this

sort of ambition and perhaps our attention should be focused more closely on the ambitions of private companies, some of whom have state sponsors. For example, Japan has been busy positioning itself as a space power. Since 2008, it has been establishing defensive capabilities, investing in rocket technologies and working to develop its own satellite-based global positioning systems. Every country recognises that space is essential to twenty-first-century economies and societies. Beyond that fundamental recognition, the drivers for this investment and activity are rooted in worries about the reliability of the US as a security partner, and fears of Chinese and North Korean aggression. Japan also sees space as a place to showcase its technological and defensive capabilities. South Korea plans to launch a new orbital rocket, Nuri (KSLV-II), in 2021 and has ambitious plans to develop its satellite industry.

The challenge for the international community is going to be whether space law can keep pace with what space powers are planning to do. The militarisation of the earth's orbit is notable while the weaponisation of outer space is for now low level. While the 1967 treaty stipulates that outer space should be used for 'peaceful purposes', it leaves plenty of scope for interpretation and doubt. There is no consensus on the way forward. Preventing an arms race in space depends on parties agreeing on what constitutes strategic competition rather than confrontation. There could be competitive struggles to secure access to earth's orbit, mineral potential and geopolitical advantage when it comes to military command, communications control and global surveillance. Rogue actors might start to jeopardise critical infrastructure via cyberattacks, such as the GPS and communication satellites that are now integral to the running of our world. It is also not clear to what lengths other operators might go to protect their corporate and private interests. In September 2014, Chinese hackers attacked US weather satellites and disrupted the transmission of data. The attacks were 'covered up' by the US authorities and the disruption was explained away as 'unscheduled maintenance'.

MANAGING WITHOUT BORDERS

Outer space will no doubt attract even more commercial, strategic and technological ambitions in the future. The space tourism industry in particular could provide its own challenges to a space without borders. Mining rights in outer space, including on celestial bodies and planets such as the moon, could be claimed by states and corporations. And increased military activity is likely if human colonisation of outer space expands. Parties living and working in space might argue about what constitutes interference with other space missions, especially if the source of the problem is cyber-hacking carried out back on earth. What has changed from the halcyon days of the International Space Station and US–Soviet detente is that there is more talk of military and space dominance, which is reminiscent of other periods of the Cold War when spy satellites and inter-continental ballistic missiles were part and parcel of global rivalries.

In the future, there will also be demands from citizens on earth to continue to develop regulatory frameworks designed to protect the increasing numbers of satellites in space, and later perhaps permanent human communities if they, as expected, are established. More international co-ordination will be needed in the management of the low-earth orbit and one would have thought there are powerful incentives to continue to share space-based information gathering. Longer term, other pressures might make themselves felt. It is possible to imagine anti-mining communities, for example, demanding that the moon be reclassified as a lunar park or protected area. If the human colonisation of the moon gathers pace, the surface might be a great deal more conflictual as we export our earthly habits to the moon. There could be demands that human rights extend to the moon and outer space: where humans go, so do their earthly rights. Otherwise, it might be that space employees, including moon residents, simply sign contracts waiving any kinds of rights. Given the inherent challenges of living and working in space, human and artificial life might have to live in an operational environment that would probably be judged to be unsafe and unhealthy on earth. We should not kid ourselves that any colonisation of space will usher in a halcyon era.

The makers of the James Bond films posited a thrilling scenario in the 1960s. In the film *You Only Live Twice* (1967), a well-resourced criminal organisation is hell-bent on kidnapping the space vessels of the Soviet Union and the United States. The British super-spy 007 has to travel to Japan to foil a fiendish plot designed to provoke a superpower confrontation. Outlandish as it appeared at the time, the film does bring to the fore prevailing concerns about how outer space is made insecure. Thankfully, Commander Bond and his Japanese ninjas frustrated the evil designs of SPECTRE. A decade later, in *Moonraker* (1979), Bond had to work with an American astronaut on board a space shuttle to save the world from deadly poison delivered by multiple satellites. This time the source of tension was a high-net-worth individual, Hugo Drax, and his private space empire. Somewhere in between, British television was producing the drama *Space: 1999* about future life on Moonbase Alpha 1. But that wasn't much fun either.

Space law is premised on members of the international community working peacefully with one another. It acts as a foil for the darker impulses of space geopolitics. The global community commits to providing emergency rescue assistance wherever possible to astronauts and be responsible for any accident-based liabilities. Administratively, the UN has worked industriously to draw up guidelines as to how nations should contribute to the safe passage of satellites, manage the growing menace of space debris, refrain from interfering in the satellite-broadcasting capabilities of other nations, and contribute wherever possible to the situational awareness of outer space. It is a tall order.

There are millions of objects whizzing around the earth's orbit at speeds of 17,500km per hour. Space debris is a real-time hazard to satellites and space vessels. In 2007, China deliberately destroyed a redundant satellite and raised troubling issues about militarising activities in space. The Chinese armed forces used ground-based ballistic missiles to carry out the task. Neighbours such as Japan and

South Korea expressed concern at such an action, and it proved to be a trigger for both of those countries to invest more in their space-based capabilities. While the missile destroyed Chinese property, it was provocative and potentially dangerous because of the altitude of the strike. It was an act of space vandalism, which carried with it risks for all parties. The following year the United States did something similar to one of their defunct satellites.

Smaller nations also worry that large space powers are compromising their right to access space. In 1976, eight equatorial nations including Brazil issued what was termed the Bogotá Declaration, stating that they should have rights to geosynchronous (a high-earth orbit that allows a satellite to match the earth's rotation) satellite slots above their territories, arguing that the orbit was a 'natural resource' of 'overhead states'. The declaration failed to find any favour with the United States and the Soviet Union but did serve to remind the international community that satellite access and radio spectrum interference is politically sensitive. No one wanted to find themselves excluded from accessing the earth's orbit for the purpose of launching and controlling their own satellites. The International Telecommunications Union has a tough working brief. The earth's orbit can only accommodate so many satellites and their orbiting tracks. Without regulation, states from the global south would have been excluded.

The 1979 Moon Treaty claimed that the moon should not become an object of international discord and thus echoes earlier treaties such at the 1959 Antarctic Treaty and the 1967 Outer Space Treaty. Article 11 of the Moon Treaty notes:

> The moon and its natural resources are the common heritage of mankind ... the moon is not subject to national appropriation by any claim of sovereignty ... Neither the surface nor sub-surface of the moon shall become property of any state.

While the Moon Treaty did secure sufficient support for its ratification into force, Article 11 proved too controversial for major space powers such as the United States and the Soviet Union. By the late 1970s, support for the 'common heritage of mankind' principle was declining in the United States, specifically in the US Senate, although it was not just a moon-related problem. There was also no support from Republican Senators in particular for the principle when it came to the deep seabed. While the Moon Treaty failed to find favour in the US and Russia, a few countries did sign it, including Romania, Chile, Morocco, Guatemala and Austria.

The opposition to common heritage is rooted in a reluctance to restrict US companies and to sign up to anything that appears to be granting the UN supranational powers. In the late 2010s, the US companies Deep Space Industries and Planetary Resources shared their plans to investigate the potential of asteroid mining. The 2015 US Commercial Space Launch Competitiveness Act (Space Act), approved by the Obama administration, subsequently made legal provision for US citizens and companies to explore and exploit asteroids that are believed to contain iron ore, nickel and precious metals. Anything that has the potential to source rocket fuel is particularly prized because it then enables further space activity without a supply chain stretching all the way back to earth. Mining, yes; sovereign appropriation, no.

Space law experts are divided as to the legality of the Act itself, and some fear that this kind of private/commercial intervention undermines the provisions of the Outer Space Treaty, which remains the legal benchmark, creating a proverbial backdoor for the US to 'claim' celestial territory via a private or commercial proxy. The relationship between space agencies such as NASA and private companies could, therefore, be complementary or competitive, depending on the situation. It is also unclear as to how citizens and companies might resolve their disputes in outer space, not only with one another but with third parties such as China. Would the international court structure back on earth be put to work for human communities involved in disputes over access to territory, resources or even intellectual property rights? Or would we have a new International Space Court, which would tackle disputes between communities living permanently beyond the earth? If nothing else, time and vast distances would clearly be major barriers to any such development.

President Trump's executive order in April 2020 encouraged the 'recovery and use of space resources' and outlines what have been termed the 'Artemis Accords'. The latter are designed to encourage a shared framework for moon-based missions and outer space operations albeit based on the US position on commercial space mining in particular. This initiative serves to remind us that the future use of the moon and outer space could be defined by a new era of exploitation and disputes over property rights, and even heritage conservation (with concerns that historic sites and artefacts of past lunar missions might not be respected by third parties). Imagine a situation where US stakeholders extract resources on the moon and other celestial bodies in the presence of neighbouring mining colonies run by the Chinese government and private companies, including those funded and supported by high-net-worth individuals. It is going to be a considerable task to keep up with these types of space activities, especially as they travel through earth and its atmosphere and then beyond.

CONGESTION WITHOUT BORDERS

For all the high jinks of James Bond movies, satellite proliferation, radio-spectrum interference and space debris are more immediate issues that do make space congested, competitive and contentious, revealing in turn how outer space becomes bordered.

As the countries in the global sout recognised in the 1970s, there are limits to how many satellites can be in geosynchronous (GEO, above 36,000km) and low-earth orbit (LEO, below 2,000km). Radio-spectrum interference acts as a border or barrier to others who might wish to come along later and launch and operate their own satellites. Given the bands of frequency and time slots, the capacity to communicate is compromised – there are only so many bands that can accommodate communication to and from outer space. You don't have to put a flag on the surface of a planet to make a point about how things are shared or not shared. Radio and television broadcasters, often associated with mainstream national media, were among the first to establish frequency rights. Over time, many more private and commercial satellite operators wanted to obtain their own frequency bands. As the LEO is filled with broadband mega-constellations like SpaceX, the struggles for access and control will intensify.

The Satellite Industry Association in its 2018 report noted that global satellite services generated around $130 billion in revenue for 2017. In the same year, some 345 satellites were launched into outer space and ground-based services generated around $120 billion for satellite providers. This would, in general, involve the generation of remote sensing imagery for agriculture, fishing, urban management, mining and national security planning from LEO satellites. Overall, the sector is valued at $270 billion per year but this will grow in the 2020s. The industry is optimistic that activity will expand with the roll-out of 5G broadband interconnectivity.

By the late 2020s, it is thought that the dispatch of satellites, big and small, via rocket launches will number in the thousands per year, with commercial operators and newer space nations eager to take advantage of outer space. This once again raises concerns about congestion in space and how the LEO is monitored and policed. Some of this conflict is occurring between commercial firms rather than states, eager to protect their 'spectrum rights' and frequencies. Keeping track of a plethora of small and comparatively cheap satellites operating in low-earth orbit and making judgements about what constitutes 'interference' is not likely to be straightforward.

Space debris is a literal barrier to entry into outer space, as even the smallest fragment can cause considerable damage to satellites and spacecraft – the speed of impact, rather than the size of the object, is the main concern. Outer space hosts the wasteful legacy of 60 years of human activity, including the 2007 Chinese anti-satellite strike, which ensured that it tops the list for worst offenders when it comes to space debris – the other biggest culprits being Russia and the United States. Debris persists in space indefinitely and only disappears if it is dragged into the earth's atmosphere, with re-entry causing it to be incinerated. As outer space becomes more populated with satellites and space vehicles, pressure might grow on the 'Big Three' to devote more attention and resources to debris collection. This problem is not just a question of garbage disposal but also relates to an array of other issues, from legal liabilities and threat perception to an ethic of care for an arena that is integral for the future of life on earth. There are two ways forward: either conflicts over space debris and radio-spectrum interference are likely to follow, or there will be powerful incentives for all to work harder to ensure the peaceful and shared usage of outer space.

FROM DATA MINING TO SPACE MINING

The Apollo missions started the practice and now China is taking data science into a new era. In January 2019, the Chinese *Yutu-2* rover landed on the moon having been deployed by the Chang'e 4 mission – China's Lunar Exploration Programme naming the mission after a Chinese moon goddess Chang'e. The mission was unique, as never before in the history of human exploration of the moon had there been a landing on its far side. The rover investigated rock samples and offered insights into the moon's genesis and evolutionary history. Academics from the Key Laboratory of Lunar and Deep Space Exploration, National Astronomical Observatories and Chinese Academy of Sciences reported in the prestigious science journal *Nature* on their findings about the lunar crust and mantle. The Chinese mission deliberately targeted an area of the moon known to have been hit by a large meteorite strike. The resulting basin offered up the tantalising prospect of the mission being able to collect evidence that will reveal clues as to the elemental composition of the moon.

The 2019 Chinese expedition was thought to be a game-changer, with the scale of its ambition being considered breath-taking by foreign observers. China is thought to be interested in space mining as well. Uranium and titanium are top of the wish list, but there is other matter, too, most notably ice and water-bearing minerals. The composition of the moon matters because, as NASA declared in November 2020, its resources include water, then this will empower, literally and figuratively, plans to occupy the moon, support human life, and inaugurate thereafter further exploration and exploitation. In 2020, the Chang'e 5 expedition was set to extract rock samples from the near side of the moon, and China might be interested in establishing a semi-permanent research station somewhere on the moon, maybe at the Lunar South Pole, in the future. But all of this is mired in uncertainty.

Space resources might be a major driver of activity in the future, but it is worth noting that some companies interested in asteroid exploitation have already come and gone (for example a US-based company Planetary Resources, which collapsed in 2018). Vice President Mike Pence declared in 2019 that the United States aimed to return to the moon and this has fuelled speculation about US intentions in the intersection of exploration, resources, strategy and space nationalism. 'Making America Great Again' is a mantra that can easily be applied to outer space too. In one speech he identified the Chinese investment in outer space as a powerful incentive, given their interest in securing what he termed the 'lunar strategic high ground'. If the US can return astronauts to the moon by 2024 then NASA hopes to construct a new base by 2028.

This return to the moon initiative will be aided and abetted by corporate and private stakeholders, such as Musk's SpaceX and Bezos's Blue Origin, which have pledged to support such efforts via their own investment in rocket technology and robotic lunar landers. Jeff Bezos has been upfront about his plans to develop not only space tourism but also permanent human infrastructure on the moon. Elon Musk is more interested in Mars and hopes, rather optimistically, to create the first human colony there by 2028. Any terraforming (to use a term coined by the novelist Jack Williamson) projects involving Mars would face formidable challenges given freezing temperatures, thin atmosphere, lack of magnetosphere, intense solar winds and low surface gravity. One can have grand designs but realising them is altogether another thing.

The ownership of space's resources and what might be appropriate in terms of usage are unclear. As we have seen, the Outer Space Treaty secured consensus on peaceful usage, universal access and non-appropriation, but space mining was not explicitly on the agenda of those negotiations in the 1960s. Space technology and geopolitical ambition have changed greatly. Coupled with ongoing climate change and a rising population on earth, plans are afoot for a very different kind of exploitation of outer space in the years to come. In the first half of the 2020s, the space-faring nations of Russia, Japan, South, India, China and the United States are all intent on expanding their lunar and outer space plans. India intends to land a module at the Lunar South Pole for the explicit purpose of collecting information on the moon's topography, elemental composition and mineral potential. Japan aims to land on the lunar poles with what it describes as its Smart Lander for Investigating the Moon. Ultimately, all of these projects in outer space are underpinned by a desire to operationalise resource exploitation.

In the future, space lawyers are going to have to grapple with a medley of developments such as asteroid and moon mining, semi-permanent human settlement and rocket fuel generation. The access, exploitation and use of space are likely to attract further controversies. As always, popular culture got there first. From the *Mars* trilogy of Kim Stanley Robinson (1992–6) to Ursula Le Guin's *The Left Hand of Darkness* (1969), published to coincide with the first humans landing on the moon, creative writers have speculated about resource conflicts and the scope for cooperative life beyond earth. For many readers, there are countless popular cultural examples, from the long-running *Star Wars* series to other films that have used the moon and Mars to postulate geopolitical dramas involving conflict, colonisation, disaster and international rescue missions. All of us appear conflicted about whether we will be able to get along with one another in outer space.

POLICING OUTER SPACE

While there are now more than 100 signatories to the Outer Space Treaty, there is no international space police to ensure that the provisions of this and other relevant treaties and agreements are respected. Whether treaties apply to outer space or to earth, they are at the collective mercy of the intent of signatories and non-signatories. Thus far, the geopolitical situation has been comparatively benign, thanks in large part to the comparative inaccessibility of outer space and the high cost of operating in 'out of earth' environments.

Outer space is integral to twenty-first-century military doctrine and is becoming even more militarised, with a strategic focus on using space to support military operations. Space is already integral to early warning systems, communication, command and control, weapons targeting, surveillance and situational awareness. China and the United States are developing ballistic missile defence and anti-satellite systems (ASAT), and Russia continues to develop plans for a space-based laser weapon system. They are not alone. India also has ASAT capabilities (Prime Minister Narendra Modi declared this in March 2019), including cyber-hacking. President Reagan oversaw plans for the Strategic Defence Initiative ('Star Wars') in the 1980s and now some three decades later we have evidence of the capacity of some countries to destroy satellites, launch increasingly long-range missiles and invest in space-based systems. But the Big Three (United States, China and Russia) are not alone in their interest in space militarisation. India has developed a Space Vision for 2025, which is based on mounting concern about what their near-neighbour China will be capable of in the future. In March 2019, India tested an ASAT weapon and in doing so became the fourth country to have tested this technology. Some might say the point of this was to signal to China in particular that it had such a technological capability. The reality of using ASAT in LEO is that there would be widespread and shared collateral damage. Cyber-hacking and jamming are far safer options for hostile parties because it does not generate the much-feared space debris.

President Trump's aforementioned statement that space will be a 'war-fighting domain' raises interesting questions about whether the president thinks (assuming that he does think about such things) the Outer Space Treaty is now hopelessly outdated. Warming to his theme, the president told various audiences that his new Space Force would be good for 'the psyche of our country'. The timing of the Space Force announcement was not apparently welcomed by the Pentagon. The Trump administration speaks about a great many things including returning astronauts to the moon but also new ballistic missile defence systems, ever mindful of what China, Russia and other strategic rivals might seek to do in outer space in the near future. All of which fits in well with a presidential determination to use defence spending to boost the US economy and restore great-power status.

The US president is not alone in this ambition. China's leadership is also eager to use space as yet another arena to put the spectre of the 'Century of National Humiliation' (1839–1949) behind it. President Xi has been crystal clear about China's ambition to be a world power on earth and beyond. From 2015 onwards, China has spoken about new technologies such as space-based solar power and space power projection. By 2045, China, according to Xi, will be the world's leading space power – but again this needs to be taken with a pinch of salt. Xi has outlined a series of targets that China should aim to meet and much of this is aimed at trying to match US technological capabilities and strategic ambition. These include developing and dispatching a Mars probe (2020), exploring asteroids (2022), launching a mission to Jupiter (2029), and introducing reusable carrier rockets and nuclear-powered space shuttles into service sometime between 2035 and 2040. As a space shopping list goes, it is formidably ambitious and expensive. The plan, in short, is to make sure that China is able to explore and exploit any resources of space in the next three decades, alongside other experiments in long-term living in extreme environments.

Recall the fictional fate that befell Matt Damon as a stranded astronaut in the movie *The Martian* (2015) and you have an idea of what the Chinese are thought to be working on: long-term endurance in space with investment in bio-regenerative life-support infrastructures either for the moon or Mars. Thus far, China has successfully established itself as an accomplished space power via its rocket technology, Chinese astronauts, Lunar Exploration Programme, satellite deployment activities, BeiDou 3 global navigation system and the soft landing of the Chang'e 4 probe on the far side of the moon. China has an annual space day on 24 April, and its official 2019 video was a very glossy affair, with the declaration at the end of the production that the country was seeking to 'pursue the space dream for the win–win cooperation'.

BORDER WARS ON AND IN THE FINAL FRONTIER

When iconic images of 'earth rising', taken in the late 1960s, began to circulate, they nourished a view that humanity shared one common home. Up in space, international boundaries disappear in favour of more elemental distinctions between land, sea and the earth's weather systems. Satellites have supplied us with forms of remote sensing and sense-making that relates to this theme of interconnectedness and 'One Earth'. And yet when you look closely, satellite imagery can provide telling visualisations of human-made borders between countries such as India and Pakistan and North and South Korea, especially at night when countries turn on their border network of security lighting. Borders are, in effect, visible from space, from the Great Wall of China to the back-garden fences of readers. But in looking downwards, we are in danger of forgetting to look around us. Satellites and space stations also provide further critical infrastructure to look at and beyond earth and think of the moon, Mars and celestial bodies as new forms of real estate to colonise and control. We have, of course, clearly been looking to the skies and heavens for millennia.

There are challenges and threats aplenty that could generate new border wars. The overwhelming impulse behind the Outer Space Treaty and the Moon Treaty was that these celestial bodies should be used in a peaceful manner and not be subject to national appropriation. This was driven by a desire to ensure that the terrestrial Cold War did not extend further into the earth's atmosphere and beyond. Several years prior to the 1967 Outer Space Treaty, the US and Soviet Union agreed to prohibit above-ground nuclear testing, with both countries recognising that the atmosphere was integral to the future health of the planet. And there have been other notable cooperative milestones, including the 2000 International Charter 'Space and Major Disasters', which although non-binding nonetheless establishes the practice that space satellite data be promptly provided to relief organisations charged with responding to disasters. Corporate, national and international space agencies are signatories to the charter and data has been shared on countless occasions in the aftermath of flooding, earthquakes, hurricanes, epidemics, and even the search for the mysterious disappearance of Malaysia Airlines Flight 370.

As the global community has become increasingly dependent on satellite-based communication networks, the capacity to disrupt telecommunications will be a perennial concern. But outer space has thus far been more or less free of conflict – international cooperation developed and even flourished through Cold War-era initiatives such as the International Space Station and Soyuz-Apollo projects. But there have always been pressures running in a less pacific direction. So much space-based technology is dual use: the ability to launch a satellite is also the ability to launch a missile. In April 2020, Iran launched its first military satellite via their own missile system, provoking concerns that the country was eager to develop further missile and space launch technology. In the recent past, Iranian satellites have been launched by Russian missions.

Future conflict could erupt over either the spectre of a new generation of anti-satellite weapons, cyber-hacking or resource potential on the moon, Mars and other celestial bodies. This might involve missile defence technology or electronic forms of warfare. If the colonisation of the moon and other celestial bodies becomes feasible, we could face the prospect of those communities seeking to break away from earthly law and politics and establishing their own models of settler colonialism. Who would stop anyone from creating their own human colony on the moon or even Mars in the future, and would that be a source of worry? Space tourism might become more accessible and affordable, and generate in the future hotel and tourist infrastructure on the moon. Would a new self-appointed president of the moon decide to declare unilateral independence from earth and pursue their own plans, some of which might threaten the earth and its inhabitants?

China's role in all of this is going to be crucial. A few years ago the Chinese head of the Lunar Exploration Programme, Ye Peijian, was quoted as saying that:

> The universe is an ocean, the moon is the Diaoyu Islands, Mars is Huangyan Island. If we don't go there now even though we're capable of doing so, then we will be blamed by our descendants. If others go there, then they will take over, and you won't be able to go even if you want to. This is reason enough.

As observers were quick to note, the reference to disputed islands (Diaoyu and Huangyan are occupied by Japan and claimed by the Philippines respectively) was a poignant reminder that outer space and celestial bodies are caught up in astropolitical calculation and strategic posturing closer to home. The future of international space law as a shared enterprise will be watched carefully.

The border wars of the future are being treated to a growing body of Chinese science fiction imagining such possibilities. In her novel *Vagabonds*, the Chinese author Hao Jingfang imagines a world in 2201 where the earth and Mars are planetary rivals with distinct economies and societies. After a major war between the two parties, what follows is a story of eventual inter-planet diplomacy and reconciliation. The grim reality is this: the forces of gravity are against those of us on earth. It is a great deal easier to send a missile towards earth than to send a missile or rocket to Mars, the moon and/or space platform.

The onset of the COVID-19 pandemic led many countries to implement emergency measures including shutting their national borders. In March 2020, the Brazilian Army started to perform public health and enhancing security screening at the Concordia International Bridge, at the border between Brazil and Uruguay.

Chapter 9

Viral Borders

In 1994, Laurie Garrett published *The Coming Plague*, a book which scoped out a world that seems eerily close to the contemporary moment. Garrett was pessimistic about the future, and imagined a wave of epidemics and pandemics ranging from yellow fever, Ebola, swine flu, AIDS and malaria to emerging menaces involving bacterial and viral infections that would in all likelihood follow. Humankind, she reasoned, was worryingly vulnerable to further infectious outbreaks not least because of scientific and logistical developments that make pandemics more likely, not less. For example, the widespread use of antibiotics, while initially touted as a wonder cure, has inadvertently stimulated more resistant microbial strains. And a medley of interventions, from DDT spraying to huge dam-building projects, set in motion a range of unintended consequences for diversity among flora, fauna and the microbial population. Urban infrastructure

– such as water-cooling towers – was also held to be responsible for local outbreaks of legionnaires' disease, in some cases within hospitals themselves. Global air travel coupled with population growth in densely populated cities will create, Garrett postulated, the perfect conditions for repeated viral hotspots to flourish.

Since the publication of *The Coming Plague*, we have had serious outbreaks of Nipah (1998), SARS (2003), swine flu (2009), Ebola (2014) and COVID-19 (2020). Climate change is widely thought to be a generator of future disease and epidemics. Warming and wetter environments are likely to lead to a new generation of pathogens and parasites. Algal blooms could easily compromise water quality and will in all likelihood place further stresses and strains on shared water supplies around the world. As soil temperatures rise, scientists worry that plants will end up ingesting more heavy-metal contaminants such as arsenic and mercury. Food and water insecurity will be a powerful source of potential border conflict in the future. Water stress exacerbates tension, especially when resources are shared by communities. What makes things even more precarious is that the water and soil that enable life itself are being poisoned and compromised by environmental degradation, pestilence and disease. Cross-border oversight in the future will require not just a shared monitoring of usage but also a collective undertaking for the biosecurity of rivers, lakes and geographical features such as floodplains and valleys in the wake of all of this – which can seem a very tall order when national governments are grappling with outbreaks of disease and associated shocks to social and political order.

It would be inconceivable, writing in 2020, to end this book without considering the COVID-19 pandemic. We will all be living with the consequences for some time to come. Very few parts of the world have been spared infections, and even the Antarctic has witnessed disruption to its logistics, science and tourism, despite having had no recorded cases thus far. Polar scientists simply wanting to return home, when other countries close to the frozen continent have closed their borders and shut down international flights, found the experience to be debilitating. But those challenges pale into insignificance when compared with the tragic consequences for those fatally infected by the disease as well as survivors living with its ravages. For governments already predisposed to closing their borders to migrants and refugees, public health strategies offer further opportunities to implement tougher public surveillance, policing and international border controls.

The COVID-19 pandemic, like outbreaks of Ebola, polio and the Zika virus before it, clearly reveals the limitations of national borders. Fundamentally, a virus is indifferent to them. However, human responses to such outbreaks of disease are not. Viral infections have the potential to undermine the absolute nature of the sovereign state and national governments around the world have faced difficult choices – do you shut down your borders completely to cross-border travel? Do you impose a strict lockdown and curfew on domestic populations? How does one coordinate with other sovereign states who may be affected by the pandemic differently or led by political leaderships that don't share the same views about its severity?

If the nation-state cannot control its own territory in the usual way, 'normal' life itself must stop. We have witnessed in many parts of the world a form of de-socialisation. What happens next depends on the country and context. In the UK, the Johnson government imposed sharp restrictions on personal mobility in late March 2020. Most shops were forced to close, with citizens being told that they were to only leave their houses to shop for food, collect medicines and undertake limited physical exercise. Borders mushroomed everywhere in our domestic lives – people wearing face masks, standing apart, and in some cases simply terrified of leaving home. While some could work at home others had to move into and out of public spaces. Meanwhile, a series of logistical scrambles ensued to organise and coordinate repatriation flights for thousands of British citizens stranded overseas as well as to secure medical equipment ranging from face masks to ventilators. Many citizens took to panic buying and hoarding of food, medicine and supplies including toilet paper.

The UK's non-essential travel advice conceded on 17 March 2020 that evidence of coordination was scant:

> This change in travel advice reflects the pace at which other countries are either closing their borders or implementing restrictive measures in response to the global coronavirus pandemic.
>
> Often there is little or no notice when countries take these steps and restrictions are also being imposed in areas where no cases of coronavirus have yet been reported. They are therefore very difficult to predict.

A public health emergency offers a powerful incentive to double-down on border security, immigration control and national surveillance. There are, unquestionably, good reasons why strict controls on assembly and movement are necessary. Citizens have accepted, largely with good grace, that civil and political rights need to be suspended in the midst of a pandemic in order to reduce the spread of disease. The right to movement, assembly and attend religious services has in various countries around the world been banned or severely curtailed. Within most countries, there has been disagreement about the trade-off between relaxing restrictions for the sake of economic revival and persevering in the name of disease control.

In the UK, it was evident from the spring and summer of 2020 that the Scottish, Welsh and Northern Irish administrations were pursuing different public health strategies to those of England. In June and July 2020, England led the way in terms of relaxing restrictions on travel within the country, as well as social gatherings and the opening of shops. Across the border in Wales, the situation was very different. Welsh residents were instructed to not travel more than 5 miles (8km) while English residents could travel the length and breadth of the nation. Scotland had the same rule as Wales. Both administrations had expressed concern about English residents crossing their respective borders and causing infections to spike. Prime Minister Boris Johnson, on the other hand, was noticeably more determined that the UK's economic life should not be 'sacrificed' in the name of prolonged social distancing rules and was eager to reduce the two-metre rule to one metre as soon as possible.

For much of the lockdown, UK citizens experienced a highly bordered form of everyday life. Friends and family were kept apart. Public transport usage plummeted as people were told to avoid using buses and trains. People were told to 'stay at home' and there was no shortage of social vigilantes eager to expose what were termed on social media #Covidiots. Public health ordinance was, however, ignored at other moments. Black Lives Matter protests and counter-protests, illegal rave parties and football championship celebrations all attracted the ire of mainstream media commentators and UK government officials. Nevertheless, for four months the UK experienced an unprecedented period of personal and collective restriction on mobility.

Around the world, we have seen very different leadership approaches and public attitudes towards restrictions, curfews, travel bans and other shutdowns. President Trump referred to the 'China virus', using the virus to make a political point. The circumspect messaging by New Zealand's Prime Minister Ardern and German Chancellor Merkel has stood in stark contrast to this. This reflects the very different approaches to the virus on the ground. Federal systems such as the United States, meanwhile, have experienced variation at state level given the decentralised power structures that allow individual states to enact their own strategies. The US has found a significant number of its citizens to be resistant to intervention. There have been protests against lockdown and a marked reluctance to introduce quarantine measures in many places. In contrast, smaller, more isolated and politically unitary island-states such as New Zealand were able to act comprehensively and decisively. Prime Minister Ardern implemented very strict border closure measures on 19 March 2020 and warned that the country's national borders were likely to remain severely restricted well into 2021. Australia matched New Zealand's closure policy and the two countries are likely to continue to coordinate their public health and border strategies given their proximity and high existing levels of cooperation and cross-border trade and immigration. In July 2020, the New Zealand immigration authorities had this simple message for visitors:

> The New Zealand border is currently closed to almost all travellers wanting to travel to New Zealand by either air or sea.

While countries might have had vastly diverging approaches, and arguments over medical supplies, health provision and welfare spending have erupted across the world, in general there has been a consensus for the need for international borders to be closed and transportation to be constrained to only the most 'essential' in order to fight the virus. Where divergence emerged was how quickly – or not – international borders were likely to reopen and whether some countries and travellers were judged to be 'safe' to admit or not. What made the decision-making harder is the high level of dependency countries such as Greece and Portugal have on inter-European tourism.

We should be careful not to focus excessively on the public health experiences of the global north when considering the pandemic. For example, in highly sensitive regions such as northern Nigeria, Pakistan and Afghanistan, disease outbreaks and vaccination programmes are shot through with geopolitical and border-security considerations. Polio eradication in particular continues to be tied up with suspicion that external authorities were using public health as a 'cover story' designed to facilitate malign intervention. In northern Nigeria religious and political leaders warned their communities that vaccination exercises were designed to harm the majority Muslim population, leading to infertility or other infections such as HIV/AIDS. In Pakistan, foreign-led public health interventions have been associated with allegations of vicarious behaviour by the United States, including the CIA-inspired hunt for Osama bin Laden in the lead-up to his death in 2011. This allows conspiratorial geopolitical narratives to flourish, where public health interventions get entangled with colonial, Cold War and War on Terror histories and the contemporary social and health experiences of vulnerable Muslim populations around the world, including the Uighurs in

China. These sorts of experiences inform public and international responses to the COVID-19 pandemic.

All of this has provoked soul-searching among those interested in global geopolitical futures. Will we see new forms of multilateral cooperation emerge in the wake of the pandemic? Or will further geopolitical fragmentation and forms of 'virus nationalism' flourish as states and their leaderships seek competitive advantage in areas of critical need such as vaccine development, medical supplies and personal protection equipment? Finally, what are the conflict lines of the future, given that this pandemic has revealed a stunning capacity to exaggerate both segregation and connection? While pandemics and disease are part and parcel of human history, the COVID-19 pandemic reveals the capacity of the viral to eviscerate the social norms of everyday life and forces states to engage in dramatic forms of emergency politics including quarantine, surveillance, detention and near-total shutdown. El Salvador, for example, introduced one of the harshest regimes with detention lasting up to 30 days for those found to have broken the lockdown rules. Eradication, quarantine and lockdown expose the political and ecological limits of our hyper-mobility, economic development and political systems.

BORDERS INSIDE AND OUTSIDE

The COVID-19 pandemic is believed to have originated in bats and jumped across species, eventually generating the first human case in China in late 2019. We might say that was the first border the pandemic crossed.

The exact timing and spread of the virus may never be known given the uncertainty over reporting (and controversy over whether China did or did not report and share that information with the wider world, including the WHO – the World Health Organization). Having revealed to the world that Wuhan province appeared to be the primary hotspot of infection, with so-called 'wet markets' being cited as a source of infection and diffusion, the Chinese authorities began in

January 2020 a series of dramatic lockdown measures, including quarantining the city of Wuhan's 11 million residents for weeks. Internal restrictions on movement were severe and the border for many citizens in China came to bear on their everyday lives. It was striking how rural Chinese villages also began to impose their own impromptu restrictions and blockades on those seeking to enter these territories. What unfolded was a series of formal and informal restrictions imposed on citizens and communities across the country, with local groups performing their own forms of surveillance and vigilantism.

Within six weeks, there were reported cases of infection in Europe, South Korea and Japan, with the earliest cases revealing how business and recreational travel, both domestic and international, was playing its part in the diffusion. In one well-publicised case, a middle-aged businessman travelling to Singapore returned to the UK and then went on a skiing holiday to France. He was described as a 'super-spreader', with his cross-border movements being unwittingly held responsible for infection in three countries. While rural residents were blocking off their villages in January and February 2020, international travellers were being asked to self-quarantine and agree to track-and-trace measures, with varying degrees of efficiency and enforcement.

By early March 2020, it was no longer possible in Europe simply to focus on some high-profile cases, often of privileged people, given the scale of new infections. Public health measures introduced severe restrictions on movement even in areas of the world where free movement is prized, such as within the EU. The EU's Court of Justice confirmed that member states have responsibility for public health and could close their borders in the name of community and national protection. Acting independently, EU members nonetheless allowed some of their citizens to travel across borders for the purpose of medical treatment and medical supply-sharing. In late March 2020, some Italian patients were treated in German hospitals because the Italian healthcare system was overwhelmed. German hospitals also took in patients from France, with regional governors in Germany noting that

this offer was designed to showcase the power of cross-European solidarity. The German military organised special humanitarian flights
from both countries.

Depending on the national-level severity of the crisis and public
healthcare capacities, the measures imposed by EU member states
varied. In Italy, attempts to contain the crisis in the north soon floun-
dered as infection spread to the south of the country, and full lockdown ensued in March 2020. In Spain, families were told not to leave
their homes and children under 14 years old in particular were kept
inside for six weeks from March to May 2020. The state of emergency
was not lifted in Spain until late June, and even at that point restrictions on shop openings and travel varied across the country depending
on reported cases. In Greece, the country's government acted quickly
to impose lockdown in late February and early March – some restrictions were eased in late April. Across Europe, there was considerable
variation in terms of access to shops, religious buildings and even
brothels. In Greece, it was possible to visit a brothel from 15 June
onwards, but only for a short visitation (a maximum of 15 minutes)
with no cash payments allowed. What might have put patrons off
returning, however, was something else. For track-and-trace public
health reasons, all customers were required to leave verifiable contact
information with the brothel owners.

In the midst of all these complicated rules of assembly, mobility
and access, others were taking to social media to complain about
being stranded in countries that were in lockdown or, in some cases,
trapped on cruise ships around the world. Airlines were forced to
operate in a capricious environment, where they might be allowed to
take off in one country but not land in another. Or, in the case of the
Irish airline Aer Lingus, were repurposed for the collection of medical
supplies with first-time flights to Shanghai in order to do so. In more
normal times, securing permission to move across air space and fly
novel routes requires consultation and processing. The normal administrative rules for borders were suspended for better and worse.

We have witnessed extreme border measures, with travel beyond
our immediate milieu severely restricted. The most immediate parallel

for some would have been the experiences of wartime conditions but for black-majority communities living in apartheid South Africa, travel passes were a reality of everyday life. Today, even pandemic-related restrictions on mobility both within a country and across borders have not been equally shared. In the UK, we had high-profile examples of government advisers being treated very differently from ordinary citizens for suspected breaches of lockdown measures.

The provision of healthcare, the management of care homes and access to medical insurance, in combination, have all been cited as drivers of the disparity in rates of disease-related mortality in different communities. In the UK, ethnic minority communities have been recorded as over-represented in deaths due to COVID-19, with anger being expressed that the phrase 'underlying health conditions', rather than inequality and poverty, was used to explain away this apparent over-representation.

We have seen medical diplomacy become a kind of international soft power. Countries have waived normal procedures in order to allow for emergency flights and deliveries of medical supplies from international donors and partners. This has in turn generated unease among some that in their desperation countries such as Italy were too swift to allow China and Russia to deliver aid and send their respective medical teams to affected areas. Italian journalists expressed concern about how closely those foreign medical teams would be scrutinised. Both countries have used medical diplomacy as a form of soft power, and their local embassies and foreign ministries used social media and hashtags to showcase their public health efforts. Journalists warned that, in the midst of the pandemic, there was a need to be vigilant about what these overseas teams were doing and to ensure that affected countries were not finding themselves tied into post-pandemic trade and financial deals that proved less beneficial. The fact remains the economic costs of the pandemic are huge, with debt ratios likely to be north of 150 per cent, which will inevitably lead to concerns that China in particular will find further opportunities to offer loans and financial assistance packages to countries that are highly exposed to debt.

TAKING ADVANTAGE OF BORDERS?

Any offers of aid, as with polio vaccination in the past, are never divorced from accusation that there might be explicit geopolitical agendas at work. During the Cold War, as we noted earlier, the US and the Soviet Union used public health to project their influence in Central and Eastern Europe and later the global south. Later, conspiracy theories began to flourish that live polio vaccination campaigns caused African communities to develop HIV/AIDS. The Americans and Soviets traded accusations with one another about rival vaccine development work. In 2011, the rumour mills were triggered once again when the CIA promoted a vaccination drive in Pakistan as a cover story for extracting DNA from members of bin Laden's family. Such subterfuge only helps to undermine 'vaccine trust' in many countries, and even led to foreign and local public health workers being assassinated. What might start out as an intervention designed to save lives often gets caught up in allegations of nefarious activities by third parties.

Disease, pandemics and virulent border nationalism also have a tendency to go hand in hand with one another. When borders shut down, nationalism, populism and nativism all receive a proverbial shot in the arm. In early nineteenth-century Australia, outbreaks of disease gave added impetus to expressions of white nationalism, as immigrants from China were blamed for being infectious. Calls for tighter restrictions on immigration followed. In 2020, Chinese immigrants faced the same threats, experiencing racism and violence in several countries as rogue citizens deemed them in some way 'responsible' for the pandemic. British-Chinese citizens and other members of the British Asian community reported hate crimes and expressions of racism and xenophobia. Around the world, Chinese communities reported anti-Chinese sentiment, with reports of harassment in public spaces and hurtful social media postings.

In the midst of the COVID-19 pandemic, emergency border control has nourished yet further anti-immigration debates. Hungary provides a stark example, where Prime Minister Viktor Orbán declared 'foreigners' were to blame for infections in the country. The temptation to blame others is huge at a time when domestic economies are shedding large numbers of jobs and there will remain long-term uncertainty about whether the virus will return either as a new 'monster wave' or simply endure as a costly burden to states. Media reports warn of 'virus nationalism' and pandemic populism, not only stirring up inter-communal tension but also dampening the willingness of countries to share information on vaccines and public health measures.

This tendency to blame others for ill-fortune is not unique to the COVID-19 pandemic. However, what the blame game does is bring 'the border' closer to those who are deemed responsible. The Chinese–Russian relationship soured in 2020. Border towns and cities are often at the forefront of all this precisely because there is a great deal of social, cultural and economic interaction between local communities. In a vast country such as Russia, a presidential decree from Moscow is felt very differently depending on whether affected people are living in major cities such as St Petersburg compared to Siberian towns on the border with China. The Chinese business and tourism sectors have provided many Russian border towns with an invaluable economic and cultural stimulus. In January 2020, Russia closed its border with China and, in April 2020, China closed its border with Russia. Each side accused the other of spreading infections, with residents of Russian far-eastern cities such as Vladivostok resenting the fact that allegedly infected Chinese citizens living in Moscow had been flown out via Vladivostok before eventually transiting to China. While conflict is unlikely over these comparatively small numbers of Chinese nationals being sent to the Russian–Chinese border, it points to possible sources of tension in the future where there is a temptation to stoke tension by blaming foreigners, accusing a rival government of spreading infection and circulating 'fake news' about the source of disease.

This all suggests that the pandemic, despite any international cooperation it might have created in some respects, might not encourage more cordial relationships and expressions of collective solidarity.

What countries such as the UK have learned, however, is that migrants often end up in frontline jobs such as health, welfare, social care, agriculture and public transport. Reclassified as 'key workers', their contribution continues to be acknowledged as integral to national recovery. In the UK, flights from Bulgaria and other Eastern European states were encouraged because British farmers were desperate for seasonal migration for agricultural work such as harvesting asparagus and soft fruit. The edge and border of a country becomes confused as countries open and close depending on community needs, sector priorities and local economic resilience. This might mean that, post-pandemic, the value of workers crossing borders to contribute to new countries will be better appreciated. However, it is undeniable that the people likely to suffer most from the discombobulation of borders during the COVID-19 pandemic are not only the world's poorest but also vulnerable communities such as refugees, asylum seekers and irregular migrants.

Countries were swift not only to close their international borders and impose travel restrictions but also to suspend the processing of asylum applications. Scores of people have been prevented from filing their claims for asylum in a range of countries from the United States and Brazil to those already hosting large numbers of migrants such as Uganda and Venezuela. Others such as Greece, already hit hard by hosting migrant communities as a result of the Syrian crisis, have maintained their detention centres but they are known to be overcrowded and injurious to health. Transit countries such as Niger are likely to be overwhelmed as many countries will continue to suspend their willingness to process new asylum applications, host migrant populations and/or lengthen detention in the name of public health protection. Opportunistic or otherwise, the fact remains that migrant groups will likely as not be trapped alongside borderlands or engage in ever-riskier journeys across mountains, deserts and seas. Public health measures such as social distancing and quarantine have little to no purchase in refugee camps and detention centres.

While there has been much change, however, it is clear that 'normal geopolitics' is not suspended entirely because of COVID-19.

Despite the costs of the pandemic to countries and their populations, long-standing geopolitical schisms do not dissipate. For example, in the case of India and Pakistan the latest source of tension between the two parties was the decision by Modi's Indian government to weaken the semi-autonomous status of Kashmir in August 2019. As a Muslim-majority state, Kashmir attracts great interest in Pakistan and both sides have accused one another of violating ceasefires, sponsoring cross-border violence and taking to social media to aggressively promote their interests. In March and April 2020, Prime Minister Imran Khan of Pakistan warned India that it risked further military confrontations if it continued to issue provocative statements about India's expectation that it will eventually take over Pakistan-occupied Kashmir (POK), a form of revanchism that could, in his words, provoke a nuclear confrontation. It is clear in this example that the pandemic had not postponed other existing border concerns.

While India has imposed quarantine and so-called 'Red Zones' in Kashmir due to infection, fears have been expressed that Pakistan has used the pandemic to muster more arms for militants. Cordon and search operations, usually conducted by India's special forces, have been suspended during the pandemic. Conspiracy narratives flourish and accusations are traded that rival factions are spreading rumours such as poultry being a carrier of coronavirus. Indian farmers have complained of falling sales and Pakistan has been blamed for inflammatory social media postings. It is not uncommon to read that military conflict might become more likely in and around Kashmir and the Punjab because of the pandemic.

While countries address the public health consequences, the pandemic does provide opportunities for geopolitical scheming. Indian media sources worry that with the US withdrawal from Afghanistan, Pakistan will be able to ramp up militant activity and encourage cross-border training and drug-smuggling operations. Pakistan's relationship with China is viewed by India as another worrying issue, as Beijing has offered medical and technical assistance to Prime Minister Khan. The recent citizenship changes in India have further emboldened anti-Indian sentiment. Pakistani social media has been used to accuse India of failing to treat its Muslim citizens fairly during the pandemic. Hindu nationalism in India offers opportunities for Pakistan to brand India as a racist, xenophobic state that is fundamentally unsafe for Muslims and other minorities. Third parties such as Turkey, which is actively re-imagining itself as a regional superpower, have expressed their support for Pakistan's depiction of India. The outlook for the Indo-Pakistan borderlands is bleak: the conflicts predating the pandemic continue to rumble, and the outbreak has found ways to create further schisms.

BORDER LEARNING FROM THE PANDEMIC

What do we learn from all of this and how does it speak to our interest in borders? First, at a time of a pandemic, hardening border controls and security is an understandable public health measure. But it has wide-ranging consequences for those caught up by border restriction and shutdown. Asylum seekers and migrants get trapped in no man's lands. Migrant workers in India, for example, could not return to their home country of Nepal because their own government closed land borders rapidly. In India, migrants, citizens and other travellers were given literally hours to respond to the prime ministerial decree that a severe lockdown was about to be imposed. Rural migrant workers and foreign labourers were trapped in cities around the world, with fears that they might bring the infection with them if they returned home. Humanitarian operations at sea will be suspended and lives lost because people become desperate and think that their chances of reaching the United States, Europe or other third destinations will only become harder after the pandemic subsides. In Scotland, a Sudanese asylum seeker stabbed several people in June 2020 and was later shot dead by armed police. Witnesses at the time reported that his mental health worsened in the weeks before, with fears expressed by charities that vulnerable people such as refugees are denied essential care and support because the focus is on responding to those with COVID-19. Lockdown for many simply makes worse a sense of isolation.

Second, it is clear that, in this public health climate, those 'smart borders' we spoke about in Chapter 7 are going to have to perform further border work. Tracking and tracing technologies will accelerate as public health and social control measures. National authorities have argued for such interventions in order to ensure that social distancing/lockdown measures can be eased completely as the human impact of the pandemic subsides (but it may never be eradicated completely unless effective mass vaccination is possible). Some of the surveillance proposals under consideration, such as the use of drones designed to monitor abnormal body temperatures, are unlikely to be efficacious (they would need to fly very close to a human subject), whereas what is more likely is that individuals will be asked to subject themselves to tracking technologies via their phone. In the UK, after a shaky start, track and trace phone apps are now widespread. In Singapore, there has been an active 'Trace Together' initiative, which had been downloaded by 20 per cent of the population by July 2020. The government of Singapore proposes to invest further and unveil a more advanced system linking national identity numbers, citizen movement and personal phones.

Your mobile phone will become part of a digital public health landscape, used to help track and trace your movements and behaviour (such as using a QR code system of checking in and out). The public health border will move with you, and no doubt differentiate between the healthy and unhealthy. What we have learned from the 2020 lockdown is that some have felt trapped inside their homes because of their 'underlying health conditions'. Public health experts have warned that we face a new epidemic of mental and physical health crises. But we also face an epidemic of borders as well, which may in turn provoke us to ask questions about whether these intimate interventions into the lives of citizens come at a tremendous cost to the liberal and democratic character of the states concerned.

Third, this pandemic has emphasised yet again the scope for great power rivalries. China is seeking now to become a global health power.

The origins of the WHO were shaped by the experience of inter-war epidemics and a liberal international order made by Euro-American wartime victors, and China's entry into this order upends decades of established hierarchies. There are two elements to this reordering work. Within the WHO, China has cultivated a close relationship with the senior leadership, profiting from the apparent lack of interest and disdain the Trump administration has displayed towards UN architecture. China has managed to persuade the WHO to block any involvement of Taiwan in the work of the organisation. Beyond the WHO, China promotes so-called 'health silk road' plans, which would sit alongside the broader One Belt, One Road initiative. Some of this work has involved the delivery of medical emergency supplies to various countries, including Malaysia and the Philippines as well as Italy and Greece, in conjunction with the Jack Ma Foundation delivering relief packages to other nations such as Uganda.

It is highly likely that China will be swift to offer follow-up support such as digital technologies to aid and abet health surveillance. All of which has important implications for China's place in the world, including its borders. Foreign aid is designed not only to bolster the legitimacy of the Communist Party in Beijing but also consolidate support for China's position on Taiwan, Tibet and contested maritime regions such as the South China Sea. It also provided China with a powerful mechanism to pressure recipient states not to follow the US in imposing tougher travel restrictions on Chinese citizens during the pandemic. We might think of all of this as a form of border screening – ensuring that China's strategic interests and vision are neither blocked nor frustrated by others. Neighbouring countries such as India and Vietnam are concerned that China will raise the military ante in areas such as the Himalayas and South China Sea, and that this might be motivated by economic factors such as speculation that hundreds of foreign companies will leave China because of COVID-19-related fears.

Finally, while we can point to the withdrawal of the US from some forms of global health leadership, this is by no means the whole story. The US Navy-funded Mercy Ship operations (mobile hospital ships that travel around the world) and influential public health funders such as the Bill & Melinda Gates Foundation will continue to provide opportunities for the US to use medical/health diplomacy as well. What will be intriguing to monitor is how other countries will be pressurised to keep their borders open to American and Chinese citizens, business and tourism.

THE FUTURE OF INTERNATIONAL COOPERATION

The pandemic has renewed concerns over the capacity of the current political system to respond in a collective and collaborative manner. While there has been evidence of scientific and technical coordination and information-sharing, the political will of governments has been patchy and in part that patchiness is due to the differing attitudes towards the pandemic itself. Another aspect of this is a wider questioning of the international order that was established in the aftermath of the Second World War. Alliances have been strained as nation-states have sought to secure their own communities and national interests.

The World Health Organization was established in 1948 and was part and parcel of the post-1945 liberal international order. Led by the United States and its allies, this order was underpinned by global institutions and the UN Charter. Designed to move the world away from dangerous rivalries and isolationism, the work of the WHO was also informed by the ravages of the 1918 Spanish flu epidemic, where the world learned to its collective cost that viruses do not care about international borders. With a death toll estimated to be at least 50 million people, this epidemic proved highly mobile and durable. The death toll accumulated over a period of three years and only Antarctica was spared. It placed a terrible burden on the poorest communities in the world, with pre-independence India losing nearly 20 million people. Many of the victims of the Spanish flu were younger people, which had a dire impact on societies around the world as some of the most economically productive elements of national populations were hit by war and pandemic within five years of one another. The task of the WHO, in short, was portentous: to ensure that member states share epidemiological data, coordinate public health measures and help to fund initiatives designed to improve vaccination and treatment.

In 2000, the UN Security Council acknowledged HIV/AIDS to be a challenge to global security and peaceful coexistence. Over the last two decades, there has been far more public recognition that infectious diseases are not only enabled by the hyper-mobility of globalisation but also enabled by the cumulative impact of humanity in terms of resource extraction, loss of biodiversity, climate change and further encroachment on the remotest wilderness regions. In the COVID-19 pandemic era, there will continue to be opportunities for both China and the US to advance their own interests. President Trump's climate change denialism and scepticism towards severe public health measures may work well with his electoral base, but this could also change if China's investment in medical-humanitarian-biodiversity leadership enables further alliance building across the world.

In recent years, the efficacy of the WHO has been questioned. Complaints have mounted about leadership and levels of funding, and administrative inertia dogged the agency during the SARS and Ebola outbreaks. While this critique of institutional efficacy is not unique to the WHO, critics point the finger at large states such as China and the United States for failing to support UN institutions and undermining their leadership. The WHO Director-General, Tedros Adhanom, has been heavily criticised for his handling of the COVID-19 pandemic. Critics point to an unwillingness to question critically China's accounting of its earliest cases. International representation also matters. Taiwanese warnings about China's public health emergency were reportedly ignored because Taiwan is not represented in the WHO (as a consequence of its long-standing dispute with China). The WHO did not declare a pandemic until March 2020, after registering the stages of animal-to-human, human-to-human and community transmission. The apparent delay to declare a 'pandemic', however, enabled others to speculate that the WHO was subject to covert Chinese pressure.

In April 2020, it was announced that China was not likely to support any investigation into the genesis of the pandemic led by WHO staff. This inevitably raises questions about how cross-border public health will be managed in the future. While sweeping reforms within the WHO were undertaken in response to criticism of its handling of the crisis, the fact remains that the UN agency is dependent on states being cooperative, which, as we've seen, hasn't always been the case during the pandemic. All the while, Chinese leadership has been eager to move the narrative away from direct Chinese culpability. Instead the leadership chooses to frame the pandemic as an opportunity to develop a 'community of common destiny of mankind'. But this narrative shift is not likely to be straightforward as rumours and conspiracies about secret Chinese laboratories are likely to recur in the United States, and trading in misinformation and disinformation remains buoyant.

The jury is out on whether this pandemic will accelerate deglobalisation, isolationism and the re-imposition of stricter border controls. Global supply chains, major industries and employers such as the tourism sector, and challenges including climate change and environmental protection, are trans-boundary and exceed the regulatory scope of any one nation – just as viruses do. The border between countries is never truly hermetic, as even New Zealand's strict border controls in 2020 contained exemptions. And there is little to no hope in assuming that political leaders can securely divide the world into connectivity that they care for (for example, the internet, visa-free travel, online trading and no trade barriers for their national exports) and things that they don't like (for example, irregular migration, viral infections and third-party interference). This will require the international community to decide, in the very immediate future, how collective security is made possible in a highly interconnected world, which is going to have to accommodate 2 billion more people, disruptive weather patterns, public health emergencies, environmental change and resource-related pressures in the coming decades.

What the pandemic might do, however, is further undermine the impulse for international cooperation and sharing. Governments might continue to use public health and pandemic management actively to harm cross-border relations, with even more resources devoted to enhancing border security and imposing harsh travel restrictions. Alternatively, it is quite possible that political leaderships sense opportunities for border adventurism. The border flare-ups in the mountainous areas of the Himalayas during the summer of 2020 are a reminder that the Chinese leadership, bruised by criticism of its handling of the pandemic, will be looking to other opportunities to demonstrate resolve and leadership. No one should be in any doubt that border disputes continue to provide plenty of opportunities for political leaders to perform sovereignty geopolitics and showcase their reputations for resolve.

Neither patriots nor globalists, to use President Trump's framing, will have the final say on the extent and intensity of sovereign protection. The protectionist measures of the present might well give way to new efforts to standardise agreement on public health, travel and mobility, and border controls. Indeed, these ideas have a far longer history of shared practice. The term 'quarantine' is derived from the Italian for 'forty' and reflects the fourteenth-century practice of ensuring that anyone arriving at a port such as Venice had to isolate for forty days. While not every port authority agreed on the exact number of days required for ship-based quarantine, the fact remained that the practice was widespread and paved the way for international agreements on public health in the nineteenth and twentieth centuries.

Accord rather than discord was enhanced, and over the centuries a common understanding of contagion and disease was coupled with recognition that no one country or empire would ever control the spread of disease on its own. In spite of the local tensions that they may expose, pandemics have a way of unifying the globe even as they reveal its inequalities. We would probably say something similar about climate change as well. Borders will continue to matter because political judgements will continue to be made about the scale and pace of the movement of things that we can control, while exposing things we cannot. The COVID-19 pandemic and its effects on borders will be with us, in some form or another, for years to come.

Georgians gathered for a peace rally held in Republic Square on September 1, 2008 in Tbilisi, Georgia. Rallies were held simultaneously across Georgia with protestors forming a human chain in Tbilisi in a display of Georgian solidarity in response to Russia's military action in Georgia and its recognition of sovereignty of breakaway regions Abkhazia and South Ossetia. Relations between Georgia and Russia remain tension and arguably more so after the annexation of Crimea by Russia in 2014.

Afterword

FOR ALL THE ATTENTION GIVEN TO BUILDING 'BEAUTIFUL WALLS', OUR experiences tell us that barriers and borders rarely work in the way their creators hope. Some walls do last for a long time but eventually they get breached – lines get crossed, violated and remade. Human communities have discovered that mountains, deserts and rivers are obstacles rather than hard barriers. Some parts of the world will continue to frustrate our desire to exercise absolute control. India and Pakistan squabble over the remotest glaciers in the Himalayas, and for all their spending and military commitment fail to impose their respective wills. A stalemate prevails, and it takes a terrible toll on those who are stationed in those frigid domains.

Border stories are integral to our everyday geopolitics because those walls and fences do work sufficiently well to prevent truly open borders. Barely a day goes by without stories of border conflicts accompanied by media sensationalism informing us about how refugees are suffering, which countries are investing more in border security, or boasting that their security plans are not being delayed by a pandemic or natural disaster. While public attention might be more focused on those seeking to cross over there are other border stories that matter as well. For decades, the international financial and business system has been quietly establishing ever more complex rules and procedures to move money and investment through an assemblage of shell companies, offshore financial centres, banking secrecy laws, passport purchasing, citizenship entitlements, and complicit governments and international institutions. Promises of financial reform notwithstanding, citizens around the world can nonetheless detect that there are vastly different border rules for multinational companies and people with high net wealth.

The COVID-19 pandemic created, temporarily at least, a mobility and border dragnet that many more privileged people usually evade. And remarkably, it also led to countries such as Denmark and Germany being very candid on the border limits of bailouts. Any companies not registered in their respective countries, for tax-purposes, were considered ineligible for government financial support. Offshoring, tax havens, flags of convenience and shell companies have all been exposed in recent years for what they are – a way of evading national tax authorities by playing elaborate hide and seek.

Criminals, especially smugglers, have also found plenty of opportunity to make money from borders. In Ukraine, for example, drones criss-cross the border with Russia, partly due to the ongoing instability in the far east of the country. Russian spy drones are integral to a military strategy designed to keep the Ukrainian–Russian borderlands under close surveillance. Further west, however, the drone is making its presence felt in a rather different way. Cigarette smuggling is big business. Cheap Ukrainian cigarettes are being smuggled across the border into countries such as Poland and Romania and sold to customers throughout Central and Eastern Europe. Border smuggling, whether of cigarettes, drugs or people, toxifies relations between neighbouring states. Border guards and smugglers alike end up in an 'arms race' with ever more investment in border surveillance and avoidance technologies.

Borders matter to states such as Russia, which remains eager to reverse the post-Cold War legacy of dissolution. While President Putin mourns the loss of the Soviet Union, his presidential legacy has been largely directed towards expanding Russia's influence in the world, whether as an energy superpower, military force or regional enforcer. In parts of Georgia, the border takes on a distinctly fluid quality and this is entirely due to ongoing tensions between the small Caucasian republic and its larger neighbour. Having fought a short-lived and rather disastrous war in 2008, the Georgian government discovered that Russia had no intention of easing off. Lasting just under a week, nearly 200,000 people were displaced from their communities. The existence of Russian-speaking enclaves (South Ossetia and Abkhazia) in the country provided President Putin with ample opportunity to postulate Russia's commitment to protect its peoples regardless of where they live and work. The net result of this commitment has found purchase on the borders between Georgia and Russia and those enclave communities. In August 2018, it was reported that the barbed-wire fences marking the current border were being moved overnight. Under the cover of darkness, fences were moved, ditches were dug and new signs established, declaring that the border had moved. According to Georgian residents, the moveable border can shift significantly, sometimes encompassing acres of previously Georgian territory. There are no signs of this type of activity abating.

The record of states in addressing cross-border challenges is mixed. States do cooperate and share responsibilities for shared environments such as glaciers, rivers and lakes, and there is an impressive portfolio of international regimes and joint authorities to which to point, ranging from prevention of pollution to the management of the world's fisheries. But these agreements are also continuously stress tested. While states and corporations want to develop and exploit resources, the location and extent of those resources (such as fish and other living creatures) is not static. As we enter an era of ongoing and intensifying climate change, existing regimes of cooperation are going to be tested further. New agreements are being sought to regulate the central Arctic Ocean, Southern Ocean and remoter areas of the sea-bed, for example. The complex interdependencies and migratory habits of fish and marine mammals don't care about our borders.

Calls for 'open borders' recognise that restricting the movement of people at borders is toxifying. In his 1987 publication *Aliens and Citizens*, Joseph Carens made a spirited defence of open borders. He posed the question: is it justifiable that people die trying to cross borders because states deny access to their national territories? Describing them as modern-day feudalism, he wrote that border controls deny the right to free movement, hard-wire privilege on the basis of birthplace and citizenship, and preclude the less fortunate from seeking physical safety and poverty reduction. Border security often ends up, as a consequence, corrupting human rights, undermining international legal obligations to refugees and asylum seekers, and ducking questions of fairness. Adopting open borders did not mean no borders, but it did mean that states should be expected to account for how and why those border controls are exercised.

Thirty years later, public discourse is a great deal more supportive in many countries regarding additional restrictions on cross-border mobility. In June 2018, the *Toronto Sun* wrote about a 'frenzy over facts'. The topic in hand was the contentious issue of separating children from migrant parents and families who enter into the US illegally. While not unsympathetic to the policy of detaining and separating, the newspaper reminded its readers that the decision to separate was actually introduced in the 1990s by the Clinton administration. The separation of migrant families has been defended on the grounds of deterrence, vetting and ease of surveillance. However, the inhumane conditions of incarceration and administrative chaos reveal the very limit of the ability of federal and state agencies to oversee the welfare of separated families. It begs the question how recipient countries will cope when global mass migration becomes a reality after sea-level rise and extremes of heat really make themselves felt. Conflict on the border will be commonplace. Borders are already well used, even overused, like a well-trodden path. Around the world we will see more and more migrant and refugee families trapped either side of a border.

The 'frenzy' is not so much over 'facts' (although these do matter) but rather is informed by competing visions of the future. Some will regard borders as indispensable while others seek a form of justice and solidarity which is indifferent to racial and settler colonial borders. Black Lives Matter is part and parcel of a wider struggle against dispossession, intrusion and oppression. Borders of every sort have been integral to that dispossessive work – from tribal reservations and redlining to closed borders, apartheid and Jim Crow laws. They have, to borrow from Virginia Woolf, acted as a 'skeleton of habit'. The flip-side is also true – borders are integral to property-owning and sovereign rights.

In the forthcoming decades, four types of 'border war' are going to be more prominent. First, there will be those that we might describe as grounded in identity politics. In her notable book, *Borderlands/La Frontera: The New Mestiza* (1987), Gloria Anzaldúa argued that:

> Borders are set up to define the places that are safe and un-safe, to distinguish us from them. A border is a dividing line, a narrow strip along a steep edge. A borderland is a vague and undetermined place created by the emotional residue of an unnatural boundary. It is in a constant state of transition.

As a self-declared Chicana (a woman of Mexican origin), she introduced a new generation of readers to the everyday realities of border experiences. She described the borderlands as an 'open wound', which seemed a more apt description of what was being experienced by those caught up in its vices.

This sense of wounding is worsening because border communities are bearing the brunt of US law-enforcement agencies seeking to tackle 'illegal migration' and protect the border. Border security language is indifferent to those who are either seeking to cross borders or find their everyday lives turned upside down. Drones are flying near-constantly along parts of the land border with Mexico and the interior of the United States. Citizens are 'discovering' surveillance cameras on their properties, while political leaders in Washington DC promise to protect homeland security. But no wall, barrier, drone or facial recognition technology is going to prevent others from wishing to cross borders.

The second type of border war that will persist is rooted in long-term conflict and its legacies. There will be readers of this book who have spent years watching and experiencing border conflicts in other parts of the world, such as on the island of Ireland and the contested contours of South Asia and the Middle East. For the peoples of Ireland, north and south, Brexit at its worst may end up disrupting cross-border living and heightening yet again surveillance and security patrolling. In South Asia, India and Pakistan continue to invest in new border technologies and find opportunities aplenty to denounce one another over multiple border infractions and security breaches. The role of China is a complicating factor in all of this because all three countries recognise that their mountainous disputes touch upon fundamental issues of water supply and strategic access to the extensive edges of their national territories.

There are many areas of the world where historic legacies receive far less attention but nonetheless reveal how border disputes fester. After the collapse of the Soviet Union in 1991, Central Asian republics found themselves with a host of unresolved border disputes with their new neighbour China. Without the proactive mantle of the Soviet armed forces, these smaller states were often forced to concede territory and sometimes the concessions ran into thousands of square kilometres of land and water. Tajikistan, for example, gave up formally around 1,000km^2 (386 square miles) in the water-rich Pamir Mountains in 2011. What makes the 'concessions' more dangerous politically speaking is that these same countries have also found themselves in the grip of virulent anti-Chinese sentiment and protest over Chinese immigration, business ownership and farming interests. Many Central Asian countries are indebted and have a dependency on Chinese investment and trade. National governments, frequent beneficiaries of Chinese largesse, have powerful incentives to keep Sinophobia under control. This could get harder in the years to come. China and Tajikistan have worked closely with one another on 'border security' projects as both countries fear 'spill-over' effects from an unstable Afghanistan. Chinese troops patrol along the shared border and have been working with Tajik counterparts inside Tajikistan. China is eager to ensure that separatism and what it considers to be religious extremism do not find purchase within and beyond the Chinese sphere of influence. As we noted at the start of this book, border matters are integral to identity politics, public cultures and national education.

The third type of border conflict will be due to new rounds of enclosure and privatisation. Borders will expand into new areas, such as the deep seabed, the high seas and the moon, because states will lay claim to territories or seek to secure exclusive access agreements to them. Resource pressures will be the key driver of this activity. As the realities of climate change continue to bite, there may even be calls to have no sovereign borders if the stewardship of the earth becomes so critical that the future of humanity is endangered. There will be fresh demands for a new global resource deal because vast areas of the ocean are no longer viable for fishing and land is simply exhausted of exploitable resources. The parts of the earth that continue to be habitable will become pressure points in the future.

US academic Stephen Walt, writing in *Foreign Policy* magazine in August 2019, posited the idea that the United States and others could intervene against countries such as Brazil if they fail to steward the Amazon effectively. He posits a future, sometime in 2025, when a US president (current governor of California Gavin Newsom rather than President Ivanka Trump) gives Brazil an ultimatum – take appropriate action to stop deforestation or face military intervention. Interestingly, he does not turn the scenario around. What about others taking action against the largest polluters in the world because they won't take mitigation seriously enough?

Walt's point is that climate change might force the international community to contemplate more coercive forms of intervention and violation of sovereign borders if states engage in ongoing reckless behaviour. The target of the ire might not just be Brazil. What about the largest polluters in the world, and when and where do you start to calculate the impact of former empires, who might now be eager to present to the world their clean and green credentials? The vulnerability of underwater communication cables might be another area that forces the global community, including leading powers such as China and the United States, to reckon with the fact that the earth is not simply a free hosting site for our critical infrastructure. Severe weather, for example, has already proven disruptive of under-sea cabling and intensifying climate change will make that even more likely.

The final type of border war will be the pushback against borders as archipelagos of incarceration. Todd Miller, in his 2019 book *Empire of Borders*, provides a devastating exposé of detention, imprisonment and expulsion. The 2018 US policy of separating families at the southern border revealed the blunderbuss nature of borders. He documents how procedures are being used to make life as unpleasant as possible for those seeking to cross borders. In 2019 alone, some 57,000 migrants were sent back to Mexico and told to wait there for their asylum cases to be heard. They might end up waiting for months in towns and cities that are unlikely to be safe. It is not implausible to imagine a world where scores of migrants simply overwhelm border infrastructure, with the assistance of domestic communities not prepared to accept closed borders, mass expulsion or widespread incarceration.

Around the world, there are thousands of detention centres, mainly in wealthier parts of the globe. The border security-detention-military complex is truly enormous and worth billions of dollars annually. From detention centres to drone technologies, a war is being waged on those judged to be illegal, irregular, unwelcome and unwanted. Borders and border management don't do discretion and subtlety well. For those working in border patrol and management, their primary responsibility is to the nation-state and homeland security. Border security is becoming ever more capacious. The US's Customs and Border Protection agency has attachés in US embassies around the world, including the Philippines and Kenya. The point, as Todd Miller reminds his readers, is to ensure that 'the border' is protected globally. The security work starts thousands of miles away from the physical borders of the United States. The US uses military training and technology transfer to encourage and support near neighbours to operate a global border system. Ultimately, for all the people who reach the southern or northern border of the country, there are many more who are deterred and detained elsewhere.

All of this could be eclipsed by other pressures. Nations without borders might be the only way we, or at least some of us, get to survive. By 2050, billions of us will be facing, in all likelihood, water shortages, sea-level rise and excessive heat. Large-scale population movement is likely. A new era of bordering and hoarding could await us, provoking no doubt an impulse to double down on border and bordering. The COVID-19 pandemic will provide opportunities, in the meantime, for states to track and trace citizens and residents in ever more intimate ways. It is not in the realm of science fiction to imagine all of us being mandated to carry mobile apps that assess our health, monitor our movements and influence our social behaviour in public places. The social contract will be re-drawn and the price for a return to some kind of normal life is enhanced smartphone-enabled surveillance. China's widespread surveillance of its minority communities provides a chilling example of what is possible, and for most of us it means that the surveillance infrastructure so often associated with strategic areas such as borderlands comes ever closer to main street.

We will need to make some fundamental decisions about the future of our deeply fragmented international system and whether it merits radical change in the face of profound planetary upheaval. Climate change is likely to provoke an escalation in hate. Populist leaders will continue to demand ever higher and tougher borders. Bordering and hoarding will become the long-term norm, with the spectre of environmental and resource conflict being used to justify more virulent anti-immigrant politics, eugenicist ideologies and the imposition of emergency governance.

It does not have to be this way. There are plans and initiatives that are seeking to delay our relentless assault on environments and resources. From new green deals to international treaties on biodiversity, there is a great deal to be hopeful about. The case will need to be made (and remade over and over again) as to why the world might be a great deal better off if our borders were more open to people and more responsive to elemental changes in land, air and water. Making borders more attuned to a world that is warmer and wetter is a first-order challenge that is ever more urgent, as so many low-lying islands and exposed coastlines face inundation. Food and fish stocks are moving, disappearing and re-emerging and many of our global agreements about allocation and distribution are in danger of becoming irrelevant. To border or not to border is a question that will demand urgent reassessment in the years ahead. And it will need to be attentive, relentlessly so, to mobile inequalities within and beyond countries. The mass movement of people will bring further inequality to the borders of others. As the environmentalists warned us fifty years ago, we only have one earth and there are some harsh choices that need to be made about our collective relationship with the biosphere.

Further Reading

There is plenty of literature, academic and more popular, on border conflicts around the world. For contemporary academic work, Reece Jones's two books, *Border Walls: Security and the War on Terror in the United States, India, and Israel* (Zed Books, 2012) and *Violent Borders: Refugees and the Right to Move* (Verso, 2017), provide an excellent introduction to the consequences of borders for human communities. On borders and their relationship to 'sensitive spaces', see Jason Cons's *Sensitive Space: Fragmented Territory at the India–Bangladesh Border* (University of Washington Press, 2016). On the idea of the border, Thomas Nail, *Theory of the Border* (Oxford University Press, 2016), is a good guide. On borders and the 'border work' that they generate for border guards, communities and refugees, see Madeleine Reeves's *Border Work: Spatial Lives of the State in Rural Central Asia* (Cornell University Press, 2014) and Nick Megoran's *Nationalism in Central Asia: A Biography of the Uzbekistan–Kyrgyzstan Boundary* (University of Pittsburgh Press, 2017). The academic field of critical border studies has been reviewed in a variety of handbooks and edited collections including Noel Parker and Nick Vaughan-Williams (eds), *Critical Border Studies: Broadening and Deepening the 'Lines in the Sand' Agenda* (Routledge, 2014), and Thomas Wilson and Hastings Donnan (eds), *A Companion to Border Studies* (Wiley-Blackwell, 2016).

Professional bodies such as the Association for Borderland Studies produce their own scholarly journals, including the *Journal of Borderland Studies*. Earlier academic literature on borders spans decades from Thomas Holdich, *Political Frontiers and Boundary Making* (Macmillan, 1916) and *Boundaries in Europe and the Near East* (Macmillan, 1918), to Victor Prescott's *The Geography of Frontiers and Boundaries* (Hutchinson University Library, 1965). The historic, even haunting, qualities of borders are captured beautifully by Kapka Kassabova, *Border: A Journey to the Edge of Europe* (Granta, 2017).

More journalistic, popular and semi-academic studies of borders include: Tim Marshall, *The Age of Walls: How Barriers Between Nations Are Changing Our World* (Simon Schuster, 2019), Alexander Diener and Joshua Hagen, *Borders: A Very Short Introduction* (Oxford University Press, 2012), and Ed Vulliamy, *Amexica: War Along the Borderline* (Vintage, 2010). Ruben Andersson's 'How fear infected the border' speaks of a 'border-security complex' in an article for *New Internationalist*, 18 February 2020, URL: https://newint.org/features/2019/12/09/how-fear-infected-border.

1 BORDER MATTERS

Alexander Murphy, *Geography: Why It Matters* (Polity, 2018), and Franck Billé (ed.), *Voluminous States: Sovereignty, Materiality, and the Territorial Imagination* (Duke University Press, 2020), provide excellent interrogations of the border and its relationship to the edge of the nation-state. Paul Richardson provides a detailed examination of the edgy quality to Russian–Japanese relations in *At the Edge of the Nation: The Southern Kurils and the Search for Russia's National Identity* (University of Hawai'i Press, 2018).

On the psychological need to build borders and 'beautiful walls', see Wendy Brown, *Walled States, Waning Sovereignty* (MIT Press, 2010), Matthew Longo, *The Politics of Borders: Sovereignty, Security, and the Citizen After 9/11* (Cambridge University Press, 2018), and Sandro Mezzadra and Brett Neilson, *Border as Method, or, the Multiplication of Labor* (Duke University Press, 2013). On the physical and emotion impact of being a border guard charged with patrolling and intercepting illegal migrants along the US–Mexico borderlands, Francisco Cantú, *The Line Becomes a River* (Riverhead Books, 2018); on the experiences of crossing those borders, Hastings Donnan, Madeleine Hurd and Carolin Leutloff-Grandits (eds), *Migrating Borders and Moving Times* (Manchester University Press, 2019); and for an examination of the cumulative legacies of borders and migration in Europe, Gabriele Proglio and Laura Odasso (eds), *Border Lampedusa: Subjectivity, Visibility and Memory in Stories of Sea and Land* (Palgrave Macmillan, 2017). Camilla Fojas, *Border Bandits: Hollywood on the Southern Frontier* (University of Texas, 2008), shows how border films played their part in helping to construct a distinctly Americanised border culture.

The link to contested borders and geopolitical cultures is explored in Gerard Toal, *Near Abroad: Putin, the West, and the Contest over Ukraine and the Caucasus* (Oxford University Press, 2016). On the gendered consequences of border violence and conflicts, see Cynthia Cockburn, *The Line: Women, Partition and the Gender Order in Cyprus* (Zed Books, 2004), Kavita Daiya, *Violent Belongings: Partition, Gender, and National Culture in Postcolonial India* (Temple University Press, 2011), and Paulomi Chakraborty, *The Refugee Woman: Partition of Bengal, Gender, and the Political* (Oxford University Press, 2018). For specific works on the Line of Control, see Happymon Jacob's engaging account, *The Line of Control: Travelling with the Indian and Pakistani Armies* (Penguin, 2018); on Beirut as a contested city see Sara Fregonese, *War and the City: Urban Geopolitics in Lebanon* (Bloomsbury, 2019), and Anne B. Shlay and Gillad Rosen, *Jerusalem: The Spatial Politics of a Divided Metropolis* (Wiley-Blackwell, 2015). For more on Partition, I recommend Aanchal Malhotra's *Remnants of Partition: 21 Objects from a Continent Divided* (Hurst Publishers, 2019), which I have quoted from in this chapter. Finally, on the Falkland Islands and South Atlantic, Graham Bound, *Fortress Falklands* (Pen and Sword Books, 2012).

On the 'everyday border' and associated bordering practices, Nira Yuval-Davis, Georgie Wemyss and Kathryn Cassidy, *Bordering* (John Wiley, 2019) and Kathryn Cassidy, '"Where Can I Get Free?"

Everyday Bordering, Everyday Incarceration', *Transactions of the Institute of British Geographers*, 44 (2019): 48–62.

2 MOVING BORDERS

Marco Ferrari, Elisa Pasqual and Andrea Bagnato, *A Moving Border: Alpine Cartographies of Climate Change* (Columbia University Press, 2019), is a highly innovative study of the moving border in the European Alps. Peter Nyers wrote an important essay on 'Moving borders: the politics of dirt' for *Radical Philosophy*, 174 (2012). Academic studies that give emphasis to the vitality of the earth and its capacity to disrupt human planning, such as border management, include Jane Bennett, *Vibrant Matter: A Political Ecology of Things* (Duke University Press, 2010), and there is a growing literature exploring the subterranean and volumetric qualities of territory and borderlands, including Eyal Weizman, *Hollow Land: Israel's Architecture of Occupation* (Verso, 2012), and Stephen Graham, *Vertical: The City from Satellites to Bunkers* (Verso, 2016).

3 WATERY BORDERS

On the United Nations Convention on the Law of the Sea, see Philip Steinberg, *Social Construction of Ocean* (Cambridge University Press, 2001), and Renisa Mawani, *Across Oceans of Law: The Komagata Maru and Jurisdiction in the Time of Empire* (Duke University Press, 2018). On aquifers and trans-boundary challenges, Gabriel Eckstein, *The International Law of Transboundary Groundwater Resources* (Earthscan, 2017), and Wolfgang Wagner, *Groundwater in the Arab Middle East* (Springer, 2011). On the prospect of water wars over a medley of challenges including ongoing dam projects, privatisation and water management, Vandana Shiva, *Water Wars: Privatization, Pollution, and Profit* (North Atlantic Books, 2016). Mark Everard provides a very readable summary of the contested politics of dams, *The*

Hydropolitics of Dams (Zed Books, 2013). On the deep seabed, John Hannigan, *The Geopolitics of the Deep Oceans* (Polity, 2016), and on the hosting properties of the seabed ('earth layer') and its relationship to underwater communication cables see Benjamin Bratton, *The Stack: On Software and Sovereignty* (MIT Press, 2015). Another fine study of sub-surface cables is Nicole Starosielski's *The Undersea Network* (Duke University Press, 2015).

4 VANISHING BORDERS

International law's relationship to the problem of disappearing territory is explored by Jenny Grote Stoutenburg, *Disappearing Island States in International Law* (Brill, 2015), and more specifically, with regard to island-states, see Alejandra Torres Camprubí, *Statehood under Water: Challenges of Sea-level Rise to the Continuity of Pacific Island States* (Brill, 2016). On the challenges posed by sea-level change and its implications for the future of vulnerable states, Kregg Hetherington (ed.), *Infrastructure, Environment, and Life in the Anthropocene* (Duke University Press, 2019). On climate refugees, see Jane McAdam, *Climate Change, Forced Migration, and International Law* (Oxford University Press, 2012), and for a more alarmist reading of sea-level change see Jeff Goodell, *The Water Will Come: Rising Seas, Sinking Cities, and the Remaking of the Civilized World* (Little, Brown, 2017).

5 NO MAN'S LAND

No man's lands have been investigated with reference to particular places, as by James Ker-Lindsay, *The Cyprus Problem* (Oxford University Press, 2011), and David Day, *Antarctica* (Oxford University Press, 2019), as well as to a network of regional spaces, as by Justin V. Hastings, *No Man's Land: Globalization, Territory, and Clandestine Groups in Southeast Asia* (Cornell University Press, 2010). On the peculiarities of no man's lands, BBC journalist John Simpson reflected on some of these via *News from No Man's Land: Reporting the World* (Pan Macmillan, 2002). Earlier studies of no man's lands such as Svalbard are also available, including William Martin Conway, *No Man's Land: A History of Spitsbergen from Its Discovery in 1596 to 1900* (Cambridge University Press, 1906). Divided cities also have their own literature, such as Jon Calame and Esther Charlesworth, *Divided Cities: Belfast, Beirut, Jerusalem, Mostar, and Nicosia* (University of Pennsylvania Press, 2011). On Antarctica, see Klaus Dodds, Alan Hemmings and Peder Roberts (eds), *Handbook on the Politics of Antarctica* (Edward Elgar, 2017).

6 UNRECOGNISED BORDERS

There are some useful general introductions to unrecognised states and entities and their borders, including Nick Middleton, *An Atlas of Countries that Don't Exist: A Compendium of Fifty Unrecognized and Largely Unnoticed States* (Chronicle Books, 2017), and Nina Caspersen, *Unrecognized States: The Struggle for Sovereignty in the Modern International System* (Polity Press, 2012), and for some interesting reflections on doing research work in unrecognised border spaces, see Bettina Bruns and Judith Miggelbrink (eds), *Subverting Borders: Doing Research on Smuggling and Small-Scale Trade* (VS Verlag, 2011). A sophisticated treatment of so-called 'invisible countries' is Joshua Keating, *Invisible Countries: Journeys to the Edge of Nationhood* (Yale University Press, 2018). Readers can follow particular case studies in Erik Jensen's *Western Sahara: Anatomy of a Stalemate?* (Lynne Rienner Publishers, 2011), and Steven Rosefielde's *The Kremlin Strikes Back: Russia and the West After Crimea's Annexation* (Cambridge University Press, 2016), and Russia's borderlands more generally in Helena Rytovuori-Apunen's *Power and Conflict in Russia's Borderlands* (I.B. Tauris, 2018).

7 SMART BORDERS

On 9/11 and the development of the smart border, see James J.F. Forest (ed.), *Homeland Security: Borders and Points of Entry* (Praeger, 2006), and Isidro Morales (ed.), *National Solutions to Trans-Border Problems? The Governance of Security and Risk in Post-NAFTA North America* (Routledge, 2016). On the expansion of the US border, Todd Miller, *Empire of Borders: The Expansion of the US Border around the World* (Verso, 2019). On Europe's use of smart border technologies, Huub Dijstelbloem and Albert Meijer (eds), *Migration and the New Technological Borders of Europe* (Palgrave, 2011). On the use of smart technology in the world's borderlands and beyond, David Lyon, *Surveillance after September 11* (Polity, 2008), Mark Salter (ed.), *Politics at the Airport* (Minnesota University Press, 2008), and Louise Amoore, *The Politics of Possibility: Risk and Security Beyond Probability* (Duke University Press, 2013).

8 OUT OF THIS WORLD

A classic statement on space geopolitics is Everett Dolman's *Astropolitik: Classical Geopolitics in the Space Age* (Frank Cass, 2005). Bohumil Doboš provides a contemporary overview in *Geopolitics of the Outer Space* (Springer, 2019). On the Apollo legacy and what it might hold for the future of the moon, Leonhard David, *Moon Rush: The New Space Race* (National Geographic, 2019). On China's ambitions in outer space, Stacey Solomone, *China's Strategy in Space* (Springer, 2013), and on the US and its strategic calculations, Joan Johnson-Freese, *Space as a Strategic Asset* (Columbia University Press, 2007) and *Heavenly Ambitions: America's Quest to Dominate Space* (University of Pennsylvania Press, 2012). Reading outer space alongside US frontier geopolitics, Daniel Sage, *How Outer Space Made America: Geography, Organization and the Cosmic Sublime* (Ashgate, 2014), and Daniel Deudney, *Dark Skies: Space Expansionism,*

Planetary Geopolitics, and the Ends of Humanity (Oxford University Press, 2020). On Elon Musk and his vision to transform other planets, Ashlee Vance, *Elon Musk: How the Billionaire CEO of SpaceX and Tesla Is Shaping Our Future* (Penguin, 2015). Finally, Daniel Deudney's *Space Expansionism, Planetary Geopolitics and the Ends of Humanity* (Oxford University Press, 2020) provides a cautionary note to those who would colonise the moon, Mars and more.

9 VIRAL BORDERS

The literature on the COVID-19 pandemic and its relationship to borders is very much a work in progress. Some of the best assessments so far have been published in magazines and journals such as *The Atlantic, Vox* and editorials in respected medical journals such as the *Lancet.* For a historic overview, John Rhodes, *The End of Plagues: The Global Battle Against Infectious Disease* (Palgrave Macmillan, 2013). On the 1918 Spanish flu pandemic, Laura Spinney, *Pale Rider: The Spanish Flu of 1918 and How it Changed the World* (Vintage, 2019). On other diseases and their relationship to borders and governance, Kevin Bardosh, *Locating Zika: Social Change and Governance in an Age of Mosquito Pandemics* (Routledge, 2019), Institute of Medicine, *Infectious Disease Movement in a Borderless World* (National Academies Press, 2010), William Summers, *The Great Manchurian Plague of 1910–11* (Yale University Press, 2012), and Frank Snowden, *Epidemics and Society: From the Black Death to the Present* (Yale University Press, 2019). Laurie Garrett, *The Coming Plague: Newly Emerging Diseases in a World Out of Balance* (New York, 1994), offers a remarkably prescient account of the dangers posed by the microbial and Reid Wilson offers a detailed reading of what we should have learned from the Ebola crisis, *Epidemic: Ebola and the Global Scramble to Prevent the Next Killer Outbreak* (Brookings Institution Press, 2018). On the relationship between fear, disease and geopolitics, Rachel Pain and Susan Smith (eds), *Fear, Critical Geopolitics and Everyday Life* (Routledge, 2016).

AFTERWORD

Gloria Anzaldúa, *Borderlands/La Frontera: The New Mestiza* (University of Texas Press, 1987). In defence of open borders', Joseph Carens, 'Aliens and citizens: the case for open borders' *The Review of Politics,* 49 (1987): 251–273, and a more recent work, *The Ethics of Immigration,* (Oxford University Press, 2013). A philosophical defence of open borders is offered by Alex Sager, *Against Borders: Why the World Needs the Free Movement of People* (Rowman and Littlefield, 2020). Stephen Walt, 'Who will save the Amazon (and how?')', *Foreign Policy* magazine, 5 August 2019. On the expansionism of the US border-security-detention complex, Todd Miller, *Empire of Borders: The Expansion of the US Border around the World* (Verso, 2019). *Toronto Sun,* 'U.S. border discussion is frenzy over facts', 20 June 2018. Achille Mbembe, 'The universal right to breathe', 13 May 2020 (translated by Carolyn Shread), critinq.wordpress.com/2020/04/13/the-universal-right-to-breathe/

Acknowledgements

The genesis of this book lay in a speculative email conversation involving me and my editor, Robyn Drury. My thanks to her for her belief coupled with some outstanding editorial stewardship. Paul Murphy and Howard Watson acted as my copy editors and did what every author hopes for: deviation, hesitation and repetition kept at bay (as the late Nicholas Parsons might have told his listeners). Martin Trotter kindly consented to the author photograph being used on the jacket cover. I thank Professors Michael Byers, Dan Deudney, Ian Klinke and Chih Yuan Woon for their expert comments on parts of the manuscript. Dr Jenni Cole provided some very helpful insights on geopolitics and health, and Ian Allen carried out a splendid proofread. Any errors of fact and interpretation are my responsibility, however. Professor Simon Dalby continues to be a source of inspiration and my thanks to him for our conversations about Anthropocene geopolitics and planetary boundaries.

This book would not have been possible without *Geographical Magazine* taking a chance on me. For over a decade, successive editors allowed me to write a monthly column on 'geopolitical hotspots' and readers were kind enough to engage with me via letter, email, social media and in person. In retrospect, I realise that I was experimenting with a writing style that I carried over to *Border Wars*. So, thank you, Geordie Torr, Paul Presley and Katie Burton. At Royal Holloway, I have been blessed by the presence of colleagues and an array of postgraduate students, past and present, who share my interests in borders and geopolitics. Special thanks to Nicola Wendt, who provided some invaluable research assistance and was excellent at locating unusual border conflict stories.

So much of this book has been informed by personal encounters with the places and communities I write about here. Academic workshops, field trips and private tours led by friends and colleagues around the world gave me access to experiences and insights that extend over some two decades. One of the most memorable was a field trip to East Jerusalem and the West Bank in 1998 and again in 2014. Other opportunities arose in large part because of generous professional networking opportunities. From the buffer zones in Cyprus and the borderlands of Arizona to the elevated heights of the Indo-Pakistani border and the cold waters of the Arctic and South Atlantic/Antarctic, an array of military personnel, diplomats, border guards and UN peacekeepers offered insights into their working lives. I also benefited from informal and off-the-record conversations and interviews with a raft of individuals working in border-security industries, mining, ocean fishing, environmental conservation and specialist international bodies such as the UN Commission on the Limits of the Continental Shelf and International Seabed Authority. Other things and opportunities such as souvenirs, trade shows, professional journals and popular culture have offered further insights into border matters.

Finally, I thank my family for tolerating the overseas travel that seems to go hand in hand with a passion for borders and geopolitics. My wife's Armenian-Lebanese family provided some compelling testimony about the enduring human costs of borders. Nothing can compare to sitting with her late grandfather in Beirut and listening to his memories of genocide, displacement, border insecurities and permanent exile.

I hope this book does some justice to some of what I heard all those years ago.

Index